RENEWALS 458-4574
DATE DUE

**WITHDRAWN
UTSA Libraries**

URBAN AFFAIRS AND URBAN POLICY

Urban Affairs and Urban Policy
The Selected Essays of Anthony Downs Volume Two

Anthony Downs
Senior Fellow, The Brookings Institution, USA

Edward Elgar
Cheltenham, UK • Northampton, MA, USA

© Anthony Downs, 1998

All rights reserved. No part of this publication may be reproduced, stored in a retrieval system, or transmitted in any form or by any means, electronic, mechanical, photocopying, recording, or otherwise without the prior permission of the publisher.

Published by
Edward Elgar Publishing Limited
8 Lansdown Place
Cheltenham
Glos GL50 2HU
UK

Edward Elgar Publishing, Inc.
6 Market Street
Northampton
Massachusetts 01060
USA

A catalogue record for this book
is available from the British Library

Library of Congress Cataloguing in Publication Data

Downs, Anthony.
   Urban affairs and urban policy / Anthony Downs.
    (The selected essays of Anthony Downs ; v. 2)
   1. City planning. 2. Urban policy. 3. Urban economics. 4. Real estate development. I. Title. II. Series: Downs, Anthony. Essays. Selections ; v. 2.
HT166.D665 1998
307.76—dc21   98–13246
                                                                                 CIP

ISBN 1 85898 734 2

Printed and bound in Great Britain by MPG Books Ltd, Bodmin, Cornwall

Contents

Acknowledgements		vii
Introduction:	*Confessions of an Economic Theorist and Urban Policy Analyst*	ix

1. 'The Law of Peak-Hour Expressway Congestion', *Traffic Quarterly*, **XVI** (3), July 1962, 393–409   1
2. 'Alternative Futures for the American Ghetto', *Dædalus*, **XCVII** (4), Fall 1968, 1331–78   18
3. 'Housing the Urban Poor: The Economics of Various Strategies', *American Economic Review*, **59** (4), Part 1, September 1969, 646–51   66
4. 'Competition and Community Schools' in *Community Control of Schools*, Henry M. Levin (ed.), The Brookings Institution, 1970, 219–49   72
5. 'The Economics of New Towns', *Dialogue*, **4** (4), 1971, 52–60   103
6. 'The Automotive Population Explosion', *Traffic Quarterly*, **33** (3), July 1979, 347–62   111
7. 'Living with Advanced Telecommunications', *Society*, **23** (1), November/December 1985, 26–34   127
8. 'A Strategy for Designing a National Housing Policy for the Federal Government of the United States' in *Building Foundations: Housing and Federal Policy*, Denise DiPusquale and Langley C. Keyes (eds), University of Pennsylvania Press, 1990, 61–112, reset   148
9. 'The Fundamental Shift in Real Estate Finance: From a Capital Surplus in the 1980s to a Capital Shortage in the 1990s', *Bond Market Research – Real Estate*, Salomon Brothers, February 1991, 1–19   165
10. 'What Have We Learned from the 1980s Experience?', *Real Estate Investment: United States Real Estate Research*, Salomon Brothers, July 1991, 1–11   184
11. 'Key Trends in the External Environment of Commercial Real Properties', *United States Real Estate Research*, Salomon Brothers, July 1994, 1–29   195
12. 'Contrasting Strategies for the Economic Development of Metropolitan Areas in the United States and Western Europe' in *Urban Change in the United States and Western Europe: Comparative Analysis and Policy*, Anita A. Summers, Paul C. Cheshire and Lanfranco Senn (eds), The Urban Institute Press, 1993, 15–54   225

Name index   265

Acknowledgements

The views in this work are solely those of the author, and not necessarily those of the Brookings Institution, its Trustees, or its members of Staff.

The author and publishers wish to thank the following who have kindly given permission for the use of copyright material.

American Economic Association for article: 'Housing the Urban Poor: The Economics of Various Strategies', *American Economic Review*, **59** (4), Part 1, September 1969, 646–51.

Brookings Institution for article: 'Competition and Community Schools' in *Community Control of Schools*, Henry M. Levin (ed.), 1970, 219–49.

Dædalus for article: 'Alternative Futures for the American Ghetto', *Dædalus*, **XCVII** (4), Fall 1968, 1331–78.

Dialogue for article: 'The Economics of New Towns', *Dialogue*, **4** (4), 1971, 52–60.

Eno Transportation Foundation Inc. for articles: 'The Law of Peak-Hour Expressway Congestion', *Traffic Quarterly*, **XVI** (3), July 1962, 393–409; 'The Automotive Population Explosion', *Traffic Quarterly*, **33** (3), July 1979, 347–62.

Salomon Brothers for articles: 'The Fundamental Shift in Real Estate Finance From a Capital Surplus in the 1980s to a Capital Shortage in the 1990s', *Bond Market Research – Real Estate*, Salomon Brothers, February 1991, 1–19; 'What Have We Learned from the 1980s Experience?', *Real Estate Investment: United States Real Estate Research*, Salomon Brothers, July 1991, 1–11; 'Key Trends in the External Environment of Commercial Real Properties', *United States Real Estate Research*, Salomon Brothers, July 1994, 1–29.

Transaction for article: 'Living with Advanced Telecommunications', *Society*, **23** (1), November/December 1985, 26–34.

University of Pennsylvania Press for article: 'A Strategy for Designing a National Housing Policy for the Federal Government of the United States' in *Building Foundations: Housing and Federal Policy*, Denise DiPusquale and Langley C. Keyes (eds), 1990, 61–112.

The Urban Institute for article: 'Contrasting Strategies for the Economic Development of Metropolitan Areas in the United States and Western Europe' in *Urban Change in the United States and Western Europe: Comparative Analysis and Policy*, Anita A. Summers, Paul C. Cheshire and Lanfranco Senn (eds), The Urban Institute Press, 1993, 15–54.

Every effort has been made to trace all the copyright holders but if any have been inadvertently overlooked the publishers will be pleased to make the necessary arrangements at the first opportunity.

Introduction: Confessions of an economic theorist and urban policy analyst

When Edward Elgar, the publisher of this volume, asked me to write an introduction to my collected articles, he urged me to make it mainly autobiographical. Yet I also wanted to explain certain basic aspects of my approaches to the two fields in which I have written. This introduction seeks to satisfy both these objectives.

My professional writings concern two distinct and very different subject areas. One set of works consists of rather abstract analyses of the political theory of democracy. These include *An Economic Theory of Democracy* (1957), *Inside Bureaucracy* (1967) and about a dozen related articles. These writings are based largely upon extensive logical deductions from a few simple premises of economic thought. The other set of works contains a much larger number of more practically-oriented studies concerning real estate and urban affairs. These include 15 books ranging from *Opening Up the Suburbs* (1973) through *Neighborhoods and Urban Development* (1981) and *Stuck in Traffic* (1992) to *New Visions for Metropolitan America* (1994) and *A Reevaluation of Residential Rent Control* (1997) plus over three hundred articles. These works are based mainly upon empirical data and inductive reasoning from field observations, research carried out by others, and my own practical experience.

These two areas of concern differ not only in subject matter, but also in the basic manner in which each is approached. Both differences are rooted in the circumstances under which I initially entered these fields, and subsequently pursued them. Yet both share two basic goals: penetrating beneath surface phenomena by understanding the most fundamental forces involved, and explaining how those forces operate in simple language comprehensible to any reader.

My initial forays into professional writing concerned sports. In high school, I was hired by the local weekly newspaper in Park Ridge, Illinois, a suburb of Chicago where I grew up, to cover local summer softball leagues. This assignment expanded into high school football and other sports, and I soon became the sports editor of that paper. My sports writing career continued on the student newspaper at Carleton College, in Northfield, Minnesota, 40 miles south of Minneapolis. There I also expanded into play-by-play broadcasting of football and basketball games on our college radio station. This experience taught me to write in language simple enough so that even local softball aficionados would understand every nuance, but colourful enough to retain the readers' attention.

While in college, I began writing articles on real estate subjects, thanks to the nepotism of my father, James C. Downs Jr. He was the editor of a magazine for property managers imaginatively titled *The Journal of Property Management*. He needed articles to fill the magazine during months when good manuscripts from the profession failed to appear. So he started giving me writing assignments. One of my first assignments was to write about the then new trend towards much larger automobile service stations. I complained that no information would be available about such a specialized subject. To my astonishment, I discovered there were two monthly magazines published solely about retail gas stations, as well as a large professional society of gas station owners and operators which held many meetings and yearly conventions. I have since learned that almost every activity in America, no matter how narrowly defined or seemingly trivial, has a similarly active following with its own societies, publications, conventions, political interests, terminology and legends.

All the articles I wrote for my father were totally practical, based upon some solid empirical data plus many anecdotes, and written to inform people working in real estate daily. He insisted on simple language and an easily-comprehensible style, to which I often added the colourful verb forms typical of sports writing (teams do not just win, they 'edge', 'crush' or 'blast' their opponents).

At the same time, two aspects of college life were pushing me towards trying to discover the fundamental forces at work concerning each subject, rather than looking only superficially at current trends. The first was a demanding English professor who assigned short essays analysing specific aspects of famous poems and plays. The second was my experience as a lowly freshman on the college debating team. I was a practising Roman Catholic, but all the other debaters – mainly upperclassmen – were sceptical agnostics contemptuous of religion in general and Catholicism in particular. They verbally assaulted my religious beliefs at every opportunity. In self-defence, I taught myself much Catholic theology by reading St Thomas Aquinas and other saints and philosophers. This required me to penetrate beneath the surfaces of daily religious practices and views to core theology and historical arguments. Moreover, I had to defend these complex ideas in relatively simple language.

One other aspect of my college life proved even more crucial to my later professional writings: this was running for president of the student body during my junior year at Carleton. I wanted to win, but I had no specific policy goals in mind. So my friends and I had to invent a whole platform just to have something to talk about. We then vigorously advocated every plank in that platform as though it had been divinely revealed to us. After I won the election, I conscientiously tried to achieve each of my ten explicit campaign goals – and accomplished almost all of them in the subsequent year.

To my chagrin, no one paid the slightest attention to my brilliant achievements in office. Student apathy towards my administration was total. Naturally, I did not want to attribute this mass ennui to my own incompetence or boring personality. Rather, I justified this outcome by concluding that students were indifferent because the results of my policies did not really affect them much. In fact, most of my policy results involved details of campus life of which they were not aware. And they were too busy doing more interesting things to worry about their student government.

So I formulated the hypothesis that voters in this particular democracy were *rationally ignorant* about their government's affairs. It was not time-efficient for them to stay well-informed about the details of student government, or whether the people they elected actually kept their promises. Doing so would not affect their lives much, but would consume a great deal of time and effort more fruitfully spent on other activities. This insight, plus the idea that candidates for office are more interested in winning than in carrying out particular policies, were two foundations of my later work *An Economic Theory of Democracy*.

After graduating from Carleton, I went to Stanford University to obtain a doctorate in economics – a subject on which I had not had a single course before arriving there. I completed my course work in three years and set about selecting a topic for my Ph.D. thesis. My first choice proved impractical, even though I had won a Social Science Research Council scholarship to pursue it. So I began casting about for an alternative subject. Professor Julius Margolis suggested that I explore an idea from Joseph Schumpeter's classic, *Capitalism, Socialism, and Democracy*. Schumpeter likened democratic governments that produced public policies to private firms that produced consumer and other products. Operators of private firms are not motivated by the desire to create specific products for society, but by the desire to create profits for themselves. Producing socially-useful products is the means by which they can attain their self-interested goal of making profits. Similarly, Schumpeter argued, politicians operating governments are not motivated by a desire to adopt or carry out specific public policies. Rather, their chief goal is to get elected so as to enjoy the power and other perquisites of office. The publicly-useful policies they advocate are simply the means by which they can attain their self-interested goal of gaining and keeping office.

This view was a radical departure from the theories of government motivation then prevailing among most economists and even among many political scientists. They contended that government officials were motivated by the desire to promote the public interest, not their own private interests. Therefore, entrusting some activity to the government automatically placed it in the hands of actors who would altruistically pursue the public interest. Those officials would not selfishly follow the type of self-interested motives that – according to prevailing economic theory – dominated private-sector decision-making among both consumers and firms. So most economic and many political theories of government decision-making focused on how to determine the public interest – often called 'maximizing public welfare'.

Schumpeter's iconoclastic idea was an appealing concept to explore, but the Social Science Research Council would not transfer my scholarship to it. So Kenneth Arrow, my thesis adviser, persuaded the Office of Naval Research to finance my thesis. I have never figured out how he convinced them that my doing so would benefit the US Navy, but I was grateful to him. I became even more grateful as he guided me through the writing of what turned out to be *An Economic Theory of Democracy*. Ken Arrow has the most brilliant and fastest-working mind I have ever encountered, and is also a wonderful adviser and a very supportive person.

However, *An Economic Theory of Democracy* might have remained an obscure Office of Naval Research manuscript if it were not for the generosity of Professor Ed Lindblom of Yale. He read a copy of my thesis and immediately persuaded three major publishers to send me signed contracts for its publication. I did not meet Ed Lindblom face-to-face until more than ten years later, but I am eternally grateful for his extending a helpful hand to an unknown graduate student whom he had never met. *An Economic Theory of Democracy* is still in print after 40 years, and produces more royalties each year than all my other books combined (unfortunately, that is not saying much!). It has sold at least 50 000 copies, been translated into several foreign languages and is one of the most frequently cited works in political science. No one could have been more surprised than I was – and still am.

Although *An Economic Theory of Democracy* is a purely theoretical book, not directly grounded in empirical research or data (it does not contain a single regression or other equation!), it does draw heavily upon my own personal experiences in student government at Carleton College, as noted above. My second book similarly drew heavily from my personal experiences – this time my three-year stint on active duty as an air intelligence officer in the US Navy. This occurred from 1956 to 1959, immediately after I finished my doctoral thesis. I left the Navy in 1959 and joined my father's consulting firm, Real Estate Research Corporation, in Chicago. In 1965, the Rand Corporation asked me to go to Santa Monica to analyse how bureaucracies make decisions.

Rand was puzzled by the seemingly irrational behaviour of two bureaucracies important to its existence: the Soviet military – its enemy – and the US Air Force – its sponsor. Rand wanted me to apply to bureaucracies the same almost cynical perspective about the behaviour of public officials – that they are significantly motivated by self-interest – that I had applied to political parties in *An Economic Theory of Democracy*. So my wife, our four children and I moved to Santa Monica for two years. I worked partly for Rand and partly for the Los Angeles office of Real Estate Research Corporation, spending alternate weeks in each place. In about two years, I managed to write the book *Inside Bureaucracy*, which was published by Little Brown Inc. in 1967.

While I was serving in the US Navy, I often lamented that my time was being wasted. I did not begrudge giving three years to my country, but the billet assigned to me did not make any use of my training as an economist. Only when I started writing about bureaucracy some six years later did I realize that the Navy had been an outstanding training ground concerning how bureaucracies work. My position as a lowly intelligence lieutenant junior grade on an aircraft carrier enabled me to observe several layers of a military bureaucracy simultaneously, discovering how they interacted and what motivated their members.

That experience convinced me that no one version of how a bureaucrat thinks and acts could encompass the great variety of different behaviours I had seen in the Navy. Therefore, instead of assuming that all bureaucrats have the same motivations, I defined five different types of bureaucrats, each with a unique set of motives and behaviours. This approach defies the usual economics assumption that a single, totally abstract utility function can serve as a theoretical vessel into which individual variations in behaviour can be poured. But it enabled me to create a much more realistic model of how bureaucrats and bureaucracies behave than would assuming that all bureaucrats act alike. This model was also superior to assuming that all bureaucrats have abstract goal-structures so empty of specific contents (such as generalized 'utility functions') that very little about day-to-day behaviour can be deduced from them. I believe similar multiple utility-function assumptions would probably greatly improve theories of consumer behaviour, and perhaps even theories of firm behaviour, compared to the continued use of totally abstract utility functions assumed to be the same for all consumers or all firms.

After I returned to Chicago in 1965 to work full-time for Real Estate Research Corporation, my activities – and interests – shifted almost entirely to real estate and urban affairs. However, I was still determined to write about my experiences in ways that drew significant and broad underlying conclusions from detailed everyday activities. The consulting business offered many opportunities to do that. It constantly exposed me to new and different problems and issues connected with business and government policies concerning land uses and demographics. Insofar as possible, I tried to turn insights gained from specific consulting assignments into publishable articles. Some were collected in 1970 into a book of essays entitled *Urban Problems and Prospects*, published by Rand McNally; a second edition was published in 1976.

Another aspect of my personal experience crucially affecting my writing was serving as a principal consultant to the National Commission on Civil Disorders (the 'Kerner Commission'), which President Lyndon Johnson appointed to investigate the urban riots of 1967. I had previously had a slight acquaintance with Victor Palmieri, the Deputy Director of the Commission's staff. I managed to persuade him and David Ginsburg, the Director of the staff, that I already knew much about the subject they were going to investigate. My persuasiveness was based upon the fact that I had just finished serving with a secret Presidential Task Force on Cities, appointed in 1965 again by President Johnson and chaired by Paul Ylvisaker. For more than two years after the 1965 Watts Riots in Los Angeles, this task force had been analysing problems of large cities. We wrote a final report predicting that large-scale racial violence would break out in many big US cities if conditions in black neighbourhoods did not improve. President Johnson suppressed this report, not even showing it to Robert Weaver, then Secretary of Housing and Urban Development. But then the Newark and Detroit riots of early 1967 exploded. So the President appointed this new Commission to look publicly into exactly what the task force had been looking into secretly for two years. I was appointed to the Kerner Commission and, working nights and weekends for months, wrote the first drafts of four of the chapters in its final report – including the chapter on the future of American cities.

This experience convinced me – as well as many others – that the racial ghettos of America posed one of our society's central problems that needed to be addressed far more powerfully than in the past. That conviction motivated me to write two books focused on this subject. One was *Racism in America – And What to Do About It*, a long booklet written for the US Civil Rights Commission and published in 1970. It is heavily based upon the ideas of John McKnight. Because he was then on the staff of the Commission, he could not be listed as a co-author, as he should have been. The second book was *Opening Up the Suburbs*, published in 1973 by the Yale University Press. It sets forth a housing strategy reflecting my profound belief that inner-city problems cannot be resolved in the long run without reducing the sizable concentrations of very poor people – mostly minorities – found in the core areas of about 50 large American cities. The book advocates creating small scattered clusters of subsidized housing throughout American suburbs, enabling many low-income households from inner-city areas to move into those units if they so wish. It pre-dated the Gautreaux Experiment in Chicago which, in 1976, started doing just that through housing vouchers rather than new construction. That Experiment has successfully moved 5000 mainly-black households out of Chicago public housing into suburban and outer-city neighbourhoods.

Among all my writings, with the possible exception of my work for the Kerner Commission, *Opening Up the Suburbs* is the one I felt the most powerful pressure from my conscience to complete, even though I had no consulting assignments related to it. I still believe its extremely unpopular message is basically correct, although its strategy has been decisively rejected by most Americans.

The strategy of turning consulting assignments into publications if at all possible resulted in two other books published in 1973 by Lexington Press. One was *Federal Housing Subsidies: How Are They Working?*, written for the National Association of Homebuilders. The second was *Achieving Effective Desegregation*, an analysis of successful school desegregation tactics written by Leanne Lachman, Al Smith and myself for the Cabinet Committee on Education in the Nixon Administration.

In 1970, my father sold the Real Estate Research Corporation to the First Chicago Corporation, the parent holding company of the First National Bank of Chicago. I continued working at Real Estate Research for seven more years, becoming chairman in 1973 when health problems compelled my father to retire. At that time, I had worked for him for 14 years and my relationship with him profoundly shaped my life in almost every way. We were not only the best of friends, but he had a realistic grasp of both my capabilities and limitations. He never entrusted me with managerial responsibility for the firm. Yet he let me 'do my own thing' in terms of creative analysis methods, taking on entirely new types of assignments, and writing about them. Also, he stood behind me when I made controversial judgements about public policies, even when doing so cost the firm dearly in terms of lost business. One example was, in the early 1970s, our complete reform of the Cook County Assessor's Office – one of the largest in the nation. Having been put in charge of this politically sensitive assignment, I insisted on doubling assessed values of the houses in Mayor Richard J. Daley's home ward – over his vehement objections – in order to bring them into line with those in the rest of the County. The Mayor never forgave me for that – even though he had personally urged me to do whatever was necessary to clean up the Assessor's Office. Consequently, the City of Chicago stopped giving our firm business when it had previously been our largest client. Yet my father – a close friend and adviser to the Mayor – never said one word to me in criticism of that decision. He was a great citizen, a great father and a great man, and both an imaginative thinker and a successful entrepreneur. Because of him, I am a firm believer in the virtues of nepotism!

In 1977, after a conflict with the then head of First Chicago Corporation, I decided to leave the Real Estate Research Corporation. The Brookings Institution had previously asked me if I was interested in going there and, fortunately for me, that offer was still open, so I took it. The family moved to McLean, Virginia, just west of Washington. I agreed to work 80 per cent of the time for Brookings, while retaining the right to spend 20 per cent as a private consultant. This change allowed me far more time to devote to individual writing projects than I had ever enjoyed in a consulting firm – while still profiting from some public speaking and consulting.

Brookings is a terrific place in which to do policy-oriented research on public issues. It has a stellar reputation that ensures its members an audience with almost anyone, and is located in the midst of the Washington government policy world. It has a fine library and computer centre, a cafeteria in which staff members can mingle and exchange ideas, and above all, other staff members of unparalleled ability in many fields. Furthermore, it permits its senior fellows to focus on major policy-oriented projects, not all of which can be supported by outside funding. This fruitful environment has enabled me to write nine books (two with co-authors), co-edit two other books (with Katharine Bradbury) and publish over 200 articles in a 20-year period, during the last few years of which I have worked half-time or less for Brookings. The rest of the time I have made speeches around the nation (25–45 per year), served on boards of directors and have undertaken a few consulting assignments.

During the 1980s, when rampant conservatism in Washington drastically reduced interest in urban problems, I decided to shift the focus of my policy analysis from inner-city ghettos to the growth of suburbs and the relationship of that growth to inner-city problems. This is the subject of my book *New Visions for Metropolitan America* and also of my current research on the costs of suburban sprawl compared with the costs of alternative forms of metropolitan growth. These topics are likely to engage the attention of key public policy decision-makers for several decades to come.

What lessons can be drawn from all this experience for others interested in policy-oriented research and publication? The following seem most important:

- *Get personally involved in activities that provide direct experience in the fields you want to write about.* If you are not so involved, it is hard to know what is really happening. Reading the literature is not enough. Neither is sitting in your office and viewing the real world from afar. If you are not a practitioner, at least go around and interact with those who are *in their home territories*. Join their trade organizations or professional societies and attend their meetings. My constant speech-making around the nation is an invaluable source of ideas that I would never have encountered if I had not met people on their home grounds and discussed local conditions with them. I have been an active member of the Urban Land Institute for 20 years, rather than being active in the American Economic Association. Doing so enabled me to get to know the nation's major real estate developers, home-builders, providers of financing, consultants, and urban public officials, and to keep informed about what they are doing and thinking. There is no substitute for such direct interactions with the people who are actually doing whatever is being done in each field of interest.
- *Tell the truth, no matter how unpopular it may be.* You do not have to be

tactless, but speaking the truth will often be so novel it will impress people with your originality. In Chicago in 1963, I wrote a housing analysis for the city that explicitly dealt with the process of neighbourhood racial transition from white to black that had dominated housing dynamics there for 20 years. Yet before then, neither race nor that neighbourhood transition process had ever been mentioned in any official city documents, so as to avoid controversy. The city government tried to suppress my study. But a reporter stole a copy from the Planning Department and printed it in daily instalments on the back page of the *Chicago Daily News*. This forced city officials at least to begin talking realistically about housing markets.

- *Write about how current and local events and trends are related to longer-run forces.* Many observers can describe what is happening on the surface, but few dig down deep enough to relate current events to long-run trends and forces.
- *Write clearly in easily-understood terms.* Most academic writers are not interested in communicating with real-world policy-makers. They only want to communicate with other academics who also understand esoteric-speak. Forget it! Use a simple word whenever a complicated one will do. Write in short sentences (though not always this short!). Break long sentences into shorter ones. If your teenage child can understand what you are saying, then it is probably clear enough. If not, keep re-writing.
- *Draw explicit conclusions about what is likely to happen and about the resulting policy implications – do not leave 'pulling it all together' up to your readers.* Analyses that conclude 'on the one hand, this, but on the other hand, that' are highly unsatisfying. If conclusions are implicit in your analysis, draw them yourself and explain them explicitly. That is why I am including this last section on lessons to be drawn!
- *Once you have generated a few really significant ideas, repeat them over and over in your writing and speaking.* Changing public opinion – even élite public opinion – about anything important is an immensely difficult task. It requires overcoming the massive inertia built into prevailing views by various self-interested structures and groups benefiting from those views. In truth, most influential thinkers and writers come up with only a small number of really good original ideas during a lifetime – a dozen would be a lot. To get those ideas widely accepted in our society of over 250 million persons requires broadcasting them constantly for years and years, perhaps changing their form slightly to disguise this repetition. Persistence – almost to the point of becoming an intellectual nuisance – is thus one of the most important virtues of an effective public policy analyst.
- *Recognize that true research consists of exploring the as-yet-unknown; so how you come out at its end may be quite different from what you expected at its beginning.* I have made an initial outline of every book I have started to write, but the finished products rarely followed those first outlines very closely. Whole sections planned at the outset were rejected along the way, and the need for entirely new sections always emerged. In two cases, a manuscript I had worked on for almost two years was judged inadequate by

outside readers. I revised one and it became one of my more successful books; the other I put aside as needing a lot more work, and it may never see the light of day. That was a blow to my ego but, upon reflection, I concluded that the outside reviewers were right. A good researcher nearly always has some basic hypotheses at the outset, but must be willing to chance failing to substantiate those theories or any other interesting conclusions!

- *Do not shrink from advocating unpopular positions if you strongly believe you are right.* Most of the great advances in social policy throughout history have started out as unpopular views of a small minority. Examples are effective voting rights for almost every group from propertyless adult males to women to African-Americans, free education for everyone, social security systems, health insurance and pensions for workers, and freedom of religion. Policies that are almost inconceivable when first promoted often become almost universally accepted after many decades of advocacy and eventual adoption. Racial desegregation of public facilities is a recent example. Someone must carry the torch for such innovations during periods when most people reject them. Such a prophetic role is a vital function performed by enlightened social policy analysts. Carrying out this role calls for both persistence and courage in the face of strong opposition.

- *Do not take yourself so seriously that you omit all humour from your work – especially speeches or lectures.* Mosts academic treatises or speeches, even those about public policies, are deadly to encounter; they quickly cause the MEGO syndrome – 'My Eyes Glaze Over'! Just telling one joke at the outset of a speech is not adequate either. I have become notorious in real estate circles for illustrating my main points with jokes or stories; I try to tell one about every three or four minutes to keep the audience alert. Even my telephone answering machine message says 'Hi there! This is the world's leading authority speaking. I am too busy thinking great thoughts to come to the phone right now. But you know what to do, so just do it!' But to use humour successfully, you must take it rather seriously. I subscribe to several joke services; frequently buy and read joke books; and read all the stories in *The Reader's Digest*, which most of my audiences consider beneath their dignity to peruse. But all that effort has greatly enhanced my audience appeal.

One last lesson is probably the most important of all, but may be difficult for many people to follow today. It is to ground your life on fundamental foundations that will continuously replenish your enthusiasm, and sustain you when things get tough. My two strongest pillars have been my wife Kay and my religion. Before we married 41 years ago, Kay and I made an implicit pact: I would earn the money, and she would operate the household and do most of the rearing of the children. She could have been an outstanding career woman, since she was working on her Ph.D. when we were married. But she chose to concentrate on our family – at least until our fifth and last child was in high school, at which point she went to law school at the age of 50. Such a family-first focus was typical of very talented women in the 1950s. It is much rarer today; now most highly-educated women pursue their own professional careers while raising a smaller family with a lot more direct help from their husbands than I provided. Yet without her outstanding management of our home and children, plus her constant support and encouragement of my own efforts, I could never have devoted so much time to writing about the projects on which I was working. I am not necessarily recommending this pattern today, but I would be remiss not to mention how significant it has been in my own life. Unfortunately, my wife has recently contracted cancer, so I must now even more strongly emphasize my role as her key supporter. I hope I can do that half as well as she has always supported me.

Similarly, I have depended greatly upon faith in a power greater then ourselves. That faith sustains not only my personal life, but also my long-run persistence in promoting often unpopular public policies that I believe would improve society. I hope to keep working at that endless task for many more years to come.

References
Joseph A. Schumpeter (1950), *Capitalism, Socialism, and Democracy*, New York: Harper and Brothers.

Writings of Anthony Downs
An Economic Theory of Democracy (1957), New York: Harper and Brothers.
Inside Bureaucracy (1967), A Rand Corporation Research Study, Boston, MA: Little, Brown and Company.
Urban Problems and Prospects (1970), Chicago, IL: Markham Publishing Company.
Racism in America and How to Combat It (1970), Washington, DC: U.S. Civil Rights Commission, U.S. Government Printing Office.
Urban Problems and Prospects, Second Edition (1976), Chicago, IL: Rand McNally College Publishing Company.
Federal Housing Subsidies: How Are They Working? (1973), Lexington, MA: D.C. Heath and Company.
Opening Up The Suburbs: An Urban Strategy for America (1973), New Haven, CT: Yale University Press.
Neighborhoods and Urban Development (1981), Washington, DC: The Brookings Institution.
Stuck in Traffic (1992), Washington, DC: The Brookings Institution and the Lincoln Institute for Land Policy.
New Visions for Metropolitan America (1994), Washington, DC: The Brookings Institution and the Lincoln Institute of Land Policy.
A Reevaluation of Residential Rent Controls (1996), Washington, DC: The Urban Land Institute.
Achieving Effective Desegregation (1973), with A. Smith and M. Leanne Lachman, Lexington, MA: D.C. Heath and Company.

[1]
The Law of Peak-Hour Expressway Congestion

ANTHONY DOWNS

Mr. Downs is Director of Retail Analysis for the Real Estate Research Corporation in Chicago, and a member of the Board of Directors of that Corporation. He holds an M.A. and a Ph.D. in Economics from Stanford University and has been a faculty member of the University of Chicago in the Economics and Political Science departments. He has published articles and reviews in his field, is a staff writer for the Journal of Property Management *and for* The National Market Letter, *and the author of* An Economic Theory of Democracy.

RECENT experience on expressways in large U.S. cities suggests that traffic congestion is here forever. Apparently, no matter how many new superroads are built connecting outlying areas with the downtown business district, auto-driving commuters still move at a crawl during the morning and evening rush hours.

To many a frustrated commuter, this result indicates abysmally bad foresight by highway planners. However, the real cause of peak-hour congestion is not poor planning, but the operation of traffic equilibrium. In fact, its results are so automatic we can even put them in the form of Downs's Law of Peak-Hour Traffic Congestion, or Parkinson's Second Law adapted to traffic: *On urban commuter expressways, peak-hour traffic congestion rises to meet maximum capacity.*[1]

Behind this law lies a complex set of forces which we can best analyze by constructing a model of commuter decision-making based on the following assumptions:

1. Every commuter seeks to minimize the total amount of time he spends en route to and from work, within four major constraints:

---

[1]. C. Northcote Parkinson, *The Law and the Profits*, Houghton Mifflin, Boston, 1960. It should be noted that this article deals exclusively with expressways which do not require their users to pay any direct tolls in order to drive upon them. The possibility of limiting congestion on such roads by introducing high tolls has been extensively discussed in the literature of economics and highway planning. However, most of the commuter expressways currently being built do not levy any direct tolls on their users. Therefore the analysis presented in this paper is relevant to the majority of cities in which commuter expressways exist, are under construction, or are being planned. For a discussion of the toll problem, see James Buchanan, "Private Ownership and Common Usage: The Road Case Re-Examined," *Southern Economic Journal*, Vol. XXII, No. 3, January 1956, 305–316.

a. *Income.* This constraint limits the means of transportation available to the commuter. Helicopters are now the technically fastest means of movement available to most commuters, but only one in a million can afford them. Thus time-minimization means seeking the shortest time that is economically feasible.

b. *Money costs of transportation.* A marked change in these costs (such as doubling of the subway fare) may shift a commuter from one means of transit to another. For purposes of our analysis, however, we will assume that no changes occur in the money costs of various forms of transportation unless specifically mentioned.

c. *Place of residence.* Some residential areas are not served by public transportation. Others have very restricted parking for automobiles. Hence, each person's choice of where to live influences to some extent what means of transportation he will select in commuting. We will take everyone's place of residence as given for purposes of our analysis, even though the level of congestion may have definite feedbacks influencing long-run choices concerning job and residence location.

d. *Personal comfort.* Some auto-driving commuters could make faster time on public transportation, but the desire to avoid crowding and to be independent of time-scheduled trips undoubtedly makes comfort a factor in commuter patterns.

2. Most commuters follow the law of inertia. That is, once a commuter has selected a means of transportation and a specific route, he continues to follow it until some alteration in his environment pushes him across his route-decision threshold.

3. Route-changing alteration in a commuter's environment consists of some event which convinces the commuter that he could reduce his travel time by shifting his route (or his means of transportation).

4. For convenience, we can classify all commuters into two basic categories: those with low thresholds (explorers) and those with high thresholds (sheep).

a. *Explorers* are imaginative, high-strung, aggressive drivers who constantly search for some new route that will save them one or two minutes' driving time.

b. *Sheep* are more placid, patient, and resigned than explorers. They tend to follow the leader and to travel the same route unless some significant change in their environment occurs.

PEAK-HOUR EXPRESSWAY CONGESTION

Every weekday morning, thousands of commuters set out from their homes for work. Within the constraints described and through a process of trial and error, they choose means of transportation and specific routes calculated to minimize their time en route. Assume that there are two routes for auto-driving commuters from Natick, Massachusetts, to downtown Boston. Both routes carry commuters over roads also traversed by many more motorists driving to Boston from other suburbs, and by other motorists driving across the downtown-bound flow of traffic. Thus the congestion experienced by commuters from Natick is a result of the decisions made by residents of a great many other parts of the metropolitan area besides Natick. Out of these myriad individual decisions comes a "typical" time consumed going downtown from Natick on Route A and another "typical" time consumed by going on Route B.

TRAFFIC EQUILIBRIUM

If these two times are about equal, then a balance is established for auto-driving Natick commuters. If they are not equal, imbalance exists. Explorers shifting from one route to the other, because of ephemeral obstacles on their usual path, will soon discover that one (say, Route A) takes less time; hence they will make Route A their normal path. Gradually word will filter around Natick and more driving commuters will shift from B to A. Similarly, commuters who live in other towns but also use routes A and B will be reacting in the same way. As the level of congestion on Route A rises and that on Route B falls, the total time required on Route A increases and that on Route B decreases. When the two travel times become equal, equilibrium has been established.

Normally, each such equilibrium is relatively stable because of the sheep, whose inertia keeps them grooved in the same route unless they receive decisive knowledge that another route is consistently faster. Since sheep outnumber explorers, the main streams of traffic on each major route remain the same day in and day out. On the margin, the explorers are ranging afield, testing other possibilities. If conditions change and they discover a faster route, they all vanish from the slower ones, and gradually some of the sheep follow. Ultimately, a new equilibrium is established.

In order to analyze the effect of a new expressway upon commuter congestion, let us assume that traffic equilibrium has been reached prior to the creation of the expressway. Then a new superhighway is opened connecting the downtown business district with outlying suburban areas. This road is a nonstop limited-access highway with multiple lanes in each direction. It has been cut through the city in such a way that its linear length is less than the length of any alternative combinations of existing streets. As a result, the no-traffic, nonstop driving time between the residential areas served by the new road and downtown is much less than on previously existing routes at any given automobile speed.

What happens to commuter congestion when such a new highway opens? To some extent, the answer depends upon what forms of public transportation are operating in the city concerned. Therefore we will consider three separate cases. We will also assume for the moment that both the total number of commuters and automobile ownership among them remain the same before and after the new expressway is opened.

CASE A: A CITY WITH AUTO-DRIVING COMMUTERS ONLY

Where all commuters travel by automobile, the opening of a new expressway reduces peak-hour traffic congestion on many previously existing streets, because large numbers of commuters shift onto the new expressway. At first, they are able to make much better time on the expressway. However, word of this time disequilibrium soon spreads, and even more commuters shift from other routes onto the expressway. Gradually the time required for commuting on the expressway rises as peak-hour congestion increases; whereas the time required on alternate routes falls as traffic on them decreases. When these two times become identical, equilibrium is restored.

At the new equilibrium point, the rush-hour level of congestion on previously existing routes paralleling the expressway is considerably lower than it was earlier. Commuting on these routes therefore requires less time than before.

However, the rush-hour level of congestion on the expressway almost always exceeds its designed optimal capacity. For example, assume that the new road is designed to move 6,000 cars per hour past a given point at a speed of 50 miles per hour. When traffic volume at the peak-hour has risen to 6,000 cars per hour, these cars will still be moving at 50 miles per hour. Since this speed is probably faster than the speed attainable on previously existing city routes marked by cross streets and stoplights, equilibrium will not have been reached. More cars will move onto the expressway from other routes until the speeds on all routes are identical. However, even at this point, equilibrium will not have been reached. The expressway is shorter than the other routes; hence motorists traveling at the same average speeds over all routes will still arrive at their destinations faster on the expressway. Therefore route-shifting onto the expressway will continue until the average speed on the expressway is reduced to *below* the average speed on alternate routes. Clearly, the expressway was designed to handle traffic at *higher* speeds than previously existing roadways; yet, at equilibrium, traffic on the expressway is moving *more slowly* than traffic on the older routes. Therefore we can say that *congestion on the expressway has risen to surpass its optimal capacity.* This result is a necessary outcome of the forces of traffic equilibrium.

It should be pointed out that the maximum capacity of an expressway is not attained at the relatively high speed at which the designers of the expressway intended it to carry traffic. As the average speed of traffic along a major road increases, the average interval between cars rises, because drivers tend to allow themselves more room for braking. This reduces the total number of cars passing a given point in any period of time. In lower ranges of speed, such increases in interval are more than offset by the fact that more cars can pass a given point during one hour because the cars are moving faster. But above 35 to 40 miles per hour, the effect of larger average intervals between cars outweighs the effect of increased speed, so the total number of cars that can pass a given point in an hour declines. Therefore, as the number of cars entering an expressway per hour rises, a point is eventually reached at which all cars must slow down to accommodate the heavier traffic going by a given point in one hour.[2]

2. For a discussion of relation between speed and hourly capacity, see Theodore M. Watson, Wilbur S. Smith, and Frederick W. Hurd, *Traffic Engineering*, McGraw-Hill Book Company, Inc., New York, 1955, p. 382. The table on the indicated page shows the following specific relationship for highways of four or more lanes:

Vehicles per lane per hour (maximum)	Speed
1,500	35–40 mph.
1,250	40–45 mph.
1,000	45–50 mph.

Since most modern expressways are designed to carry traffic at 50 miles per hour or faster, the number of vehicles they can carry past a given point per hour at this optimal speed is smaller than the maximum number which they can carry by this point in an hour. Therefore, when traffic volume rises markedly, the commuters' average speed is forced below this optimal speed, and congestion surpasses the optimal capacity of the expressway. As we pointed out above, this is exactly what happens in our theoretical model of commuter behavior.

The only way in which such heavy congestion could be avoided is through creation of a single expressway or system of expressways with such an enormous capacity that all the commuters formerly driving on parallel conventional streets could use the new facilities and still maintain optimal speeds. Furthermore, such facilities would have to be wide enough to carry most of these commuters *simultaneously*. Some auto-driving commuters attempt to avoid peak-hour congestion by leaving earlier or later than the period of greatest crowding. However, even if a new expressway were wide enough to carry *all* the peak-period traffic formerly moving on conventional streets, a telescoping of this "spreading out" over time would probably occur after the expressway opened. Drivers who previously left earlier or later than the peak moment to avoid maximum crowding would soon discover that they could depart closer to the peak moment, since the new expressway would reduce congestion at that moment. Therefore more and more commuters would tend to leave right at or around the moment of maximum convenience (assuming most government offices and businesses continued to open and let out at about the same time). This would tend to push the level of crowding at that moment back to where it was before the expressway was opened, although it would also make the total peak period of shorter duration. Thus convergences in commuters' *time schedules* as well as their *route schedules* tend to force the level of congestion on an expressway during peak hours upwards to the maximum capacity of the expressway. In pure theory, only a road or system of roads wide enough to carry every commuter simultaneously at an optimal speed would be sufficient to eliminate all peak-hour congestion. It is obvious that no such roads are practical unless we convert our metropolitan areas into giant cement slabs.

Therefore Downs's Law still holds: congestion at the peak hour will rise until the commuters' average speed is forced below the optimal speed for which the expressway was designed.

In summary, a new expressway serving the downtown district of a city in which all commuters travel by car will have the following effects:

1. It will reduce traffic on existing streets, thereby decreasing the average journey time on those streets for the commuters who still use them.

2. It will carry very heavy traffic loads during rush hours, heavier than its optimal capacity; hence serious congestion will be created. Nevertheless, commuters using the expressway will have faster commuting trips than they did before it was opened.[3]

3. It will shorten the duration of the period of peak traffic congestion.

Whether the total time savings experienced in a city after a new expressway is opened—plus other benefits, such as greater safety—are sufficient to balance the cost of constructing the road depends upon the particular factors involved in each city; hence we cannot reach any conclusion about it here.

CASE B: A CITY WITH BOTH AUTO-DRIVING AND BUS-RIDING COMMUTERS

A great many U. S. cities have extensive bus networks (some including fixed-rail streetcars) which carry thousands of commuters to work each day. How will the effects of a new suburbs-to-downtown expressway in such a city differ from its effects in a city with only auto-driving commuters?

Right after the expressway is introduced, congestion on all existing streets falls, as described in the first case above. This enables buses as well as cars to move faster at peak hours, thus providing better service to bus riders. However, in relative terms, bus service does not speed up as fast as commuting by automobile. Buses must stop and start to pick up and discharge passengers. Such delays take about the same time no matter how much traffic exists on the streets. The total amount of time thus consumed is a "fixed cost" of

---

3. For some evidence verifying this conclusion, see Paul T. McElhiney, "Evaluating Freeway Performance in Los Angeles," *Traffic Quarterly*, Vol. XIV, No. 3, July 1960, 296–312.

each bus route. For express buses which load in a few stops in outlying areas and run nonstop downtown (vice versa in the evening), this fixed cost constitutes a relatively small proportion of total trip time. But for local buses which stop every few blocks throughout their route, this fixed cost may consume a considerable portion of total trip time.

Therefore, even though the time cost of both bus and automobile commuting falls when the expressway opens, the time cost of bus commuting falls considerably less than that of automobile commuting. As a result, some commuters shift from buses to driving their own cars. This causes a rise in congestion that partially offsets the initial improvement in travel speed effected by the opening of the expressway.

The extent to which this feedback tends to return traffic congestion on city streets to its pre-expressway level depends upon such factors as (1) the percentage of commuters who traveled by bus on routes paralleling the expressway before the latter was opened; (2) the percentage of such bus commuters who used local as opposed to express bus service; (3) the incomes of bus commuters; and (4) the availability and cost of terminal parking facilities in the downtown area.

If any large number of commuters abandon buses and start driving to work, a second feedback occurs: the cost of bus travel per person rises. As passenger revenues fall, bus lines find themselves under increasing pressure to reduce service or to raise fares. Either move has the effect of driving more bus commuters to using their automobiles, thus worsening the bus revenue situation.

This second feedback has two possible outcomes. In the most drastic case, each attempt by the bus line to adjust to lower passenger revenues by raising fares or cutting service causes so many more passengers to switch to automobiles that another adjustment is required, which causes more passengers to quit riding, thus requiring another adjustment, etc., until the bus line goes bankrupt and ceases operation.[4] However, it is unlikely that construction of any one expressway in a city will cause its bus lines to go bankrupt. Each expressway serves only a part of the entire metropolitan area; whereas its bus routes usually serve a much larger portion of the area. Therefore a very slight fare increase over the whole bus system would probably compensate for a very large withdrawal of cutomers in the section competing with the expressway. For this reason, the shifts in modes of transportation caused by the opening of one new expressway are likely to bring about a new equilibrium at a point where most of the bus service extant before the expressway appeared is still in effect.

But completion of a whole series of new expressways in one city may produce a very serious cumulative effect upon the city's bus system. If all of these expressways together serve almost the entire area also served by the bus system, the total withdrawal of commuting bus passengers into private automobile commuting may be very large indeed. Hence the downward spiral into bankruptcy described above may actually occur. Because not many U. S. cities have whole networks of expressways serving commuters in all parts of their metropolitan areas, the results of this process are not yet clear. Of course, insofar as any revenue losses induced by new expressways are made up through subsidies to the bus lines, no spiral effect such as that described above will occur.

Assuming that some bus lines are still operating after a new equilibrium point is established, this equilibrium will have the following characteristics in relation to the pre-expressway situation:

1. Commuting time will be less than before the expressway opened for all commuters.

2. A smaller proportion of all commuters will ride buses to and from work, and a larger proportion will use automobiles.

3. Either the per person, per mile cost of providing bus service will have risen because of fewer passengers, or total bus service will have been curtailed, or both.

4. Because more automobiles will be used in commuting than formerly, a smaller improvement in traffic congestion (and hence a smaller reduction in commuting time) will have occurred than

4. The ultimate equilibrium point (even if it occurs only when the bus operator becomes bankrupt) is essentially determined by the immediate shift in the demand for bus service caused by the opening of the new expressway. If the demand curve for bus service shifts completely to the left of the average total cost curve of the bus company, bankruptcy will inevitably result eventually. If not, equilibrium will eventually be established with some buses still running. The spiral of repeated fare increases and passenger losses which I have described is simply the process by which the bus company discovers the new equilibrium point (which may be bankruptcy). The spiral thus does not *cause* such an equilibrium to come into being. I am indebted to Professor Donald Bear of the University of Chicago for pointing out this relationship.

would have been the case if the same number of commuters used automobiles as before the expressway was opened.

CASE C: A CITY WITH SEGREGATED TRACK PUBLIC TRANSIT AND AUTO-DRIVING COMMUTERS

The third major type of commuter transportation (besides autos and buses) employed in the United States is transit with segregated tracks. That is, its rails or roadways are separated from other land uses and other forms of transportation (including streets) by elevation, depression, or fencing. Such transit includes subway trains, elevated trains, and steam and diesel-electric railroad trains. These forms of transportation all have one crucial characteristic in common: since their rights-of-way are completely separated from automobile traffic, the level of automobile congestion has no direct effect upon their speed or efficiency.

In a city served by such segregated track transit facilities, the effects of the opening of a new expressway are initially the same as those described in the two preceding sections. Traffic congestion falls on all city streets, and the expressway experiences heavy peak-hour congestion, but all street-using commuters (including those on buses and streetcars) spend less time en route than they did before the expressway opened. However, because the fall in traffic congestion on city streets has no effect whatsoever on the speed of vehicles using segregated tracks, commuters riding such vehicles experience no reduction in commuting time. *Thus there is a sharp change in the relative desirability of automobiles versus segregated track transit—a change favoring automobiles.* Consequently, many commuters who formerly used segregated track transit shift to automobiles.

Furthermore, the expressway cuts even more deeply into the segregated track system's noncommuter traffic. During rush hours, the expressway becomes extremely crowded, as indicated in previous sections of this analysis. But between rush periods, the expressway provides a relatively congestion-free, high-speed means for shoppers and other noncommuting travelers to move to and from the downtown area; hence it constitutes a dramatic improvement over pre-existing streets or other means of transit. This improvement creates a sharp disequilibrium in the previous distribution of noncommuting passengers among means of transportation—one proportionally much greater than the corresponding disequilibrium concerning commuters. Therefore a great many non-peak-hour travelers shift from fixed-rail transit to automobiles. As a result, the total passenger load of the fixed-rail, segregated track system becomes more and more concentrated in rush hours.

The New York subway system provides a striking illustration of this tendency. In the period from 1948 to 1956, the number of subway passengers entering the Manhattan business district on a typical business day during the morning rush hours (from 7:00 A.M. to 10:00 A.M.) fell 11.7 per cent. But during the other 21 hours of the day, inbound passenger loads dropped 20.8 per cent. These figures reflect both impacts of increased automobile usage upon segregated track transit: a decline in over-all traffic, and a much heavier concentration of the remaining traffic in a few peak hours.[5]

These two impacts reduce both the total revenue accruing to the system and its efficiency in terms of cost per passenger per mile. As revenues fall and costs rise, the system finds itself in a perilous "squeeze." Its usual reactions are increases in fares and reductions in service or both. As with bus travel, these adjustments often cause further withdrawals of passengers from the system.

A dramatic example is provided by the Chicago and Northwestern Railway. Often cited in recent years as a model of commuter service modernization, the Chicago and Northwestern was making a small profit on its suburban passenger business before two new expressways opened in late 1960. Each of these superroads paralleled a set of existing Chicago and Northwestern tracks connecting downtown Chicago with outlying areas. Within three months after these two expressways opened, the railroad's suburban passenger traffic declined 9.6 per cent. Furthermore, this fall in traffic shifted the results of over-all suburban passenger operations from a profit to a loss.[6]

5. Edgar M. Hoover and Raymond Vernon, *Anatomy of a Metropolis*, Harvard University Press, 1959, Cambridge, p. 218.
6. Figures taken from a statement made by Mr. Larry S. Provo, Vice President and Comptroller, at a hearing before the Interstate Commerce Commission concerning the future of the Chicago and North Shore Railroad. Mr. Provo emphasized that the loss of passengers indicated was not a result of the general economic recession of 1960–1961, since the number of suburban passengers on the Chicago and Northwestern Railway had been rising in the recession months before the expressways opened, and also rose during the previous recessions of 1953–1954 and 1957–1958.

In any city where the number of nonautomobile commuters is relatively large, the shift from other means of commuting to automobiles may become extremely significant, especially if a whole network of expressways is built converging on the downtown area. Some of our larger metropolises still have sizable pools of such potential "shifters" riding segregated track transit. In Chicago, about 45 percent of all persons entering the central business district on a typical day in 1959 used such transit.[7] In New York, 66 percent of all persons entering the Manhattan business district on a typical business day in 1956 traveled on segregated track facilities.[8] However, the number of persons using this type of transit is steadily declining as the automobile gains in popularity. Thus the percentage of persons entering Manhattan's central business district by auto and taxi rose from 15.7 in 1948 to 22.2 in 1956; whereas the percentage using segregated track transit fell from 72.4 to 66.4 during the same period.[9]

As more and more commuters start using their automobiles to reach work, the level of traffic congestion begins to return to the level existing before the expressway improved traffic conditions. Theoretically, such shifting could continue until the original automobile commuting time was re-established in spite of the added capacity introduced by the expressway

Since the time required for commuting by rail is not changed by the introduction of the expressway, it would seem that the original equilibrium would reappear when the initial automobile commuting time was again required. But the original situation can never return. The new expressway has absorbed a great many former riders of segregated track transit, thereby permanently lowering the number of passengers using such transit. Therefore, even if congestion on the expressway rises so high that the original automobile commuting time is restored, the number of passengers riding segregated track transit at that point is much lower than it was before the expressway opened. Because of the high fixed costs in transit operations, such a fall in total traffic almost always raises

---

7. *Chicago Area Transportation Study*, Volume II. Study conducted under the sponsorship of the State of Illinois, County of Cook, and City of Chicago in cooperation with the U.S. Department of Commerce. Chicago, 1961.

8. Hoover and Vernon, *op. cit.*, 217.

9. *Ibid.*

PEAK-HOUR EXPRESSWAY CONGESTION

the average cost per passenger. Thus when total passenger traffic falls, and that which remains becomes more concentrated during peak hours, segregated track transit firms are forced to raise fares or reduce service or both, as noted before. These changes diminish the attractiveness of their service compared to automobile transportation.

If a very large number of persons shift from segregated track transit to automobiles, the cost of such transit per passenger may rise so high that its attractiveness is drastically reduced. In such a case, congestion on the highways may have to become slightly worse than it was before the expressway was opened before automobile travel becomes just as undesirable as segregated track transit travel. But only the marginal equality of these two undesirabilities can establish a new equilibrium. We thus arrive at the paradoxical conclusion that the opening of an expressway could conceivably cause traffic congestion to become worse instead of better, and automobile commuting times to rise instead of fall!

In fact, this result is almost a certainty if the segregated track transit firms are caught in the kind of downward spiral into bankruptcy described in connection with buses. For if these firms actually go bankrupt and are forced to withdraw their services from the market altogether, all commuters formerly riding them will have to use automobiles or buses, and congestion on the streets will rise to record levels. The recent bankruptcy of the New York, New Haven and Hartford Railroad shows that this analysis is by no means purely theoretical. Of course, if government agencies or public receivers take over the bankrupt transit facilities and run them at a loss, this drastic outcome would be prevented.

However, it is probably likely that a new equilibrium will be established before highway traffic congestion has reached its pre-expressway level. But even in such cases, the expressway will be extremely crowded during peak hours—almost certainly loaded beyond its optimal capacity. Therefore the basic "Law" propounded at the beginning of this article—congestion rises to meet maximum capacity—will still hold true.

When a new equilibrium is finally established, it will have the following characteristics in relation to the pre-expressway situation:

1. A larger proportion of all commuters will use automobiles,

and a significantly smaller proportion will use segregated track transit.

2. Passenger loads on segregated track transit will not only be smaller; they will also be more heavily concentrated during peak travel hours.

3. The aforementioned load changes will raise the per person, per mile cost of providing segregated track transit.

4. Segregated track transit facilities will have made a stable adjustment to their higher costs and lower revenues in one of the following ways:

a. By raising fares.

b. By reducing service.

c. By accepting lower profits (or greater losses), whether or not compensated by more subsidies.

d. By some combination of the above.

e. By going out of business.

5. Peak-hour congestion and average commuting time per trip on city streets other than the expressway may be less than, equal to, or greater than it was before the expressway opened, depending upon the shift of commuters from nonautomobile to automobile commuting.

6. Peak-hour congestion on the new expressway will surpass its optimal capacity; hence the average *speed* of commuters using it will probably be lower than the average speed of those using alternative routes on older city streets (although the total commuting *time* for both will be the same), even if the average commuting *time* for all auto-driving commuters has fallen.

MORE PEOPLE AND MORE CARS

Throughout the preceding analysis, we have assumed that both the number of commuters and automobile ownership among them were the same before and after the expressway was opened. Removal of these two assumptions raises still further the probability that a new expressway will be overcongested during rush hours.

In spite of the explosive population growth in most U.S. metropolitan areas during the past twenty years, the number of persons in each major city commuting daily between outlying areas and the central business district has not always risen. In Chicago, for example, the total number of persons entering the central business district during a typical day in May declined from 1947 to 1959 by about 8 percent. However, the number of persons using automobiles to enter the same area during the same periods has risen about 15 percent.[10] Figures for New York City show similar trends.[11] This greater use of automobiles for commuting is only partly the result of new expressways. Actually, Chicago's two largest nonstop expressways for commuters were not opened until late in 1960; hence they have just begun to affect commuting patterns and are not reflected in the above statistics.

The primary causes of the shift to automobiles shown by these statistics are (1) higher automobile ownership and use and (2) the isolation of new areas of population growth from nonautomobile transit. From 1947 to 1959, automobile registration in the City of Chicago rose 67 percent; whereas total population did not rise at all. Within all of Cook and Du Page counties (including Chicago), automobile registration jumped 96 percent, whereas population increased only about 22 percent.[12] For the nation as a whole, motor vehicle registration from 1945 to 1959 rose by 130 percent to a total of 71.5 million vehicles, but population increased by only 33 percent.[13]

Thus, throughout the nation, the tremendous increase in ownership of automobiles during the postwar period has markedly raised the inclination of commuters to drive to work. Furthermore, low-density suburban housing has spread across the landscape into many areas quite distant from the nearest nonautomobile transportation. In such places, use of automobiles for getting at least part way to and from work is absolutely essential.

If we introduce into our model of commuting behavior analogous changes in (1) automobile ownership, (2) total population, and (3) population distribution, our conclusions regarding peak-hour overcrowding on expressways are strongly reinforced. Furthermore, automobile ownership is expected to continue rising rapidly,

10. *Cordon Count Data of the Central Business District*, Bureau of Street Traffic, City of Chicago, 1961. Table 3.
11. Hoover and Vernon, *op. cit.*, 217.
12. *Chicago Area Transportation Study, op. cit.*
13. U.S. Bureau of the Census, *Statistical Abstract of the United States: 1960.* 81st edition. Washington, D.C., 1960, pp. 5, 560.

especially if real incomes continue to increase. The conclusion is inescapable that peak-hour traffic congestion on commuter expressways is likely to increase throughout the foreseeable future.

All of the preceding analysis is based upon the axioms concerning commuter behavior stated early in this article. If those axioms accurately describe the way commuters behave in the real world, our analysis leads to the following major conclusions:

1. Peak-hour traffic congestion on any expressway linking a central business district and outlying areas will almost always rise to surpass the optimal capacity of the expressway.

2. Therefore, in relatively large metropolitan areas, it is impossible to build expressways wide enough to carry rush-hour traffic at the speed and congestion levels normally considered optimal for such roads. The forces of traffic equilibrium will inevitably produce enough overcrowding to drive the actual average speed during peak hours to a level below the optimal speed.

3. Commuters driving on expressways should resign themselves to encountering heavy traffic congestion every day, even though they may spend less time commuting than they did before using expressways.

4. Since urban expressways cannot be designed large enough to eliminate rush-hour traffic congestion, other design goals must be employed to decide how large a capacity each such expressway should have. The only goal regarding commuting which is feasible is reduction of the average amount of time spent by commuters per trip. Low congestion and optimal speeds during nonpeak hours probably constitute much more practical goals for the design of urban expressways than any goal connected with rush-hour traffic movements.

5. Under certain conditions, the opening of an expressway may make rush-hour traffic congestion worse than before the expressway was built. This outcome can occur only in cities in which a high proportion of commuter traffic is carried by segregated track transportation facilities before the expressway is opened.

6. Thus any program of expressway planning and construction must be integrated with similar programs concerning other forms of transit in the area if it is not to cause unforeseen and possible deleterious effects upon the level of automobile traffic congestion

PEAK-HOUR EXPRESSWAY CONGESTION

therein. In particular, marked improvement of roads without any improvement in segregated track transit may cause automobile traffic congestion to get worse instead of better. Since the U. S. has already launched a massive road improvement program, which includes construction of many urban expressways, continued failure to undertake an analogous program for other forms of urban commuter transit may result in a generally higher level of rush-hour automobile traffic congestion in those cities which now have extensive segregated track transit facilities serving commuters. Therefore such possibilities as the charging of direct tolls on expressways and the expenditure of auto toll collections or gasoline tax revenues on segregated track transit should be thoroughly explored as means of developing a *balanced* urban transportation system.

[2]

ANTHONY DOWNS

Alternative Futures for the American Ghetto

IN THE past few years, the so-called "ghetto" areas of large American cities have emerged as one of the major focal points of national and local concern. Yet there have been very few attempts to develop a comprehensive, long-run strategy for dealing with the complex forces that have created our explosive ghetto problems.

Historically, the word "ghetto" meant an area in which a certain identifiable group was compelled to live. The word retains this meaning of geographic constraint, but now refers to two different kinds of constraining forces. In its *racial* sense, a ghetto is an area to which members of an ethnic minority, particularly Negroes, are residentially restricted by social, economic, and physical pressures from the rest of society. In this meaning, a ghetto can contain wealthy and middle-income residents as well as poor ones. In its *economic* sense, a ghetto is an area in which poor people are compelled to live because they cannot afford better accommodations. In this meaning, a ghetto contains mainly poor people, regardless of race or color.

Considerable confusion arises from failure to distinguish clearly between these different meanings of the word "ghetto." In the remainder of this analysis, I will use the word in its racial sense unless otherwise noted.[1]

The Population of Ghettos

In March 1966, there were 12.5 million nonwhites living in all U.S. central cities, of whom 12.1 million were Negroes. Since the Negroes were highly segregated residentially, this number serves as a good estimate of the 1966 ghetto population in the racial sense. Approximately 39 per cent of these racial ghetto residents had incomes below the "poverty level" (the equivalent of $3,300

1331

per year for a four-person household), based upon data for 1964 (the latest available).[2]

On the other hand, in 1964 the total number of persons with incomes below the "poverty level" in all U.S. central cities was about 10.1 million. Approximately 56 per cent of these persons were white and 44 per cent were nonwhite.[3] Since there were about 11.3 million nonwhites altogether in central cities in 1964, the ghetto in its purely economic sense contained about 11 per cent fewer people than in its racial sense. Moreover, about 4.4 million persons were doubly ghetto residents in 1964—they were central-city citizens who were both poor and nonwhite.[4]

No matter which ghetto definition is used, it is clear that the population of ghettos is a small fraction of total U.S. population—less than 7 per cent. Moreover, future growth in the ghetto population will be dwarfed by future growth in the suburbs of metropolitan areas, which are predominantly white. From 1960 through 1980, those suburbs will gain about 40.9 million persons.[5] Thus the *growth* of suburban population in this period will be almost twice as large as the *total size* of all U.S. ghettos by 1980.

Any policies designed to cope with the ghetto must recognize that the concentrations of Negro population in our central cities are growing rapidly. In 1950, there were 6.5 million Negroes in central cities. In 1960, there were 9.7 million. This represents an increase of 49.2 per cent, or an average of 320,000 persons per year. In the same decade, the white population of central cities went from 45.5 million to 47.7 million, an increase of 2.2 million, or 4.8 per cent. However, in the largest central cities, the white population actually declined while the Negro population rose sharply.[6]

Since 1960, the growth of nonwhite population in central cities has continued unabated. White population growth in all those cities taken together has, however, ceased entirely. In 1966 the total Negro population of all central cities was about 12.1 million. This is a gain of 2.4 million since 1960, or about 400,000 persons per year. Thus the *absolute* rate of growth of ghettos per year has gone up to its highest level in history. In contrast, the white population of central cities in 1965 was 46.4 million, or 1.3 million *less* than in 1960. So for all 224 central cities considered as a whole, all population growth now consists of gains in Negro population.[7]

Moreover, nearly all Negro population growth is now occurring in ghettos, rather than in suburbs or rural areas. From 1960 to 1966,

Alternative Futures for the American Ghetto

89 per cent of all nonwhite population growth was in central cities, and 11 per cent was in suburbs. Nonmetropolitan areas (including the rural South) actually *lost* nonwhite population. This indicates that heavy out-migration from rural areas to cities is still going on.[8]

Future Ghetto Growth If Present Policies Continue

All evidence points to the conclusion that future nonwhite population growth will continue to be concentrated in central cities unless major changes in public policies are made. Not one single significant program of any federal, state, or local government is aimed at altering this tendency or is likely to have the unintended effect of doing so.[9] Moreover, although nonwhite fertility rates have declined since 1957 along with white fertility rates, ghetto growth is likely to remain rapid because of continued in-migration, as well as natural increase.

Recent estimates made by the National Advisory Commission on Civil Disorders indicate that the central-city Negro population for the whole U.S. will be about 13.6 million in 1970 and could rise to as high as 20.3 million by 1985. These estimates assume continued nonwhite in-migration at about the same rate as prevailed from 1960 to 1966. But even if net in-migration is reduced to zero, the 1985 central-city Negro population would be about 17.3 million.[10]

Within individual cities, rapid expansion of segregated ghetto areas will undoubtedly continue. Our 1967 field surveys in Chicago show that about 2.9 city blocks *per week* are shifting from predominantly white to nonwhite occupancy, mainly on the edge of already nonwhite areas. This is somewhat lower than the 3.5 blocks-per-week average from 1960 to 1966, but above the average of 2.6 from 1950 to 1960.[11] If such "peripheral spread" of central-city ghettos continues at nearly the same rate—and there is no present reason to believe it will not—then a number of major central cities will become over 50 per cent Negro in total population by 1985. These cities include Chicago, Philadelphia, St. Louis, Detroit, Cleveland, Oakland, Baltimore, New Orleans, Richmond, and Jacksonville. Washington, D.C., Newark, and Gary are already over 50 per cent Negro. The proportion of nonwhites in the public school systems in most of these cities now exceeds 50 per cent. It will probably be approaching 90 per cent by 1983—unless major changes in school programs and districting are adopted before then.¹²

This future growth has critical implications for a great many policy objectives connected with ghettos. For example, it has been suggested that school district boundaries within central cities should be manipulated so as to counteract *de facto* segregation by creating districts in which many Negroes and many whites will jointly reside. This solution is practical over the long run only when there is reasonable stability in the total size of these two groups. But when one group is rapidly expanding in a city where there is no vacant land to build additional housing, then the other group must contract. The only alternative is sharp rises in density which are not occurring. Therefore, as the Negro population expands in such cities, the white population inevitably falls. So possibilities for ending *de facto* segregation in this manner inexorably shrink as time passes. For this and other reasons, no policy toward ghettos can afford to ignore this rapid expansion of the Negro population.

The Complexity of the Ghetto Population and Ghetto Problems

To be accurate, every analysis of ghettos and their problems must avoid two tempting oversimplifications. The first is conceiving of the ghetto population as a single homogeneous group, all of whose members have similar characteristics, attitudes, and desires. Thus, because many ghetto residents are unemployed or "underemployed" in low-paying, transient jobs, it is easy—but false— to think of all ghetto households as plagued by unemployment. Similarly, because some ghetto residents have carried out riots and looting, whites frequently talk as though *all* ghetto dwellers hate whites, are prone to violence, or are likely to behave irresponsibly. Yet all careful studies of recent riots show that only a small minority of ghetto residents participated in any way, a majority disapprove of such activity, and most would like to have more contact with whites and more integration.¹³

In reality, each racial ghetto contains a tremendous variety of persons who exhibit widely differing attitudes toward almost every question. Many are very poor, but just as many are not. Many have radical views—especially young people; many others are quite conservative—especially the older people. Many are "on welfare," but many more are steadily employed.

Alternative Futures for the American Ghetto

This diversity means that public policy concerning any given ghetto problem cannot be successful if it is aimed at or based upon the attitudes and desires of only one group of persons affected by that problem. For example, take unemployment. Programs providing job training for young people could, if expanded enough, affect a large proportion of ghetto dwellers. But the inability of many adult ghetto men to obtain and keep steady, well-paying jobs is also a critical ghetto problem.[14] Also, many women with children cannot work because no adequate day-care facilities are available. Thus, public policy concerning every ghetto problem must have many complex facets in order to work well.

A second widely prevalent oversimplification of ghetto problems is concentration of remedial action upon a single substandard condition. For instance, improving the deplorable housing conditions in many slums would not in itself eliminate most of the de-humanizing forces which operate there. In fact, no single category of programs can possibly be adequate to cope with the tangled problems that exist in ghettos. Any effective ghetto-improvement strategy must concern itself with at least jobs and employment, education, housing, health, personal safety, crime prevention, and income maintenance for dependent persons. A number of other programs could be added, but I believe these are the most critical.[15]

The Location of New Jobs

Most new employment opportunities are being created in the suburban portions of our metropolitan areas, not anywhere near central-city ghettos.[16] Furthermore, this trend is likely to continue indefinitely into the future. It is true that downtown office-space concentrations in a few large cities have created additional jobs near ghettos. But the out-flow of manufacturing and retailing jobs has normally offset this addition significantly—and in many cases has caused a net loss of jobs in central cities.

If we are going to provide jobs for the rapidly expanding ghetto population, particularly jobs that do not call for high levels of skills, we must somehow bring these potential workers closer to the locations of new employment opportunities. This can be done in three ways: by moving job locations so new jobs are created in the ghetto, by moving ghetto residents so they live nearer the new jobs, or by creating better transportation between the ghetto and the locations of new jobs. The first alternative—creating new jobs in the ghetto—will not occur in the future under normal free-market conditions, in my opinion.

That nearly all *new* job opportunities will be located in suburbs does not mean that central cities cannot provide *any* employment to their Negro residents. There are still millions of jobs located in central cities. Just the turnover in workers regarding those jobs will open up a great many potential positions for Negro central-city residents in the future—if employers and other workers cease racial discrimination in their hiring and promotion practices. Nevertheless, as the total number of Negro central-city job-seekers steadily rises, the need to link them with emerging sources of new employment in the suburbs will become more and more urgent as a means of reducing unemployment in Negro neighborhoods.

Recently, a number of proposals have been advanced to create public subsidies or guaranteed profits encouraging free enterprise to locate new jobs in ghettos.[17] It is possible that they might work to some extent if the promised profits are high enough to offset the risks and disadvantages involved. Any ghetto improvement strategy must, however, face the problem of linking up persons who need employment with those firms which can provide it or those public agencies assigned to create it.

The Future "Cost Squeeze" on Local Governments

Traditionally, individual productivity has risen faster in the manufacturing, mining, construction, and agricultural sectors of our economy than in sectors where personal services are dominant —such as finance, insurance, and real estate; retailing; services; and government. The ability to employ larger amounts of capital per worker, coupled with technological change, has caused much larger increases in hourly output-per-worker in the former sectors than in the latter.

All sectors compete with one another for talent and personnel, and all use many of the same products as basic inputs. This means that wages and salaries in the service-dominated sectors must generally keep up with those in the capital-dominated sectors. This tends to place a "squeeze" on the cost of those activities for which individual productivity is hard to increase.

A recent analysis of the performing arts by economists William

Alternative Futures for the American Ghetto

Baumol and William Bowen highlighted this type of "cost squeeze" as the major reason why it is so difficult to sustain theaters, opera, symphonies, and ballet companies on a self-supporting basis.[18] A pianist cannot perform Chopin's Minute Waltz in 30 seconds, or spend half as much time learning how to play it, to improve efficiency. Yet his salary and the salaries of all the electricians, accompanists, administrators, and others needed for the performing arts are constantly raised to keep their living standards comparable with those of people in the sectors where wage gains can be offset by productivity increases.

Baumol has argued that a similar "cost squeeze" is one of the reasons why state and local expenditures have risen so fast in the postwar period. They increased 257 per cent from 1950 to 1966, as compared to 159 per cent for Gross National Product and 206 per cent for federal expenditures.[19] Moreover, Baumol believes that this pressure to increase service-oriented wages and salaries faster than real output-per-man-hour in the service-oriented sectors will generate an even bigger "explosion" of local and state government costs in the future. For one thing, a higher fraction of society is now and will be employed in public activities than ever before. So there is a steady increase in the proportion of persons whose compensation tends to rise faster than their real output. This reflects both rapid automation in non-service-oriented sectors and an increasing shift of consumer demand toward such services as education, entertainment, and government activities of all types.

The resulting upward pressure on local and state government costs—and tax needs—will undoubtedly be offset to some extent by two forces. The first is greater automation of services themselves through use of computers, closed-circuit TV, duplicating machines, and other devices. The second is the partial substitution of semiskilled and low-skilled assistants for highly-skilled professionals. For example, teachers' aids could relieve professional teachers of immense amounts of administration and paperwork, thereby freeing the latter for more effective use of their time.

Nevertheless, the huge future growth of suburban population will almost certainly force a continuance of the trend toward rising local and state taxes that has now gone on for twenty years. Similar upward pressure on revenue needs will be felt even more strongly by central-city governments. Center cities will contain ever higher proportions of low-income residents who need more services per capita than wealthier suburbanites.

This future "cost squeeze" is important to our analysis because of its impact upon the willingness of suburban taxpayers to help finance any large-scale programs aimed at improving ghetto conditions. Such programs would almost certainly require significant income redistribution from the relatively wealthy suburban population to the relatively poor central-city population. Yet suburbanites will be experiencing steadily rising local and state tax burdens to pay for the services they need themselves.

The "Law of Dominance"

The achievement of stable racial integration of both whites and nonwhites in housing or public schools is a rare phenomenon in large American cities. Contrary to the views of many, this is *not* because whites are unwilling to share schools or residential neighborhoods with nonwhites. A vast majority of whites of all income groups would be willing to send their children to integrated schools or live in integrated neighborhoods, *as long as they were sure that the white group concerned would remain in the majority* in those facilities or areas.

The residential and educational objectives of these whites are not dependent upon their maintaining any kind of "ethnic purity" in their neighborhoods or schools. Rather, those objectives depend upon their maintaining a certain degree of "cultural dominance" therein.[20] These whites—like most other middle-class citizens of any race—want to be sure that the social, cultural, and economic milieu and values of their own group dominate their own residential environment and the educational environment of their children. This desire in turn springs from the typical middle-class belief of all racial groups that everyday life should be primarily a *value-reinforcing* experience for both adults and children, rather than primarily a *value-altering* one. The best way to insure that this will happen is to isolate somewhat oneself and one's children in an everyday environment dominated by—but not necessarily exclusively comprised of—other families and children whose social, economic, cultural, and even religious views and attitudes are approximately the same as one's own.

There is no intrinsic reason why race or color should be perceived as a factor relevant to attaining such relative homogeneity. Clearly, race and color have no necessary linkage with the kinds of social, cultural, economic, or religious characteristics and values that can have a true functional impact upon adults and children. Yet I believe a majority of middle-class white Americans still perceive race and color as relevant factors in their assessment of the kind of homogeneity they seek to attain. Moreover, this false perception is reinforced by their lack of everyday experience and contact with Negroes who are, in fact, like them in all important respects. Therefore, in deciding whether a given neighborhood or a given school exhibits the kind of environment in which "their own" traits are and will remain dominant, they consider Negroes as members of "another" group.

It is true that some people want themselves and their children to be immersed in a wide variety of viewpoints, values, and types of people, rather than a relatively homogeneous group.[21] This desire is particularly strong among the intellectuals who dominate the urban planning profession. They are also the strongest supporters of big-city life and the most vitriolic critics of suburbia. Yet I believe their viewpoint—though dominant in recent public discussions of urban problems—is actually shared by only a tiny minority of Americans of any racial group. Almost everyone favors at least some exposure to a wide variety of viewpoints. But experience in our own society and most others shows that the overwhelming majority of middle-class families choose residential locations and schools precisely in order to provide the kind of value-reinforcing experience described above. This is why most Jews live in predominantly Jewish neighborhoods, even in suburbs; why Catholic parents continue to support separate school systems; and partly why so few middle-class Negro families have been willing to risk moving to all-white suburbs even where there is almost no threat of any harassment.

However demeaning this phenomenon may be to Negroes, it must be recognized if we are to understand why residential segregation has persisted so strongly in the United States, and what conditions are necessary to create viable racial integration. The expansion of nonwhite residential areas has led to "massive transition" from white to nonwhite occupancy mainly because there has been no mechanism that could assure the whites in any given area that they would remain in the majority after nonwhites once began entering. Normal population turnover causes about 20 per cent of the residents of the average U.S. neighborhood to move out every year because of income changes, job transfers, shifts in life-cycle position, or deaths. In order for a neighborhood to retain any given character, the persons who move in to occupy the resulting vacancies must be similar to those who have departed.

But once Negroes begin entering an all-white neighborhood near the ghetto, most other white families become convinced that the area will eventually become all Negro, mainly because this has happened so often before. Hence it is difficult to persuade whites not now living there to move in and occupy vacancies. They are only willing to move into neighborhoods where whites are now the dominant majority and seem likely to remain so. Hence the whites who would otherwise have moved in from elsewhere stop doing so.[22] This means that almost all vacancies are eventually occupied by nonwhites, and the neighborhood inexorably shifts toward a heavy nonwhite majority. Once this happens, the remaining whites also seek to leave, since they do not wish to remain in an area where they have lost their culturally dominant position.

As a result, whites who would be quite satisfied—even delighted—to live in an integrated neighborhood *as members of the majority* are never given the opportunity to do so. Instead, for reasons beyond the control of each individual, they are forced to choose between complete segregation or living in an area heavily dominated by members of what they consider "another group." Given their values, they choose the former.

Many—especially Negroes—may deplore the racially prejudiced desire of most white middle-class citizens to live in neighborhoods and use schools where other white middle-class households are dominant. Nevertheless, this desire seems to be firmly entrenched among most whites at present. Hence public policy cannot ignore this desire if it hopes to be effective. Moreover, this attitude does not preclude the development of racial integration, as long as whites are in the majority and believe they will remain so. The problem is convincing them that their majority status will persist in mixed areas in the face of past experience to the contrary. Even more difficult, the people who must be persuaded are not those now living in a mixed area, but those who must keep moving in from elsewhere to maintain racial balance as vacancies occur through normal population turnover.

Clearly, the dynamic processes related to this "Law of Dominance" are critical to any strategy concerning the future of American ghettos. They are especially relevant to strategies which seek to achieve stable residential or educational integration of whites and nonwhites, instead of the "massive transition" and "massive segregation" which have dominated the spatial patterns of nonwhite population growth in the past twenty years. Such stable integration will occur in most areas only if there is some way to guarantee the white majority that it will remain the "dominant" majority. This implies some form of "quotas" concerning the proportion of nonwhites in the facility or area concerned—even legally supported "quotas."

Unless some such "balancing devices" are *explicitly* used and reinforced by public policies and laws to establish their credibility, whites will continue to withdraw from—or, more crucially, fail to keep entering—any facility or area into which significant numbers of nonwhites are entering. This means a continuation of *de facto* segregation and a reinforcement of the white belief that any nonwhite entry inevitably leads to "massive transition." Even more importantly, it means continued failure to eliminate white perception of race as a critical factor by encouraging whites and nonwhites to live together in conditions of stability. Thus, in my opinion, the only way to destroy the racial prejudice at the root of the "Law of Cultural Dominance" is to shape current public policy in recognition of that "Law" so as to encourage widespread experience that will undermine it.[23]

The Concept of Social Strategy

Americans typically do not attempt to solve social problems by means of behavior patterns that could reasonably be considered "strategies." The concept of strategy implies development of a single comprehensive, long-range plan to cope with some significant social problem. But U.S. decision-making concerning domestic issues is too fragmented and diffused to permit the formulation of any such long-range plan regarding a given problem. Instead, we approach most social problems through a process which has been aptly labeled "disjointed incrementalism."[24] Each decision-maker or actor makes whatever choices seem to him to be most appropriate at that moment, in light of his own interests and his own view of the public welfare. For two reasons, he pays little attention to most of the consequences of his action upon others—especially the long-run consequences. First, no one has the detailed knowledge and foresight necessary to comprehend all those consequences. Second, no one has the time nor the energy to negotiate in advance with all others likely to be affected by his actions. So instead he acts "blindly" and waits for those who are hurt to complain or those who are benefited to applaud.

A process of mutual adjustment ensues. Those who are unduly harmed by each decision supposedly recoup their losses by exercising whatever economic, moral, or political powers are available to them. Those who benefit use their powers to encourage more of the same. Presiding over this melee is a set of mainly "reactive" governments and other public agencies. They keep altering the "rules of the game" and their own programs and behavior so as to correct any grievous imbalances that appear.

There is no guarantee that the checks and balances built into this uncoordinated process will effectively counteract every destructive condition or trend that emerges from it. It is certainly possible that each individual will be motivated by the incentives facing him to take actions that, when combined with those taken by others acting in a similar individualistic fashion, will lead to collective disaster.

So far in history, the system has been remarkably effective at avoiding such outcomes. Part of this success undoubtedly results from society's ability to generate in most of its citizens a single set of basic values and even broad policy objectives that exert a cohesive influence on their supposedly individualistic decisions. But another important ingredient in the system's success is the ability of enough significant actors in it to perceive threatening trends in time to formulate and carry out ameliorating policies.

This means they must accurately forecast any potentially dire outcome of current trends. They must also visualize alternative outcomes that would be preferable and are within the capabilities of society. Finally, they must devise policies and programs that will shift individual incentives so one of those alternatives will occur. In some cases, the ongoing trends that threaten society are strongly entrenched in its institutional structure. If so, alternatives that avoid the pending threats may not be attainable without fundamental changes in institutions. Those changes in turn may be possible only if a preponderance of powerful people in society share at least a broad concept of the need for change and the kinds of objectives motivating it. This concept closely resembles a social strategy. It visualizes a certain desired outcome, implies a wide range of policies by various actors necessary to attain that outcome, and serves as a "hidden coordinator" of seemingly individualistic behavior.

Alternative Futures for the American Ghetto

The above reasoning implies two conclusions crucial to this analysis. First, strategic thinking about social problems can play a vital role in stimulating social change even where decision-making is dominated by disjointed incrementalism. Second, the alternative outcomes conceived in such thinking can usefully include some which could not be achieved without major changes in existing institutions or values. For example, some of the strategies discussed herein require a highly coordinated set of policy decisions. Such coordination is unlikely to occur in the presently fragmentalized governmental structures of our metropolitan areas unless major changes in the incentives facing these governments are created.

I will therefore formulate several alternative strategies for coping with the problems posed by future ghetto growth, even though carrying out some of them would require a far more consciously coordinated development of social change than has been typical of America in the past.

Formulation of Major Alternative Strategies

Because of the immense complexity of our society, an infinite number of alternative future strategies regarding ghettos could conceivably be designed. But for purposes of practical consideration, this number must be narrowed drastically to a few that highlight the major choices facing us. Selecting these few is inescapably arbitrary—there is no "scientific" way to do it. I believe, however, that the narrowing of alternative ghetto futures can best be accomplished by focusing upon the major choices relating to the following three questions:

> To what extent should future nonwhite population growth be concentrated within the central cities, as it has been in the past twenty years?
>
> To what extent should our white and nonwhite populations be residentially segregated from each other in the future?
>
> To what extent should society redistribute income to relatively depressed urban areas or population groups in society in a process of "enrichment"?

Each of these questions can be answered with any one of a whole spectrum of responses from one extreme to the other. But for purposes of analysis, I believe we can usefully narrow these answers down to just two points on the spectrum for each question. This allows us to reduce the alternatives to the following:

Degree-of-Concentration Alternatives
1. Continue to concentrate nonwhite population growth in central cities or perhaps in a few older suburbs next to central cities. *(Concentration)*
2. Disperse nonwhite population growth widely throughout all parts of metropolitan areas. *(Dispersal)*

Degree-of-Segregation Alternatives
1. Continue to cluster whites and nonwhites in residentially segregated neighborhoods, regardless of where they are within the metropolitan area. *(Segregation)*
2. Scatter the nonwhite population, or at least a significant fraction of it, "randomly" among white residential areas to achieve at least partial residential integration. *(Integration)*

Degree-of-Enrichment Alternatives
1. Continue to provide relatively low-level welfare, educational, housing, job training, and other support to the most deprived groups in the population—both those who are incapable of working, such as the vast majority of public-aid recipients, and those who might possibly work, but are unemployed because of lack of skills, discrimination, lack of desire, or any other reason. *(Non-enrichment)*
2. Greatly raise the level of support to welfare, educational, housing, job-training, and other programs for the most deprived groups, largely through federally aided programs. *(Enrichment)*

Even narrowing the alternatives in this fashion leaves a logical possibility of eight different combinations. A number of these can, however, be ruled out as internally inconsistent in practice. For example, I believe it is extremely unlikely that any strategy of dispersing the nonwhite population throughout metropolitan areas could be accomplished without provision of substantially greater incentives to both nonwhites (to get them to move) and whites (to increase their willingness to accept large numbers of nonwhite in-migrants without strong resistance). Thus no combination of both dispersal and non-enrichment need be considered.

Alternative Futures for the American Ghetto

Similarly, in the very long run, concentration of future nonwhite population growth within central cities is probably inconsistent with integration. Many of those cities will become so preponderantly nonwhite that integration within their borders will be impossible. Admittedly, it may take two or more decades for this to occur in some central cities, and it might never occur in others. Nevertheless, some types of integration (such as in the public schools) will become impossible long before that if a concentration policy is followed. For these reasons, I will consider only one special combination containing both concentration and integration. This consists of continued concentration, but a build-up of a gradually expanding inner-city core of fully integrated housing and public facilities created through massive urban renewal. For reasons explained below, this strategy would require a significant enrichment program too.

This whole process of elimination leaves five basic alternative strategies relevant to future development of ghettos. For convenience, each has been assigned a short name to be used throughout the remainder of this article. These strategies can be summarized as follows:

1. *Present Policies:* concentration, segregation, non-enrichment.

2. *Enrichment Only:* concentration, segregation, enrichment.

3. *Integrated Core:* concentration, integration (in the center only), enrichment.

4. *Segregated Dispersal:* dispersal, segregation, enrichment.

5. *Integrated Dispersal:* dispersal, integration, enrichment.

Before these strategies are examined in detail, two things about them should be emphasized.

First, they apply to individual metropolitan areas. Therefore, it would be at least theoretically possible to adopt different strategies toward the ghetto in different metropolitan areas. There are, in fact, some convincing reasons why this would be an excellent idea.

Second, these strategies are formed from relatively extreme points on the relevant ranges of possibilities. Hence they could actually be adopted in various mixtures, rather than in the "pure" forms set forth above. This further strengthens the case for using a variety of approaches across the country. For purposes of analysis, however, it is fruitful to examine each of these strategies initially as though it were to be the sole instrument for coping with ghetto problems in all metropolitan areas.

The Present-Policies Strategy

In order to carry out this strategy, we need merely do nothing more than we do now. Even existing federal programs aimed at aiding cities—such as the Model Cities Program—will continue or accelerate concentration, segregation, and non-enrichment, unless those programs are colossally expanded.

I do not wish to imply that present federal and local efforts in the anti-poverty program, the public housing program, the urban renewal program, health programs, educational programs, and many others are not of significant benefit to residents of ghettos. They are. Nevertheless, as both recent investigations and recent violence have emphasized, existing programs have succeeded neither in stemming the various adverse trends operating in ghetto areas nor in substantially eliminating the deplorable conditions there. Therefore, the strategy of continuing our present policies and our present level of effort is essentially not going to alter current conditions in ghettos.

This may make it seem silly to label continuation of present policies as a specific anti-ghetto strategy. Yet failure to adopt effective policies is still a strategy. It may not be a successful one, but it nevertheless is an expression of society's current commitment and attitude toward the ghetto.

Thus, if we maintain our current programs and policies, segregated areas of residence in our central cities will continue to expand rapidly and to suffer from all the difficult problems inherent in both racial and economic ghettos.

The Enrichment-Only Strategy

The second fundamental ghetto future strategy I call "enrichment only." This approach is aimed at dramatically improving the quality of life within the confines of present ghetto areas and those nearby areas into which ghettos will expand in the future if concentration continues. I presume that any such policy would apply to the poverty meaning of ghetto more than the racial one—that is, any enrichment strategy would aim at upgrading the lowest-income and most disadvantaged citizens of our central cities, regardless of race. Nevertheless, a sizable proportion of such persons are nonwhites. Moreover, programs aimed at reducing racial discrimination in employment and in the quality of public services would form an important part of any strategy aimed at upgrading the most deprived groups. So the enrichment-only strategy would still concentrate upon the same areas as if it were to follow a racial policy.

The basic idea underlying the enrichment-only strategy (and part of every other strategy involving enrichment) is to develop federally financed programs that would greatly improve the education, housing, incomes, employment and job-training, and social services received by ghetto residents. This would involve vastly expanding the scale of present programs, changing the nature of many of them because they are now ineffective or would be if operated at a much larger scale, and creating incentives for a much greater participation of private capital in ghetto activities. Such incentives could include tax credits for investments made in designated ghetto areas, wage subsidies (connected with on-the-job training but lasting longer than such training so as to induce employers to hire unskilled ghetto residents), rent or ownership supplements for poor families, enabling them to rent or buy housing created by private capital, and others.[25]

It is important to realize that the enrichment-only strategy would end neither racial segregation nor the concentration of nonwhites in central cities (and some older adjoining suburbs). It would help many Negroes attain middle-class status and thus make it easier for them to leave the ghetto if they wanted to. Undoubtedly many would. But, by making life in central-city ghettos more attractive without creating any strong pressures for integration or dispersal of the nonwhite population, such a policy would increase the in-migration of nonwhites into central cities. This would speed up the expansion of racially segregated areas in central cities, thereby accelerating the process of "massive transition" of whole neighborhoods from white to nonwhite occupancy.

The Integrated-Core Strategy

This strategy is similar to the enrichment-only strategy because both would attempt to upgrade the quality of life in central-city ghettos through massive federally assisted programs. The integrated-core strategy would also seek, however, to eliminate racial segregation in an ever expanding core of the city by creating a socially, economically, and racially integrated community there. This integrated core would be built up through large-scale urban renewal programs, with the land re-uses including scattered-site public housing, middle-income housing suitable for families with children, and high-quality public services—especially schools.

All of these re-uses would be based upon "managed integration" —that is, deliberate achievement of a racial balance containing a majority of whites but a significant minority of Negroes. Thus, the integrated-core strategy could be carried out only if deliberate racial discrimination aimed at avoiding *de facto* segregation becomes recognized by the Supreme Court as a legitimate tactic for public agencies. In fact, such recognition will probably be a necessity for any strategy involving a significant degree of integration in public schools, public housing, or even private residential areas. This conclusion was recently recognized by the Chicago Board of Education, its staff, and its consultants, who all recommended the use of quotas in schools located in racially changing neighborhoods to promote stable integration.[26]

The integrated-core strategy essentially represents a compromise between an ideal condition and two harsh realities. The ideal condition is development of a fully integrated society in which whites and Negroes live together harmoniously and the race of each individual is not recognized by anyone as a significant factor in any public or private decisions.

The first harsh reality is that the present desire of most whites to dominate their own environment means that integration can only be achieved through deliberate management and through the willingness of some Negroes to share schools and residences as a minority. The second harsh reality is the assumption that it will be impossible to disperse the massive Negro ghettos of major central cities fast enough to prevent many of those cities from eventually becoming predominantly, or even almost exclusively, Negro in population. The development of predominantly Negro central cities, with high proportions of low-income residents, ringed by predominantly white suburbs with much wealthier residents, might lead to a shattering polarization that would split society along both racial and spatial lines.

This strategy seeks to avoid any such polarization by building an integrated core of white and nonwhites in central cities, including many leaders of both races in politics, business, and civic

Alternative Futures for the American Ghetto

affairs. Negro leadership will properly assume the dominant position in central-city politics in many major cities after Negroes have become a majority of the municipal electorates there. By that time, integration of leadership within those cities will, it is to be hoped, have become a sufficient reality so that leaders of both races can work together in utilizing the central city's great economic assets, rather than fighting one another for control over them.

Thus, the integrated-core strategy postulates that a significant movement toward racial integration is essential to keep American society from "exploding" as a result of a combined racial-spatial confrontation of central cities vs. suburbs in many large metropolitan areas. It also postulates that development of integration in the suburbs through massive dispersal cannot occur fast enough to avoid such a confrontation. Therefore, integration must be developed on an "inside-out" basis, starting in the core of the central city, rather than in the suburbs.

The Concept of Dispersal

The two dispersal strategies concerning the future of ghettos are both based upon a single key assumption: that the problems of ghettos cannot be solved so long as millions of Negroes, particularly those with low incomes and other significant disadvantages, are required or persuaded to live together in segregated ghetto areas within our central cities. These strategies contend that large numbers of Negroes should be given strong incentives to move voluntarily from central cities into suburban areas, including those in which no Negroes presently reside.

To illustrate what "large numbers" really means, let us postulate one version of dispersal which I call the "constant-size ghetto strategy." This strictly hypothetical strategy aims at stopping the growth of existing central-city ghettos by dispersing enough Negroes from central cities to the suburbs (or to peripheral central-city areas) to offset potential future increases in that growth. Taking the period from 1970 through 1975, estimates made by the National Advisory Commission on Civil Disorders show that the nonwhite population of all U.S. central cities taken as a whole would, in the absence of any dispersal strategy, expand from about 13.6 million to about 15.5 million.[27] Thus, if dispersal of nonwhites were to take place at a scale large enough to keep central-city racial ghettos at their 1970 level during the five subsequent years, there would have to be an out-movement of 1.9 million Negroes into the suburbs. This amounts to 380,000 per year.

From 1950 to 1960, the suburban Negro population of all U.S. metropolitan areas grew a total of only 60,000 per year. In that decade, the white population of suburban portions of our metropolitan areas (the so-called "urban fringe") increased by about 1,720,000 persons per year. Thus, 96.6 per cent of all suburban population growth consisted of whites. From 1960 to 1966, the Negro population growth in all suburban areas declined sharply to a rate of 33,300 per year. In fact, there was actually in-migration of Negroes from suburbs to central cities. But the white population in all suburbs went up an average of 1,750,000 per year. Thus the proportion of suburban growth made up of whites climbed to 98.1 per cent—an even higher fraction than in the decade from 1950 to 1960.[28] Undoubtedly, some of this white population increase was caused by an exodus of whites from central cities in response to the growth therein. If future Negro population growth in central cities were stopped by a large-scale dispersion policy, then white population growth in the suburbs would be definitely smaller than it was from 1950 through 1966. The size of the resulting decline would depend upon the fraction of white exodus from central cities that occurs in response to Negro growth, as opposed to such other factors as rising incomes, the aging central-city housing stock, and shifts in life-cycle position. If whites leave central cities in a one-to-one ratio with the expansion of Negro population therein, then a cessation of Negro ghetto growth would result in a large drop in white suburban growth. In that case, future suburban population increases would consist of about 23 per cent Negroes (based on very rough calculations). This contrasts with proportions of less than 5 per cent from 1950 through 1960 and less than 3 per cent from 1960 through 1966.

Clearly, such dispersal would represent a radical change in existing trends. Not only would it stop the expansion of Negro ghettos in central cities, but it would also inject a significant Negro population into many presently all-white suburban areas. It is true that policies of dispersal would not necessarily have to be at this large a scale. Dispersal aimed not at stopping ghetto growth, but merely at slowing it down somewhat could be carried out at a much lower scale. Yet even such policies would represent a marked departure from past U.S. practice.

Alternative Futures for the American Ghetto

Such a sharp break with the past would be necessary for any significant dispersal of Negroes. Merely providing the *opportunity* for Negroes to move out of ghettos would, at least in the short run, not result in many moving. Even adoption of a vigorously enforced nationwide open-occupancy law applying to *all* residences would not greatly speed up the present snail's-pace rate of dispersion. Experience in those states that have open-occupancy ordinances decisively proves this conclusion.

Hence, positive incentives for dispersion would have to be created in order to speed up the rate at which Negroes voluntarily move from central cities and settle in suburban areas. (Certainly no policy involving *involuntary* movement of either whites or Negroes should ever be considered.) Such incentives could include rent supplements, ownership supplements, special school-support bonus payments linked to the education of children moving out from ghettos, and other devices which essentially attach a subsidy to a person. Then, when the person moves, he and the community into which he goes get credit for that subsidy. This creates incentives both for him to move and for the community to accept him gladly. Both of the strategies involving dispersal would thus represent radical changes in existing practices.

Segregated vs. Integrated Dispersal

One of the fundamental purposes of any dispersal strategy is providing Negro Americans with real freedom of choice concerning housing and school accommodations. The experience of other ethnic groups indicates that Negroes would exercise that choice in suburban areas in a combination of two ways. Some individual Negro households would become scattered "randomly" in largely white residential areas. But other Negro households—probably a larger number—would voluntarily cluster together. This would create primarily Negro neighborhoods, or even primarily Negro suburban communities. Such a combination of both *scattering* and *clustering* would occur even if Negro households had absolutely no fears of hostility or antagonism from white neighbors. It is unrealistic to suppose, however, that *all* prejudice against Negro neighbors can be eliminated from presently all-white suburbs in the immediate future. As a result, even if a dispersal strategy is carried out, there will still be some external pressure against Negro newcomers. This will encourage an even higher proportion of in-coming Negro households to cluster together than would do so in the absence of all fears and antagonism. Moreover, public policies to accomplish dispersion might include deliberate creation of some moderate-sized clusters of Negro families, as in scattered-site public housing developments.

Once all-Negro clusters appear in previously all-white suburbs, there is a high probability that they will turn into "ghetto-lets" or "mini-ghettos." The same forces that produced ghettos in central cities are likely to repeat themselves in suburbs, though in a much less pathological form. Those pressures are a rapidly expanding Negro population, the "Law of Cultural Dominance" among whites, and at least some restriction of Negro choice in areas far removed from existing all-Negro neighborhoods. Therefore, once a Negro cluster becomes large enough so that Negro children dominate a local elementary school, the typical phenomenon of white withdrawal from the local residential real-estate market is likely to occur. This has already taken place regarding Jews and gentiles in many suburban areas. Thus, any dispersal strategy that does not explicitly aim at preventing segregation, too, will probably create new segregated neighborhoods in the suburbs.

This new form of *de facto* segregation will, however, have far less damaging effects upon Negroes than existing segregation concentrated in central cities. In the first place, if Negro clusters are deliberately created in almost all parts of the metropolitan area at once, whites will be unable to flee to "completely safe" suburbs without accepting impractically long commuting journeys. This will strongly reduce the white propensity to abandon an area after Negroes begin entering it. Moreover, the presence of some Negroes in all parts of suburbia will also make it far easier for individual Negro families to move into all-white neighborhoods on a scattered basis. Thus any dispersal policy that really disperses Negroes in the suburbs will immediately create an enormous improvement in the real freedom of residential choice enjoyed by individual Negro families. This will be true even if most of those families actually choose to remain in Negro clusters.

Second, any dispersal strategy would presumably be accompanied by strongly enforced open-occupancy laws applying to all housing. At present, these laws do not lead to scattering, but they would in the climate of a dispersal strategy. Then Negro willingness to move into all-white areas would rise sharply, and white antagonism toward such move-ins would drop.

Alternative Futures for the American Ghetto

Third, *de facto* residential segregation need not lead to segregated suburban schools. In relatively small communities, such as most suburbs, it is easy to bus students to achieve stable racial balance. Thus, the formation of clustered Negro housing would not have to cause the quality-of-education problems that now exist in central-city ghettos. True, if a given suburb became predominantly Negro, its schools might become quite segregated. In that case, school systems in adjoining suburbs might have to merge or at least work out student exchange procedures with the segregated community in order to counteract segregation. This may be difficult to accomplish (though in the climate of a dispersal strategy, it would be at least thinkable). Hence it is possible that some segregated school systems might appear in suburban areas. But Negro families would still have far more opportunities than they do now to move to areas with integrated schools.

A dispersal strategy that did not succeed in initially placing Negro households in almost all parts of the metropolitan area would be more likely to generate "ghetto-lets." Hence, if dispersal tactics call for initially concentrating on dispersion only to a few suburbs, it is quite possible that segregated dispersal would result. This implies that integrated dispersal could be attained in only two ways. Either the initial dispersal strategy must place Negroes in almost all suburban communities, or specific integration-furthering mechanisms—such as school and residential quotas—must be adopted.

The speculative nature of the above discussion illustrates that society needs to do much more thinking about what dispersal really means, how it might be achieved, what alternative forms it might take, and what its consequences would be.

In an article of this length, it is impossible to present an adequate analysis of each of the strategies described above. Certain factors will, however, have a crucial influence on which strategy actually prevails. These factors should be at least briefly mentioned here.

The Possibility of a Spatial-Racial "Confrontation"

Society's existing policies toward the ghetto are, by definition, those called for by the present-policies strategy. Yet there are strong reasons to believe that maintenance of these policies in ghettos is not possible. The striking increase in violence in big-city ghettos is probably related to a combination of higher aspirations, reduced sanctions against the use of violence, and continued deplorable slum conditions. If so, persistence of the present-policies strategy may continue to spawn incidents, riots, and perhaps guerrilla warfare. Then existing local police forces might have to be supplemented with para-military forces on continuous alert. Thus, the present-policies strategy might lead to further polarization of whites and Negroes and even to the creation of semi-martial law in big cities.

Moreover, when Negroes become the dominant political force in many large central cities, they may understandably demand radical changes in present policies. At the same time, major private capital investment in those cities might virtually cease if white-dominated firms and industries decided the risks of involvement there were too great. In light of recent disorders, this seems very likely. Such withdrawal of private capital has already occurred in almost every single ghetto area in the U.S. Even if private investment continues, big cities containing high proportions of low-income Negroes would need substantial income transfers from the federal government to meet the demands of their electorates for improved services and living conditions.

But by that time, Congress will be more heavily influenced by representatives of the suburban electorate. The suburbs will comprise 41 per cent of our total population by 1985, as opposed to 33 per cent in 1960. Central cities will decline from 31 per cent to 27 per cent.[29] Under a present-policies strategy, this influential suburban electorate will be over 95 per cent white, whereas the central-city population in all metropolitan areas together will be slightly over 60 per cent white. The suburban electorate will be much wealthier than the central-city population, which will consist mainly of Negroes and older whites. Yet even the suburbs will be feeling the squeeze of higher local government costs generated by rising service salaries. Hence the federal government may refuse to approve the massive income transfers from suburbs to central cities that the mayors of the latter will desperately need in order to placate their relatively deprived electorates. After all, many big-city mayors are already beseeching the federal government for massive aid—including Republicans like John Lindsay—and their electorates are not yet dominated by low-income Negroes.

Thus the present-policies strategy, if pursued for any long period of time, might lead to a simultaneous political and economic

Alternative Futures for the American Ghetto

"confrontation" in many metropolitan areas. Such a "confrontation" would involve mainly Negro, mainly poor, and fiscally bankrupt larger central cities on the one hand, and mainly white, much wealthier, but highly taxed suburbs on the other hand. Some older suburbs will also have become Negro by that time, but the vast majority of suburbs will still be "lily white." A few metropolitan areas may seek to avoid the political aspects of such a confrontation by shifting to some form of metropolitan government designed to prevent Negroes from gaining political control of central cities. Yet such a move will hardly eliminate the basic segregation and relative poverty generating hostility in the urban Negro population. In fact, it might increase that population's sense of frustration and alienation.

In my opinion, there is a serious question whether American society in its present form could survive such a confrontation. If the Negro population felt itself wrongly "penned in" and discriminated against, as seems likely, many of its members might be driven to supporting the kind of irrational rebellion now being preached by a tiny minority. Considering the level of violence we have encountered already, it is hard to believe that the conditions that might emanate from a prolonged present-policies strategy would not generate much more. Yet the Negro community cannot hope to defeat the white community in a pitched battle. It is outnumbered 9 to 1 in population and vastly more than that in resources. Thus any massive resort to violence by Negroes would probably bring even more massive retaliation by whites. This could lead to a kind of urban *apartheid*, with martial law in cities, enforced residence of Negroes in segregated areas, and a drastic reduction in personal freedom for both groups, especially Negroes.

Such an outcome would obviously violate all American traditions of individual liberty and Constitutional law. It would destroy "the American dream" of freedom and equal opportunity for all. Therefore, to many observers this result is unthinkable. They believe that we would somehow "change things" before they occurred. This must mean that either the present-policies strategy would not lead to the kind of confrontation I have described, or we would abandon that strategy before the confrontation occurred.

Can the Present-Policies Strategy Avoid "Confrontation"?

What outcomes from a present-policies strategy might prevent this kind of confrontation? For one thing, if incomes in the Negro community rise rapidly without any additional programs, the Negro population of central cities may enter the middle class at a fast rate. If so, the Negro electorate that comes to dominate many major central cities politically by 1985 under the present-policies strategy may consist largely of stable, well-to-do citizens capable of supporting an effective local government.

To test this possibility, we have done some projections of incomes in the nonwhite population on a rough basis through 1983, assuming a present-policies strategy. These indicate that about two thirds of the nonwhite population at that time will have incomes *above* the existing poverty level—about the same fraction as at present. Since nonwhites will then form a much larger share of total central-city population, however, the percentage of *total* central-city population below the present poverty level might actually *rise* slightly. It is possible that nonwhite incomes might increase faster than in this forecast. Yet it is almost certain that the substitution of a relatively poor nonwhite group for a middle-income white group in central cities under a status-quo strategy will counterbalance likely increases in the incomes of nonwhites.

As a result, the electorate that will exist in major cities when Negroes become a majority will probably be just as poor as it is now (in real income terms). In contrast, the population in surrounding suburbs will be much wealthier than it is now. Thus, even if nonwhite incomes rise rapidly, there is still likely to be a significant "gap" between central-city and suburban income levels at that time—probably larger than at present.

Yet even under *present* conditions, many large central cities are critically short of revenue. Furthermore, in a generally wealthier society, it is highly probable that most central-city electorates will demand higher-than-existing levels of public service. Finally, the general cost of all government services will have risen sharply because of the productivity trends explained earlier. Hence, future central-city governments will have much higher costs, but not much greater resources than they do now. So rising incomes among nonwhites will not remove the fiscal pressure on central-city governments that is a key ingredient in the "confrontation" described above.

Moreover, the population group most responsible for violence and disturbances in central cities appears to consist of young Negro men between fifteen and twenty-four years of age. A high

Alternative Futures for the American Ghetto

proportion of these people are unemployed because they lack skills (many are high school dropouts) and elementary training and motivation. This group will undoubtedly grow larger through natural increase and in-migration. Its problems are not likely to be solved under a status-quo strategy. Hence, even if the vast majority of nonwhites in central cities have increasing reason to abhor violence and riots, the *absolute size* of this more alienated group in 1975 will be 40 per cent larger than in 1966, and even larger by 1985.[30] This implies that at least part of this group might start actions forcing the kind of "confrontation" I have described.

Most of the other possible developments under a non-enrichment strategy that would avoid any major "confrontation" involve abandoning concentration of Negroes in central cities. Thus, some observers argue that members of the Negro middle class will increasingly move out to suburban communities as their incomes rise with no further encouragement from public programs. In this way, Negroes would be following the precedent of other ethnic groups. Up to now, there is no evidence that this has started to occur, even though a large Negro middle class already exists. But if such a pattern did evolve, it would amount to dispersal rather than the concentration implicit in the present-policies strategy.

Can Present Policies Be Sustained?

In any event, there appears to be significant probability—which I subjectively judge to be at least 25 per cent and perhaps as high as 75 per cent—that the present-policies strategy will prove unsustainable. If adopted, it would probably generate major repercussions that would force it to be abandoned. Society would be compelled either to suspend traditional individual rights and adopt martial law in cities or to institute major programs to improve ghetto conditions or to move toward wider dispersal of the Negro population, or some combination of these. Admittedly, there is no certainty that the present-policies strategy will lead to these outcomes. Nevertheless, I believe the probability that it will is high enough to make this strategy essentially self-defeating. Modern life is too dynamic for the status quo to be preserved for long.

Yet the present-policies strategy is the one society has so far chosen. Almost all current public policies tend to further concentration, segregation, and non-enrichment, as mentioned earlier. The few supposedly anti-concentration devices adopted, such as open-occupancy laws, have proved almost totally ineffective. All we have to do to confirm our choice of this strategy is to continue existing policies. In fact, avoiding this strategy will be difficult, because doing so will require major changes in present attitudes as well as in existing resource allocations.

The "Black Power" Case for the Enrichment-Only Strategy

The enrichment-only strategy is consistent with a current ideology that has come to be called the "Black Power" viewpoint. This viewpoint has been criticized by many, and some of its proponents have misused it to incite violence. Yet it is certainly an intellectually respectable and defensible position containing some persuasive elements.

The "Black Power" argument states that the Negro American population needs to overcome its feelings of powerlessness and lack of self-respect before it can assume its proper role in society. It can do so only by exerting power over the decisions that directly affect its own members. According to this view, a fully integrated society is not really possible until the Negro minority has developed its own internal strength. Therefore, the ideal society in which race itself is not an important factor can only come much later. It could exist only after Negroes had gained power and self-respect by remaining in concentrated areas over which they could assume political and economic control and direction. Hence this view contends that a future in which central cities become primarily Negro and suburbs almost entirely white would be an advantage rather than a disadvantage.

The "Black Power" view has several notable strong points. First, such assumption of local power would be fully consistent with the behavior of previous nationality groups, such as the Irish in New York and Boston. They, too, came up from the bottom of the social and economic ladder, where they had been insulted and discriminated against. And they did it by gaining political and economic control over the areas in which they lived.

Second, it is unquestionably true that one of the two most important factors providing Negroes with all their recent gains in legal rights and actual welfare has been their own forceful presentation of grievances and demands. (The other factor has been high-level prosperity in the economy in general.) Negro-originated

Alternative Futures for the American Ghetto

marches, demonstrations, protests, and even riots have had immensely more impact in improving their actual power, income, and opportunities than all the "purely voluntary" actions of whites combined—including those of white liberals.

Third, time is on the side of the "Black Power" argument if current population growth and location trends continue. As pointed out earlier, Negroes are likely to become a majority of the electorate in many large American cities within the next fifteen years, unless radically new policies are adopted. By giving Negroes political control over these cities, this trend would provide them with a powerful bargaining position in dealing with the rest of society—a tool they now sorely lack.

Fourth, the "Black Power" viewpoint provides many key ideological supports for Negro self-development. It stresses the need for Negroes to become proud of their color and their history, more conscious of their own strengths. It also focuses their attention on the need for organizing themselves economically and politically. Hence it could provide a focal point for arousing and channeling the largely untapped self-development energies of the Negro American population. One of the greatest difficulties in improving ghettos is discovering effective ways in which the lowest-income and most deprived residents can develop their own capabilities by participating more fully in the decisions and activities that affect them. Such "learning by doing" is, in my opinion, a vital part of the process of bringing deprived people into the main stream of American society. Insofar as "Black Power" proponents could develop such mechanisms, they would immensely benefit American society.

There are, however, also significant flaws in the "Black Power" argument. First, Negroes do not in fact have much power in the U.S. Nor is it clear just how they can obtain power solely through their own efforts, particularly in the near future. "Black Power" advocates constantly talk about "taking what is rightfully theirs" because they are dissatisfied with what "whitey" is willing to turn over to them voluntarily. They also reject the condescension inherent in whites' "giving" Negroes anything, including more power. But what bargaining power can Negroes use to compel whites to yield greater control over the economic and political decisions that affect them?

There are two possible answers. First, they could organize themselves so cohesively that they would become a potent political and economic force through highly disciplined but fully legal action. Examples would be block voting and economic boycotts. So far, nearly all efforts at such internal organization have foundered on the solid rocks of apathy, lack of funds, internal dissension, and disbelief that anything could be accomplished.

Second, Negroes could launch direct action—such as demonstrations and marches—that would morally, economically, or physically threaten the white community. This approach has so far proved to be the most successful. But many Negroes believe it has not improved their situation as fast as is necessary. Hence, there is a tendency to shift the form of threat employed to more and more violent action in order to get faster and more profound results. This tendency need only influence a small minority of Negroes in order to cause a significant escalation of violence. Yet such an escalation might result in massive retaliation by the white community that would worsen the Negroes' position. What is needed is enough of a threat to cause the white community to start changing its own attitudes and allocation of resources in ways far more favorable to Negroes, but not so much of a threat as to cause withdrawal of all white cooperation and sympathy.

This conclusion points up the second flaw in the "Black Power" case: Ultimately, U.S. Negroes cannot solve their own problems in isolation, because they are fully enmeshed in a society dominated by whites. The solution to Negro problems lies as much in the white community as in the Negro community. This is especially true because whites control the economic resources needed to provide Negroes with meaningful equality of opportunity. Hence, any strategy of action by Negro leaders that totally alienates the white community is doomed to failure.

Yet "Black Power" advocates are probably correct in arguing that Negroes must develop an ideology that focuses upon self-determination and therefore has some "anti-white" tinges. They need an "enemy" against which to organize the Negro community. History proves that organization *against* a concrete opponent is far more effective than one *for* some abstract goal. They also need an abrasive ideology that threatens whites enough to open their eyes to the Negroes' plight and their own need to do something significant to improve it. The question is how they can accomplish these goals without going too far and thereby creating violent anti-white hostility among Negroes and equally violent anti-Negro sentiment among whites.

Alternative Futures for the American Ghetto

In the past few years, many Negro Americans—including prominent community leaders—have shifted their sights away from direct racial integration as a goal. Instead they have focused upon other goals more consistent with the "Black Power" viewpoint. They want better housing, better schools, better jobs, and better personal security within all-Negro areas—and a much stronger Negro voice in controlling all these things. These enrichment-only objectives have apparently eclipsed their desire for greater ability to enter directly into white-dominated portions of the society. This rather dramatic change in values appears to rule out much possibility of Negroes' accepting either dispersal strategy.

In my opinion, the main cause of this shift in objectives is the failure of white society to offer any real hope for large-scale integration. After years of seeking equality under the law, Negro leaders have discovered that even removal of legal barriers is not producing much progress toward a true sharing in the life of white-dominated society. Why should they keep knocking on the door if no one will answer? Why not turn instead to existing all-Negro communities and try to improve conditions there? Indeed, I believe continued white refusal to engage in meaningful, large-scale integration will make it impossible for any self-respecting Negroes to avoid espousing some version of the "Black Power" viewpoint. Understandably, they will not be able to accept the conclusion that most of the millions of Negroes whom whites force to live racially segregated lives must therefore be condemned to inferior educations, housing, culture, or anything else.

Rather, they will reason, there must be some way to make the quality of life in all-Negro portions of a racially segregated society just as good as it is in the all-white portions. And if equality in terms of the indices of desirability accepted by whites cannot be achieved, then some of these "Black Power" advocates will be willing to attain at least nominal equality by denouncing those indicators as specious. They will further claim—with some justification—that life in all-white portions of society cannot be better and may be morally worse because whites suffer from racial blindness.

The reason why this argument is and will be advanced so strongly is certainly understandable. Those who advance it would hardly be human if they were not at least tempted to do so. As long as present white attitudes and behavior persist, adopting any other view amounts to despairing of any chance at equality for most Negroes.

Can the Enrichment-Only Strategy Create "Separate But Equal" Societies?[31]

The "Black Power" viewpoint essentially argues that racially separate societies in America can provide equal opportunities for all their members if Negroes are able to control their own affairs. Yet there is a great deal of evidence that this argument is false.

Certainly concerning employment, equality of opportunity for Negroes cannot possibly be attained in a segregated labor market. Negroes must be provided with full freedom and equality regarding entry into and advancement within the white-dominated enterprises that are overwhelmingly preponderant in our economy. Only in this way can they have any hope of achieving an occupational equality with whites.

In education, the evidence is far more ambiguous. The recent reports of the Office of Education and the Civil Rights Commission contend that both racial and economic integration are essential to the attainment of educational equality for Negroes.[32] Yet critics of these reports point out that many types of enrichment programs were not tested in the studies conducted by the authors. Unfortunately, most alternative approaches have not yet been tried on a scale large enough to determine whether any of them will work. Yet one conclusion does seem reasonable: Any real improvement in the quality of education in low-income, all-Negro areas will cost a great deal more money than is now being spent there, and perhaps more than is being spent per pupil anywhere.

Thus, society may face a choice between three fundamental alternatives: providing Negroes with good-quality education through massive integration in schools (which would require considerably more spending per pupil than now exists), providing Negroes with good-quality education through large-scale and extremely expensive enrichment programs, or continuing to relegate many Negroes to inferior educations that severely limit their lifetime opportunities. The third alternative is what we are now choosing. Whether or not the second choice—improving schools in all-Negro areas—will really work is not yet known. The enrichment alternative is based upon the as-yet-unproven premise that it will work.

Regarding housing, the enrichment-only strategy could undoubtedly greatly improve the quantity, variety, and environment of decent housing units available to the disadvantaged population

Alternative Futures for the American Ghetto

of central cities. Nevertheless, it could not in itself provide Negroes of *any* economic level with the same freedom and range of choice as whites with equal incomes have. Clearly, in this field "separate but equal" does not mean *really* equal. Undoubtedly, all-white suburban areas provide a far greater range and variety of housing and environmental settings than can possibly be found in central cities or all-Negro suburbs alone.

Moreover, there is an acute scarcity of vacant land in many of our largest central cities. Therefore, greatly expanding the supply of decent housing for low-income families in those cities at a rapid rate requires creating many new units for them in the suburbs too.

Thus, if society adopts one of the many possible versions of the enrichment-only strategy, it may face the prospect of perpetuating two separate societies—one white and one Negro—similar to those that would develop under the present-policies strategy. If the enrichment programs carried out proved highly effective, then the gap between these two societies in income, education, housing, and other qualities of life would be nowhere near so great as under the present-policies strategy. Hence, the possibility of a potentially catastrophic "confrontation" between these two societies sometime in the next twenty years would be greatly reduced.

Nevertheless, I do not believe it will really be possible to create two separate societies that are truly equal. Therefore, even if the enrichment-only strategy proved extraordinarily successful at improving the lot of disadvantaged central-city residents of all races and colors (which is by no means a certainty), it would still leave a significant gap in opportunity and achievement between the separate white and Negro societies which would continue to emerge over the next twenty years. This gap would remain a powerful source of tension that might lead to violence, for experience proves that men seeking equality are not placated by even very great absolute progress when they perceive that a significant gap remains between themselves and others in society who are no more deserving of success than they. And that would be precisely the situation twenty years from now under the enrichment-only strategy—whether linked to "Black Power" concepts or not.

Why Dispersal Should Be Seriously Considered

As pointed out earlier, either of the two dispersal strategies would require radical changes in current trends and policies concerning the location of Negro population growth. Moreover, it is likely that massive dispersal would at present be opposed by *both* suburban whites and central-city Negroes. Many of the former would object to an influx of Negroes, and many of the latter would prefer to live together in a highly urbanized environment. Why should we even consider a strategy that is not only socially disruptive, but likely to please almost nobody?

In my opinion, there are five reasons why we should give enrichment plus dispersal serious consideration. First, future job-creation is going to be primarily in suburban areas, but the unskilled population is going to be more and more concentrated in central-city ghettos unless some dispersion occurs. Such an increasing divergence between where the workers are and where the jobs are will make it ever more difficult to create anything like full employment in decent jobs for ghetto residents. In contrast, if those residents were to move into suburban areas, they would be exposed to more knowledge of job opportunities and would have to make much shorter trips to reach them. Hence they would have a far better chance of getting decent employment.

Second, the recent U.S. Office of Education and U.S. Civil Rights Commission reports on equality of achievement in education reach a *tentative* conclusion that it is necessary to end the clustering of lower-income Negro students together in segregated schools in order to improve their education significantly.[33] As I understand these reports, they imply that the most significant factor in the quality of education of any student is the atmosphere provided by his home and by his fellow students both in and out of the classroom. When this atmosphere is dominated by members of deprived families, the quality of education is inescapably reduced—at least within the ranges of class size and pupil-teacher ratios that have been tried on a large scale. Therefore, if we are to provide effective educational opportunities for the most deprived groups in our society to improve themselves significantly, we must somehow expose them to members of other social classes in their educational experience. But there are not enough members of the Negro middle class "to go around," so to speak. Hence this means some intermingling of children from the deprived groups with those from not-so-deprived white groups, at least in schools. Because of the difficulties of bussing large numbers of students from the hearts of central cities to suburban areas, it makes sense to accomplish this objective through some residential dispersal. This consideration tends to support the integrated-dispersal strategy to some extent, even though these reports have received significant criticism, as noted above.

Third, development of an adequate housing supply for low-income and middle-income families and provision of true freedom of choice in housing for Negroes of all income levels will require out-movement of large numbers of both groups from central cities to suburbs. I do not believe that such an out-movement will occur "spontaneously" merely as a result of increasing prosperity among Negroes in central cities. Even the recently passed national open-occupancy law is unlikely to generate it. Rather, a program of positive incentives and of actual construction of new housing in suburban areas will be necessary.

Fourth, continued concentration of large numbers of Negroes under relatively impoverished conditions in ghettos may lend to unacceptably high levels of crime and violence in central cities. The outbreak of riots and disorders in mostly nonwhite areas in our central cities in the past few years is unprecedented in American history. As the report of the National Advisory Commission on Civil Disorders indicates, continuing to concentrate masses of the nonwhite population in ghettos dominated by poverty and permeated with an atmosphere of deprivation and hopelessness is likely to perpetuate or intensify these disorders. This could lead to the disastrous outcome already discussed in connection with the present-policies strategy.

Fifth, a continuation of ghetto growth will, over the next three or four decades, produce a society more racially segregated than any in our history. We will have older, blighted central cities occupied by millions of Negroes, and newer, more modern suburban areas occupied almost solely by whites. Prospects for moving from that situation to a truly integrated society in which race is not a factor in key human decisions are not encouraging. In fact, by that time we will be faced with a fantastically more massive dispersal problem than the present one if we really want to achieve a society integrated in more than just words.

Thus, only the two enrichment-plus-dispersal strategies explicitly seek to create a single society rather than accepting our present perpetuation of two separate societies: one white and one Negro. Dispersal would involve specific policies and programs at least starting us toward reversal of the profoundly divisive trend now so evident in our metropolitan areas. It may seem extraordinarily difficult to begin such a reversal. But however difficult it may be now, it will be vastly more difficult in twenty years if the number of Negroes segregated in central cities is 8 million larger than it is today.

The Difficulty of Gaining Acceptance for Dispersal

I am fully aware that any strategy involving significant dispersal may now seem wholly impractical to responsible politicians and social leaders. The voluntary movement of large numbers of Negroes from ghettos to the suburbs encouraged by federal programs presupposes radical changes in existing attitudes among both suburban whites and central-city Negroes.

In spite of our social mobility, Americans are extremely sensitive to class differentiations. We have deliberately developed class-stratified suburban areas. Residents of each suburb use zoning, tax rates, lot-size requirements, and other devices to exclude persons considered farther down the ladder of social and economic prominence. As each group and each family moves upward in our mobile society, they become more concerned about creating social distance between themselves and those now below them—including those who were once equal to them.

I certainly do not deplore the historic traditions of self-improvement and protection of amenities and privileges that have been won through hard work and perseverance. These traditions should and will continue in some form, because it is proper for successful people to enjoy the fruits of their efforts.

Nevertheless, it is at least possible that the social objective of upgrading the lowest and most deprived groups in our society cannot be accomplished if we simultaneously insist upon excluding those groups from nearly all daily contact with other more fortunate people—as we do now—by maintaining extremely rigid class distinctions by geographic area. Thus, the best dispersal policy might be one that promoted day-to-day inter-class and inter-racial experiences without changing the dominant socio-economic character of the receiving suburban areas. This would allow persons moving out from the inner city to benefit from the existing character of those suburbs. Such a policy implies that the newcomers would comprise a minority in each area into which they went. This means that an integrated-dispersal strategy might ultimately provide the most desirable form of dispersal. It would enable the group that was already there to maintain nearly intact their conception of the proper standards for that community, while sharing the benefits of those standards with others.

Even this change in attitude, however, presupposes a shift in values of profound magnitude among white middle-class Americans. Furthermore, I doubt that most Negroes today want to live in white communities in which they would be relatively isolated from other Negroes. Hence they might prefer a segregated-dispersal strategy, if they were willing to accept dispersal at all. Yet, since most suburban areas are already incorporated into predominantly white communities, where and how could such a strategy be initiated?

Some Tactical Mechanisms for Encouraging Dispersal

Any attempt to achieve dispersal must involve specific answers to two basic questions:

> What *mechanisms* can be designed to encourage voluntary out-movement of large numbers of Negroes into the suburbs and their peaceful acceptance and welcome by whites there?

> What *incentives* can be developed leading particular interest groups in society to press politically for—or at least support—employment of those mechanisms?

Let us consider the mechanisms first. Americans have always used one basic approach to get people to overcome inertia and make voluntarily some socially desirable change. It consists of providing a significant economic or other reward for persons who behave in the desired manner. That reward might be free land (as for homesteaders and railroads in the nineteenth century), or tax reductions (as for homeowners or investors in equipment in the past few years), or direct payments (as for farmers), or services and income supplements tied to participation in specific programs (as for users of the G.I. Bill in education).

In the case of dispersion, I believe the system of rewards used should probably have the following characteristics[34]:

1. Advantages should accrue both to the Negro households moving out from central cities and to the suburban households into whose communities the newcomers move.

2. Whenever possible, these advantages should consist of rewards administered under metropolitan-area-wide organizations specifically set up for such a purpose. These organizations could be quasi-private bodies able to cooperate directly with existing local governments and other geographically limited organizations. Hence they would *not* be metropolitan governments.

3. Advantages to out-moving households might include the following:

   The possibility of sending their children to top-quality schools that receive special grants because of participation in programs involving out-moving children.

   Home-buying or renting financial aids available only to out-moving families or at least with assigned proportions of their total funding available only to such families.

   Top-priority access to special programs concerning employment and on-the-job training in suburban industrial and other firms. In my opinion, such programs might be effectively built around the self-selection principle embodied in the G.I. Bill—that is, eligible persons would be given certificates enabling those firms who hire them to receive special benefits to compensate for their lower productivity or training costs. Such benefits might include tax credits or direct payments. The persons receiving these certificates would then make their own choice of employers among firms participating in such programs. This would preserve maximum individual choice among program participants.

4. Advantages to households already living in the receiving areas might include:

   Special aid to schools receiving children of out-moving Negro families. Such aid should consist of funds linked to the students in such families (as Title I funding under the Elementary and Secondary Education Act is now linked to low-income families). But the per-student amount of aid given should greatly exceed the added direct cost of teaching each out-moving student. Hence the school district concerned would have a positive incentive to accept such students because of the financial "bonuses" they would bring with them. Those bonuses could be used to upgrade the entire receiving school or cut locally-borne costs therein.

"Bonus" community financing to participating suburban local governments. Again, the payments involved should significantly exceed the added costs of servicing in-coming families, so that each participating community would be able to improve other services too.

Giving higher priority in other federal programs to communities participating in out-movement programs than to those refusing to participate. These related programs could include sewer and water financing, planning aid, and selection as locations for federal installations.

5. Benefits available for out-moving families and receiving areas could be restricted by geographic area to avoid either paying people discriminately by race or wasting funds paying families who would move out anyway. A precedent for giving residents of certain neighborhoods special benefits already exists in the urban renewal and Model Cities programs. Thus, specific ghetto neighborhoods could be designated "origination" areas and largely white suburban communities designated "receiving" areas. Benefits would accrue only to persons moving from the former to the latter or to residents of the latter participating in reception programs.

6. If these programs were part of an integrated-dispersal strategy, they could be linked to quota systems concerning newcomers to each school or community involved. Thus, the special bonus aids would be available only up to a certain fraction of the total school enrollment or residential population of a given receiving community. This restriction would be aimed at retaining in the schools or communities concerned the dominance of the groups originally residing there. It is to be hoped that the result would be suburban integration, rather than a shift of massive neighborhood transition from central cities to suburbs.

The above suggestions are highly tentative and exploratory. Yet

I hope they at least indicate that practical mechanisms can be created that might achieve a substantial amount of peaceful Negro out-movement—*if* they were adopted in a general atmosphere of social encouragement to dispersal.

Some aspects of the basic approach described above may seem terribly unjust. In particular, this approach rewards the advantaged (those already living in suburbs) as well as the disadvantaged (those moving out of deprived areas into suburbs) in order to get the former to accept the latter. Yet that is a key mechanism, one which free-enterprise systems have always employed when they seek to attain high-priority ends through voluntary action. Our society abounds with arrangements that provide special economic advantages to those who are already privileged, presumably in order to evoke socially desired behavior from them. Examples are oil depletion allowances, stock option plans for top executives, profitable contracts for defense firms, lower tax rates on capital gains, and subsidy payments to wealthy farmers. I am defending neither the equity nor the effectiveness of these particular examples. Yet they illustrate that we often adopt public policies that pay the rich to undertake behavior which presumably benefits society as a whole.

A second aspect of the approach to dispersal I have described which might seem harsh is that no benefits apparently accrue to disadvantaged persons who fail to move out to the suburbs. As stated earlier, however, I believe dispersal programs should only be undertaken simultaneously with large-scale ghetto enrichment programs. The latter would provide comparable, or even greater, benefits for those "left behind" in central cities—who will undoubtedly comprise the vast majority of Negroes in our metropolitan areas for many years to come.

Developing Political Support for Dispersal

The concept of dispersal will remain nothing but an empty theory unless a significant number of Americans decide their best interests lie in politically supporting specific dispersal mechanisms. It is conceivable that such support might result from a massive "change of heart" among white suburbanites. They might view dispersal as a way to "purge themselves" of the kind of "white racism" which the National Advisory Commission on Civil Disorders described. I do not think this will occur. In fact, I believe

Alternative Futures for the American Ghetto

recent urban violence has tended to make white suburbanites more hostile than ever to the idea of having Negroes live next door to them.

Yet, on the other hand, several specific groups in society are beginning to realize that dispersal might benefit them immensely. The motivation of persons in these groups varies widely, from pure moral guilt to sheer self-interest. But almost all significant social change in the United States has occurred because a wide variety of different types of people with diverse motives have formed a coalition to accomplish something. In my opinion, only through that kind of process will any of the basic strategies I have described (except the present-policies strategy) ever be achieved.

I believe the groups favorable to dispersal now include, or soon will include, the following:

> Suburban industrialists. In many metropolitan areas, they are experiencing acute labor shortages, particularly of unskilled workers. They will soon be willing to provide open and powerful political support for the construction of low-income and moderate-income housing for Negro workers and their families in currently all-white suburbs.

> Downtown-oriented retailers, bankers, restaurant operators, hotel operators, and other businessmen in our larger cities. In cities where disorders have penetrated into central business districts (such as Milwaukee and Washington), many former patrons have stopped visiting these areas altogether—especially at night. If disorders in these areas get worse, the impact upon both consumer patronage and future capital investment in big-city downtowns could be catastrophic. Those whose enterprises are "locked in" such areas will soon realize they must vigorously support both stronger law enforcement and positive programs aimed at alleviating Negro discontent. At first, these programs will consist primarily of ghetto enrichment, but these groups will soon begin to support dispersal too.

> Home builders. They would benefit from any large-scale programs of housing construction. But the delays and difficulties of carrying out such programs within central

cities are much greater than they are on vacant suburban land. Hence they will eventually exert at least low-level support for dispersal if it means large-scale subsidy of privately built homes.

White central-city politicians in large cities. As the populations of their cities shift toward Negro majorities, they will be more and more willing to support some dispersal policies, as well as the enrichment programs they now espouse.

Businessmen in general with plants, offices, or other facilities "locked in" large central cities. An increasing number of such persons will realize that they will emerge losers from any major "confrontation" between black-dominated central cities and white-dominated suburbs, as described earlier.

Persons of all types whose consciences influence them to accept the National Advisory Commission's conclusion that dispersal of some kind is the only way to avoid perpetuating two separate societies, with the Negro one forever denied equality.

Since these groups now constitute a small minority of Americans a great many other Americans must change their existing values considerably if large-scale dispersal is ever to occur. Yet the alternatives to such a strategy—especially the one we are now pursuing—could conceivably lead us to equally grave changes in values. For example, if there is an extremely significant increase in violence in Negro ghettos which spills over into all-white areas, the white population might react with harshly repressive measures that would significantly restrict individual freedoms, as noted above. This, too, would call for a basic shift in our values. But it is a shift which I regard with much more alarm than the one required by a dispersal strategy. In fact, in this age of rapid technological change, it is naïve to suppose that there will not in the future be significant alterations in attitudes that we presently take for granted.

The Scale of Efforts Required

The foregoing discussion emphasizes that any strategy likely to have a significant impact upon ghettos will require a very much

Alternative Futures for the American Ghetto

larger effort than we are now devoting to this problem. Even a "pure" ghetto-enrichment strategy, which does not eliminate or even slow down the growth of the racial ghetto, would require a significantly greater allocation of financial and manpower resources to coping with the problems of the urban poor. A dispersal strategy that addresses itself to breaking up or at least slowing down the growth of the racial ghetto would also require even more profound changes in values and attitudes. Only the first strategy—that of continuing our present activities—requires no immediate change in effort or values. But it may eventually result in significant value changes too—and perhaps far less desirable ones than are required by the other two alternatives.

Thus, there is simply no easy way to cope with this problem. In my opinion, past federal programs and many currently suggested approaches have suffered from the desire to find a cheap solution to what is an extremely expensive problem. The problem is expensive in terms not only of money, but also of our national talents and our willingness to change our basic values. In one way or another, we must and will accommodate ourselves to this problem. We cannot evade it.

Creating the Programs and Incentives Necessary to Achieve Any Desired Ghetto Future

Each strategy contains two basic parts: a desired outcome and a set of actions designed to achieve that outcome. I have not placed equal emphasis on these two parts in discussing each of the five strategies concerning ghetto futures. For example, the present-policies strategy as I have described it is essentially a set of actions—the continuation of present policies. Hence it does not emphasize a desired outcome. In fact, I have pointed out several reasons why its outcome might be quite undesirable. Conversely, my discussion of the enrichment-only strategy has focused upon its outcome. Hence I have not made many suggestions about how that outcome might be brought about. Similar emphasis upon the outcome rather than the means of attaining it also marks the discussion of the integrated-core strategy. Even my tentative analysis of how dispersal might be carried out hardly represents a complete blueprint for action.

Any strategy is really just wishful thinking until it links the outcome it envisions with some feasible means of attaining that outcome. This is especially true regarding several of the ghetto futures I have described, since they embody such radical changes in society. They are likely to remain largely fantasies, rather than real alternatives, until specific programs for achieving them can be defined. I have made some program suggestions in connection with dispersal strategies in order to prove that dispersal is not totally unrealistic. Unfortunately, the complexity of developing similar suggestions for the other strategies involving social change prevents my attempting to do so in this article.

Nevertheless, there are five basic principles crucial to formulating such programs.

1. No proposed "solution" to ghetto problems that is not eventually supported by the majority of the white middle class can possibly succeed.[35]

2. The actions designed to bring about any desired outcome must be linked to incentives that will appeal both to the self-interest of all groups concerned and to their consciences. In fact, the most difficult part of implementing any strategy (other than the present-policies strategy) will be providing effective incentives for the relatively well-off white majority. This group must be persuaded to expand many resources, and alter its own traditional behavior, in order to produce outcomes that appear to benefit mainly a small minority of the population. As indicated in the discussion of dispersal, each segment of the white majority (such as business, labor, suburbanites, senior citizens, farmers, and so forth) must be presented with arguments and incentives which appeal specifically to its interests. An example is the argument that business suffers great losses of potential profits and output because of the failure of poor Negroes to engage in high-level consumption and the inability of poorly educated Negro workers to help meet high demands for skilled labor.

3. Any program designed to achieve a given outcome should involve significant action by the private sector. Otherwise, society may relegate ghettos to a position of dependency upon government that is inconsistent with full equality in American life. On the other hand, it is naïve to suppose that the private sector can or will bear the huge expense of

coping with ghetto problems unaided. Society as a whole must pay the extra costs of on-the-job training programs, new factories located in ghettos, union training of unskilled Negro apprentices, and other actions aimed at helping the unskilled or otherwise "left out" enter the main stream of our economy. These actions must be carried out by non-governmental organizations, but financed by the government through direct payments, tax credits, or other means.

4. No program involving ghettos can be effective unless it involves a high degree of meaningful participation by ghetto residents, and significant exercise of power and authority by them. We must realize that ghettos cannot be drawn into the main stream of American life without some redistribution of authority and power, as well as income, for equality in America means exercise of significant self-determination. Admittedly, lack of skill and experience may cause that exercise to be disorderly, inefficient, and even corrupt at first—as it was among the Irish, Italians, Jews, and others in the past. Therefore, turning over more power in ghetto areas to local residents may actually cause a short-run decline in the professional quality of government there—whether in schools, the police, or local government in general. Yet it will greatly alter the attitudes of residents toward those institutions and begin to draw them into the real functioning of our society. So it should and must come.

5. The more benefits that most ghetto residents receive through programs aimed at helping them, the more dissatisfied and vocally discontent certain small parts of the ghetto community are likely to become. This makes the problem of persuading the white majority to support large-scale aid programs doubly difficult. It also means that socio-economic programs will have to be accompanied by greatly enlarged and improved law-enforcement efforts, particularly those in which ghetto leaders themselves play significant roles. Yet emphasis on improving law enforcement alone, without massively trying to meet the other needs of ghetto residents, will probably prove disastrous. Such one-sided emphasis on "law and order" could easily provoke steadily rising violence shifting in form toward guerrilla warfare. The need to avoid

this outcome further emphasizes the importance of relying more and more on ghetto communities to develop their own internal controls of violence, with outside aid, as is consistent with the preceding principle of greater self-determination.

Merely stating these principles emphasizes how far we are from having designed practical programs to achieve most of the outcomes set forth in this article. In my opinion, one of the most important tasks facing us is the formulation and public discussion of the specific ingredients needed for such programs. But even that cannot be done until we have recognized more explicitly the various possible futures of American ghettos and weighed their relative advantages and disadvantages.

At present, most public discussion and thought about racial and ghetto problems in America suffer from a failure to define or even to consider explicit possible long-range outcomes of public policy. This is one reason why such discussion seems so confused, inchoate, and frustrating. I hope that the ideas set forth in this article can serve as a nucleus for more fruitful public discussion of this crucial topic, for the future of American ghettos will determine to a large extent the future of America itself.

REFERENCES

1. The first draft of this article was written in the early summer of 1967. Subsequently, the author became a consultant to the National Advisory Commission on Civil Disorders. In that capacity, he wrote the rough drafts of several chapters in the Commission's final report. One of these (Chapter 16) contains many of the ideas set forth in this article. Nevertheless, there are sufficient differences between the contents and presentation of Chapter 16 in the Commission's Report and this article to warrant separate publication of the latter. The contents of this article express the thoughts of its author only and do not necessarily represent the views of either the National Advisory Commission on Civil Disorders or Real Estate Research Corporation.

2. Data from the Social Security Administration.

3. *Report of the National Advisory Commission on Civil Disorders* (Washington, D. C.; March 1, 1968), p. 127. This document will hereafter be referred to as the *NACCD Report*.

4. *Ibid.*, pp. 121, 127.

5. Based upon the Census Bureau's Series D projections of future population—the ones assuming the lowest of the four levels of future fertility used by the Census Bureau. See U. S. Bureau of the Census, *Statistical Abstracts of the United States, 1967* (88th Edition; Washington, D. C., 1967), pp. 8-10.

6. *NACCD Report*, p. 121.

7. *Ibid.*

8. *Ibid.*

9. Open-occupancy legislation appears to be aimed at shifting the location of some future nonwhite growth to presently all-white areas. Experience in those states which have had open-occupancy ordinances for some time indicates, however, that they have little, if any, impact in altering the distribution of nonwhite population growth.

10. *NACCD Report*, p. 227.

11. Surveys conducted annually by Real Estate Research Corporation, results unpublished.

12. *NACCD Report*, p. 216.

13. See Raymond J. Murphy and James M. Watson, *The Structure of Discontent*, Mimeographed, Los Angeles: University of California at Los Angeles, June 1, 1967.

14. *NACCD Report*, pp. 123-31.

15. Specific recommendations concerning these subjects are set forth in the *NACCD Report*, Chapter 17.

16. See John F. Kain, "The Distribution and Movement of Jobs and Industry," in *The Metropolitan Enigma*, ed. James Q. Wilson (Washington, D. C., 1967).

17. These include legislative proposals made by Senator Javits, the late Senator Robert Kennedy, and Senator Percy.

18. William Baumol and William Bowen, *The Performing Arts: The Economic Dilemma* (New York: 20th Century Fund).

19. *NACCD Report*, p. 217.

20. Insofar as I know, this principle was first formulated by my father, James C. Downs, Jr.

21. Two well-known urban specialists with such views are Jane Jacobs and Victor Gruen. See Jane Jacobs, *The Life and Death of Great American Cities* (New York, 1961), and Victor Gruen, *The Heart of Our Cities* (New York, 1964).

22. This phenomenon explains why it is so difficult to halt "massive transition" from white to nonwhite occupancy once it begins. It tends to continue

even when whites originally living in the area concerned do not "panic" at all. As long as normal turnover continues to produce vacancies, and only nonwhites fill them, such transition is inescapable. The key persons whose behavior must be affected to stop transition are not the whites living in the area at the outset, but those living scattered elsewhere in the metropolitan area or even other parts of the nation. They are the persons who must move into the areas as vacancies appear in order to maintain racial balance therein. Thus, attempts to organize existing white residents so as to prevent them from fleeing almost always fail to halt transition. Organizers can rarely identify "the whites who aren't there yet," so they cannot influence the decisions of these potential future occupants, and transition continues relentlessly.

23. The U. S. Supreme Court will soon have to face up to the consequences of this "Law." In order to attack *de facto* segregation effectively, it must recognize racial discrimination in the form of school quotas as Constitutional. At present, our society cannot achieve integration or end segregation without deliberate and explicit racial discrimination by public authorities. This is true in relation to other public facilities besides schools, including hospitals and housing.

24. This term and usage were coined by Charles E. Lindblom. See Lindblom and David Braybrooke, *The Strategy of Decision* (New York, 1963).

25. See the *NACCD Report*, Chapter 17.

26. See their statements as quoted in the Chicago *Daily News*, August 25, 1967.

27. *NACCD Report*, p. 227.

28. *Ibid.*, p. 121.

29. These figures are based upon the Census Bureau's Series D population projections. If higher fertility projections are used, the suburbs would contain slightly higher proportions of total population in 1985. See the reference cited in footnote 5.

30. *NACCD Report*, pp. 216-17.

31. This section of the article was written after Chapter 16 of the *NACCD Report* had been completed and closely parallels the contents of certain parts of that chapter.

32. See James Coleman *et al.*, *Equality of Educational Opportunity* (Washington, D. C., 1966), and the U. S. Civil Rights Commission, *Racial Isolation in the Public Schools* (Washington, D. C., 1967).

33. *Ibid.*

34. Many of the programs described in this section have been recommended by the National Advisory Commission on Civil Disorders. See the *NACCD Report*, Chapter 17.

35. This fact is recognized by most Negro leaders not committed to zealously militant separatism. For example, see Kenneth Clark, *Dark Ghetto* (New York, 1965), p. 222.

[3]
Housing the Urban Poor: The Economics of Various Strategies

By ANTHONY DOWNS*

Helping to provide decent housing for low-income households is a worldwide challenge to national governments, especially in countries where most citizens are adequately fed. However, it would be euphemistic to use the term strategies to denote public policies concerning the housing situation in most countries, particularly those dominated by free markets. Their governments simply do not have well reasoned, realistic, long range policies for coping with housing needs. Nevertheless, for purposes of analysis, it is useful to view the public efforts to improve the housing of low-income households in each nation as resulting from at least an implicit strategy.

I. *Key Background Factors and Relationships*

The analysis requires understanding of the following key background factors and relationships:

A. *Quality Standards for New Construction*

I will arbitrarily define three different quality standards actually used by various nations to control new housing construction (as distinct from those verbally professed). High standards are equivalent to the housing consumed by upper middle-class families in terms of unit size, land per unit, quality of construction, and utilities. In the United States, all new urban housing construction must meet high standards. Moderate standards embody far more modest quality levels, but still qualify as decent housing. They govern new construction in most European nations. Zero standards mean that any type of new housing construction is allowed, including crude shacks built by squatters. Zero standards prevail in most of the world.

B. *Relationships Among Housing Standards, Housing Costs, and Public Subsidies*

The public subsidy necessary to enable the average low-income household to live in a newly built decent home is much larger if high quality standards are required than if moderate quality standards are required. (If zero standards are required, the housing units concerned are not decent in quality.) Therefore, requiring high standards means that (1) a higher proportion of households in the economy cannot buy new housing without subsidies; (2) fewer badly-housed poor households can be provided with "decent" new housing per million dollars of public subsidy; (3) the total cost of providing all presently ill-housed poor households with "decent" housing is vastly greater; and (4) among middle class voters, political opposition to large scale housing subsidies is greater, since many appear to be paying taxes to put poor people in housing better than their own. Also, the higher the standards required for new housing, the more citizens of all incomes must resort to debt financing in buying homes. Therefore, the higher the fraction of total cost they pay that goes to interest instead of direct construction. In contrast, zero standard housing can be paid for entirely out of current income without debt financing, especially because the land is often expropriated.

C. *Effects of Rising Incomes and Rising Occupancy Costs*

If real incomes rise faster than housing occupancy costs (which include land, interest, and construction costs), then most households upgrade their housing. They do so either by moving into higher quality units, or improving the units they now occupy. Improvement without movement is most likely where: social class mixture and racial mixture in any given neighborhood are common and socially accepted; zero standard construction is common, so residents can gradually upgrade initially skimpy housing by adding improvements wholly financed out of

* Real Estate Research Corporation, Chicago.

current income; there is an acute overall shortage of housing; or housing is rationed by public authorities who control the supply, or at least control all new units. Where opposite conditions prevail, upgrading is usually accomplished by moving to a better neighborhood, as in the United States. If occupancy costs rise faster than real incomes, then little upgrading occurs, and the amount of subsidy required per household to put ill-housed families into decent housing rises.

D. *The Impact of Population Growth and Migration upon Local Housing Conditions*

In any given metropolitan area or neighborhood, the number of households can normally fluctuate much more rapidly, both up and down, than the total supply of "decent" quality housing units. Thus, rapid natural increase in population plus heavy inmigration can lead to an acute local housing shortage. This situation absolutely compels one or more of the following indecent housing conditions to result at least temporarily: overcrowding of existing "decent" units, division of such units into smaller substandard units, construction of many new substandard units (or even zero standard units), or households living in the streets or in the open without housing. Public authorities may attempt to prevent such outcomes by prohibiting migration into a given metropolitan area. However, experience throughout the world, even in totalitarian nations, shows that such prohibitions are ineffective if strong pressures are driving people out of rural areas. Hence a critical factor influencing housing conditions in any locality is the pressure of population growth on the local housing supply. Where such growth occurs mainly among poor households, the only way to prevent the above indecent results from lasting a long time is through huge public housing subsidies, since the new households cannot afford to purchase new housing on the free market.

E. *The Importance of Public Policies in Stimulating Total Housing Production*

In any locality, the relationship between the total supply of decent housing units and the total number of households determines to what extent the indecent housing conditions described above will occur. Any rapid increase in total supply relative to total needs, even consisting solely of more new luxury units, tends to loosen the entire housing market, thereby eventually improving conditions for all households, even the poorest. Unless demolition offsets new building, the prices of all units decline relative to incomes, and more options are available to all households, though frictions may weaken this effect in poor areas. Thus, any public policies which stimulate total housing production tend to improve housing conditions among the poor to at least some extent, other things being equal. Clearly, the bigger the total direct public subsidy put into housing, the more new units will be built. In addition, because so much new housing employs debt financing, national monetary and fiscal policies that reduce interest rates can greatly increase the amount of new housing produced in free markets.

F. *The Effects of Varying Public Housing Subsidy Distributions*

Public housing subsidies have two effects which improve housing conditions among poor households: they always increase total housing output, thereby tending to loosen the entire housing market; and they may provide direct access to new housing for poor households if they focus upon aiding such households. But the amount of subsidy per household needed to close the gap between a household's own ability to pay and the cost of a new decent unit is larger, the lower the household's income. Therefore, any given sized public housing subsidy can generate more new production of decent units if concentrated upon middle-income and upper-income groups than if concentrated upon the poorest groups. True, the frictions of the housing market mean that the immediate impact of such larger outputs upon the poorest households will be far less than a lower total output directly distributed to them. Yet focusing housing subsidies upon middle-income groups (as in the United States) enables the government to assist more households per million dollars of subsidy, and therefore may be considered politically more efficient than direct housing aid to the poor.

G. Approaches to Second Best Solutions

In all nations and all historic periods, providing decent housing for every household has been far too expensive for society to achieve without sacrificing other objectives which it considers more desirable. Hence a variety of second best solutions have been tried. Where the poorest groups are politically powerful, there is usually a combination of (1) allowing urban squatters to expropriate housing sites without payment, especially on publicly owned land; (2) allowing large amounts of zero standard housing to be built privately by poor urban squatters; and (3) building some publicly subsidized decent units for poor households in large cities. Where middle-income groups are politically dominant, there is more pressure to prevent squatting and zero standard new construction, and to shift subsidies to directly benefiting middle-income or high-income households.

H. The Location of Low-Income Households in Urban Areas

Throughout the world, most new urban construction occurs on vacant land at the edges of existing built-up areas. It is almost always much cheaper and faster to build on vacant sites than to acquire existing properties, relocate their occupants, demolish them, and then build on their sites. Also, where acute housing shortages prevail, it is politically difficult to destroy existing units because it is so hard to relocate their occupants.

The edge of most urban areas lies on the outskirts relatively distant from the central business district. However, in some cities, more close-in areas have remained vacant because of undesirable features that caused earlier developers to bypass them. For example, in Caracas, close-in hillsides were skipped by early urban developers because of the high costs of building on steep slopes.

In societies which cope with rapid increases in low-income population by housing poor households in new units, the poorest people tend to live at these edges of the developed area, mostly on the periphery, but sometimes also on initially bypassed hillsides, public parks, or swamps. Since it is too expensive to provide decent new units for most such households, the majority usually live in zero standard shacks clustered around these outskirts.

In contrast, societies which prohibit zero standard new construction generally cannot afford to house all or even most low-income population growth in new units. Instead, poor households must concentrate in the lowest price existing units. These tend to be the most dilapidated and obsolete houses, which are usually the oldest in the area. Almost all cities were historically built up in concentric rings outward from their points of origin. Hence the oldest units are close to central commercial areas. Thus, prohibiting poor households from building new zero standard or low standard housing on vacant land radically shifts the spatial concentration of the poor from the outer periphery of a metropolitan area to the inner core, as in the United States. Conversely, in these societies, only relatively affluent families or those receiving public subsidies can afford to occupy the decent new units built on vacant land at the edge of the urban area. True, a few very wealthy households live close to the center in older units they rehabilitate, or new units created through clearance. But these are exceptions to the general rule that whoever lives in new construction occupies the outer portions of a metropolitan area, and whoever lives in older units dominates the near-core area.

II. Basic Strategies for Providing Housing for Low-Income Urban Households

Using the background factors and relationships described above, we can systematically analyze the basic strategies employed in various nations to provide housing for low-income urban households. Each such strategy occurs in a setting influenced by three key exogenous factors: the rate of population growth and population migration patterns; the rate of change of average real income per household; and the rate of change of occupancy costs per household for newly built decent housing units. Variations in these factors influence both the selection of particular housing strategies by public authorities, and the outcomes of whatever strategy is selected. Clearly, a myriad of other exogenous factors can influence these things too, but these three are especially critical.

For purposes of analysis, I will arbitrarily view each basic housing strategy as containing four main elements: the quality standards actually enforced regarding new housing construction, the degree of overall public stimulation of total new housing production, the total amount of public subsidy for housing, and the way this public subsidy is allocated among income groups. A huge number of possible combinations and variations of these elements can be conceived of. But I believe it is useful to narrow down these possibilities to the following three major types of strategies:

Filtering strategies involve strict enforcement of high or moderate quality standards for all new construction, and either (a) no public housing subsidies at all or (b) public subsidies focused mainly on middle-income or high-income households. Thus, nearly all new housing units are occupied by non-poor households. Poor households receive decent units through filtering down of older units from higher income households.

Low-income subsidy strategies also involve strict enforcement of high or moderate quality standards (usually the latter) for all new construction, but include large scale public housing subsidies allocated directly to low-income households. High standard versions require either larger total public subsidies or reach fewer poor households than moderate standard versions. The latter are better able to use the economies of mass produced or industrialized housing.

Minimal standard strategies involve only partial enforcement of any housing quality standards in urban areas, primarily in existing good quality neighborhoods. A great deal of the new construction under such strategies consists of zero standard units built by their occupants. Any housing subsidies employed can be either concentrated on the poor or spread over all income groups.

Additional variations of these strategies can result from differences in the magnitude of both total stimulation of housing production and total public housing subsidies.

III. *The Likely Results and Effectiveness of These Strategies*

The key results and effectiveness of these strategies can be assessed in terms of their locational outcomes and how well they cope with large scale migration of poor households to urban areas.

A. *Their Locational Outcomes*

Filtering strategies cause a concentration of low-income households in or near the central cores of urban areas. Moreover, poor households can gain more housing units only by taking over those formerly occupied by wealthier households. Therefore, if the low-income population in an urban area expands rapidly, it must progressively displace more and more somewhat wealthier households through gradual outward expansion of the areas it occupies. This displacement or transition process causes systematic instability in residential occupancy patterns. It also tends to generate antagonism between the poor newcomers and those groups pressured to leave their existing neighborhoods. If older parts of the urbanized area are under a political jurisdiction different from newer peripheral parts (as in the United States), the concentration of poor households in the older parts can cause major political and fiscal disparities between the core and periphery in the urbanized area.

In contrast, since the other two strategies provide new housing for poor households, those households become concentrated on the outskirts of the urbanized area. Under a minimal quality strategy, nearly all poor households are located in shacks at least partially encircling older built-up areas. But under a low-income subsidy strategy, total subsidies are almost never large enough to house all badly housed poor urban households in new decent housing built on vacant land. Hence at least some poor households, often a large fraction of all those newly entering the urban area, must still concentrate in older existing units near the central core, as in a filtering strategy.

These locational variations have important social class impacts. Where all housing for low-income groups is provided through filtering (as in the United States), the poor are almost completely spatially separated from middle-income and upper-income groups. The central core becomes dominated by the former, and outlying growth areas by the latter. An opposite pattern of spatial segregation occurs in minimal quality strategies, with the poor living outboard of middle- and upper-class groups. However, many households who start out in shacks may gradually improve them as their incomes rise, thereby remaining in a primarily poor neighborhood. But in low-income subsidy strategies (as in Sweden and the Soviet Union), the new units occupied by low income groups are likely to be spatially close to or intermixed with those occupied by higher income groups.

Consequently, any attempt to introduce strong elements of low income subsidy into what has long been a nearly "pure" filtering strategy (as the Department of Housing and Urban Development is proposing) requires moving from strong social class segregation (and in the United States, racial segregation) to much greater spatial mixture of social classes in peripheral areas. The political acceptability of this aspect of the strategy shift may be more important in determining its success than either the physical availability of sites or the cost of required subsidies.

B. *Coping with Large-Scale Urban Inmigration*

Large scale movement of low-income households from rural areas into urban centers has been a worldwide phenomenon in the past few decades. How well can these strategies cope with such movement, and what are the differences in their effectiveness?

During periods of really rapid inflow of poor people into a given urban area, none of the strategies can provide decent housing for all the newcomers, even in the wealthiest nations. Hence there is an inescapable surplus housing need which must somehow be met. If public authorities still prohibit construction of new zero standard or sub-standard units, this need is met through overcrowding or cutting up existing units. Sometimes public authorities themselves build new lower standard units on a temporary basis (such as the Veterans Housing at U.S. universities right after World War II). Where a minimal quality strategy is official policy (usually because the nation cannot afford any other), whole cities of new shacks spring up on the edge of existing urban areas.

No one really knows whether it is more desirable to overcrowd or cut up existing units than to build new substandard ones. Therefore, it is hard to compare the effectiveness of these different approaches. However, low-income subsidy strategies are clearly far more effective than filtering strategies at remedying these conditions among low-income households per million dollars of total public and private investment in housing. This is true because the former provide new decent units directly to poor households. On the other hand, the resulting interference with free markets tends to spread the impact of the housing shortage to middle-income and upper-income groups too, and to distort normal allocations of resources in the economy.

C. *Some Tentative Policy Implications*

Space limitations prohibit any extensive analysis of the strategies summarized above, or their many policy implications. However, two related policy suggestions can be tentatively derived from them. Both spring from the undesirable results of a society's trying to require poor urban households to meet housing quality standards which are in reality beyond their capacity, or the society's, to achieve.

For example, in the U.S. filtering strategy, rigid prohibition of any new construction at less-than-high quality standards forces many poor urban households to live in overcrowded slum conditions. Thus, unrealistic insistence upon high quality in fact produces more low quality than is necessary.

The low-income households concerned would be much better off if the United States allowed construction of new moderate standard units. Then the limited subsidies voted by Congress for direct housing aid to poor households would generate far more units. Also, Congress might be willing to increase those subsidies because it would not seem to be putting poor people into better units than those occupied by the taxpayers providing the subsidies. The widespread insistence of poor households themselves upon very high standards for public housing thus requires them to endure miserable housing conditions longer than would acceptance of moderate quality standards. Some observers hope that Congress will provide large enough direct public subsidies to put every badly housed poor family in a high quality unit in the foreseeable future, or that the filtering process will work well enough to do so without huge direct subsidies. In my opinion, these hopes are largely wishful thinking.

Many poorer nations could also benefit from similarly accepting lower-than-optimal housing quality standards because they produce better results than unrealistically seeking higher standards. Some governments concentrate upon production of a small number of moderate quality subsidized units for the poor, while thousands more zero standard units are built in completely unregulated fashion. The net result would be superior if more public attention were focused upon trying to achieve even extremely low level standards regarding all housing, including shacks. For example, public funds might provide minimum-sized lots for shacks in selected locations, with streets, water and electricity available. This could help control the location of zero standard development so as to conform to urban planning, while allowing room on each lot for future upgrading and immediately providing minimal utilities for all residents.

Hopefully, other policy implications can be derived from the housing strategy model set forth above by examining the impacts of varying both key exogenous factors and the basic elements of each strategy.

[4]
ANTHONY DOWNS

Competition and Community Schools

To an economist, many of the criticisms recently made against big-city public school systems have a familiar ring: they are identical with the complaints that consumers have leveled against monopolies for centuries. Since big-city school boards, administrations, and teachers' organizations are all essentially monopoly organizations, this similarity of discontent is no coincidence.

The classic antidote to monopoly is competition. By introducing alternative sources of supply, competition expands the choice available to consumers. Moreover, these alternative sources are likely to use different methods and approaches, or even to develop wholly new products. Thus, greater variety makes expanded choice really meaningful. Since consumers can shift their trade from suppliers who do not please them, suppliers have a strong incentive to provide what the consumers want. This attitude also means competitors regard innovations positively, as potential means of winning more business (if they can protect new ideas from instant duplication by other competitors). In contrast, monopolists usually view innovations negatively, as a bother designed to upset established routines for no good reason. Clearly, if greater competition causes these results in general, it might produce some tremendous improvements in big-city school systems.

Community schools could represent a limited form of competitive influence within such systems if these new types of schools were organized, operated, and related to other schools in certain ways.

219

The shifting of power in education from a single, monolithic administration to many decentralized boards would be quite similar to the breaking up of a monopoly into many competitors—that is, if consumers really had the power to choose among the competitors, and did not merely find themselves faced by many small monopolists rather than one big one. In this chapter, I will examine some of the possibilities, implications, and problems of introducing more competition into big-city public school systems, and will show how they can be related to community schools.

Requirements for Effective Competition

In order to provide the major benefits of competition, any system of production must possess certain fundamental characteristics. It is not possible to explore all of these here. Instead, five key characteristics will be described and related to existing conditions in most big-city school systems.

MEANS FOR CONSUMERS TO EVALUATE OUTPUTS

If consumers cannot tell a good product from a bad one, they cannot exercise consumer sovereignty to pressure the production system into giving them what they want. In our highly technological society, it is often difficult for consumers to evaluate the quality of products offered them. Is a Ford station wagon better or worse than a Chevrolet station wagon of comparable size and cost? Few people are expert enough to determine the answer. However, since both Fords and Chevrolets are readily available, consumers can directly compare certain measurable traits, such as size, design, and accessories. They can even hire experts to make impartial tests of more complex things, such as acceleration, braking, speed, and stability under loads.

Similar comparisons of more abstract products—such as schooling—require the same basic ingredients. That is, there must be well-defined outputs from different producers; those outputs must be measurable in some way; such measurements must be made; and information about those measurements must be available to consumers. Unfortunately, none of these conditions prevail in today's big-city public school systems. There are few agreed-upon definitions of what public school systems are supposed to produce; measuring those products that can be identified is extremely hard; they are rarely measured because doing so is expensive and potentially threatening to many teachers, administrators, and parents; and such rare information as does exist is usually a closely guarded secret.

Nevertheless, some information is available about the quality of education provided in different parts of the nation. It has generated strong discontent among many parents of children in low-income, big-city areas, especially those where ethnic minorities live, because it shows how poor are the results of public schools there as compared to other areas. But effective competition within, or outside, big-city public school systems can never be stimulated without vastly improving the quality and quantity of information evaluating the outputs of different schools and educational methods. How this can be done will be discussed later.

THE EXISTENCE OF ALTERNATIVE SUPPLIERS

Few "perfect" monopolies exist. Most consumers can usually find some alternative source of supply if they look hard enough, and users of big-city school systems are no exception. Parents living in big cities can send their children to private schools, buy entry into suburban schools without moving (in some cases), or actually move into the jurisdictional area of some other school within the big-city system or into a suburban system. But these alternatives are far more expensive than using the neighborhood public school. Therefore, low-income households cannot employ such alternatives. And even middle-income nonwhite households are restricted from moving into many all-white areas where superior schools are found. Thus, for thousands of households in big cities, there are no educational choices available except sending their children to that public school which has a district encompassing their residence.

Creating realistic alternative choices for these households will not be easy. Even placing control of local schools in the hands of many decentralized school boards will not expand real choices if each family must still use the nearest public school. Consumers—including the lowest-income consumers—must be able to choose among several, at least two and preferably more, alternatives if competition is to have any real effects. Therefore, individual schools must have attendance areas that overlap to some degree. For example, consider an area containing five elementary schools run by a single board of education. Each of these schools exclusively serves an attendance area surrounding it; that is, all students living in that area must attend that school, whereas no one living outside the area can attend that school. Now assume that control of these schools is shifted from a single centralized board into five decentralized boards. This does not create any expansion of choice for individual families if the same attendance policy is retained. However, such an expansion could be achieved by merging all five attendance areas into a single inclusive area, in which each family could apply to attend any school. Additional public schools (perhaps run by outside firms or agencies) could be introduced into the area and assigned attendance areas overlapping those of the original five schools. These expansions of choice would have to be accompanied by some scheme providing public payment of the extra transportation costs resulting from parents' sending their children to schools other than the ones closest to their homes. Otherwise, low-income families would be under economic pressure to continue using the nearest school, even if other options were theoretically available to them.

Inescapably, awarding consumers some freedom of choice creates uncertainty among producers concerning what "share of the market" each school will actually "capture." For example, if each of the five schools served 20 percent of all students initially, allowing consumers free choice might result in 40 percent applying for entry into one school, and only 10 percent into another. Coping with such an outcome raises difficult administrative and capital-planning considerations relevant to the next two requirements for effective competition.

FREEDOM TO OFFER SIGNIFICANTLY VARYING PRODUCTS

Multiplicity of outlets does not guarantee true competition concerning a given product; it must be accompanied by freedom among several producers to vary the nature of the products they offer. If every car dealer sold only red Ford two-door sedans all with the same accessories and at the same price, vastly increasing the number of dealer outlets would not expand consumer choice. Similarly, providing parents with the ability to choose among several schools for their children would not really increase their freedom of choice if exactly the same subjects, approaches, types of teachers, and materials were used in all the schools. True, individual personality differences among principals and teachers always produce some differences among schools, even when they are all governed by identical regulations. But a meaningful range of variation in educational contents and quality can be offered to parents only if principals of individual schools, or supervisors of relatively small districts, have real freedom to vary the products they offer consumers. Thus, decentralization of control over a significant part of what goes on in individual schools is an essential prerequisite for effective competition in education. Moreover, such decentralization must cover most of the key elements of educational contents. It is a sham to announce that individual principals or district superintendents are free to innovate and then retain centralized and standardized control over hiring and firing of teachers, teachers' salary levels, selection of textbooks, allowable classroom sizes, a large part of the curriculum, most administrative procedures, and capital expenditures for new buildings and equipment.

This means that competition among several schools for students cannot be the force that generates decentralized control of those schools. Allowing parents to choose among different schools might set up much stronger pressures accentuating those limited product differentiations that could be developed within existing centralized rules and regulations. But those rules and regulations must be greatly relaxed to allow wide variation among individual schools before competition can exert its maximum impact. To create fully effective competition requires overcoming all the frustrating and difficult obstacles that have so far blocked significant decentralization of control in most big-city systems.

Nevertheless, I do not believe it is feasible to wait for complete decentralization before initiating major experiments in greater competition. At least a few competitive units in which the local board, the principal, or individual teacher had significant autonomy could initially be set up outside the existing public school system, or as special, additional units supplementing it in certain areas. Similarly, competition among units within the system could be started even though only marginal decentralization of control existed (though this is inferior to the proposal just mentioned). But to postpone using competition until "perfect" decentralization is achieved is to forgo using it forever—even though it could be an immediate force exerting at least some added pressure to create greater decentralization of control.

CONSUMER CONTROL OVER SIGNIFICANT RESOURCES

In a free enterprise economy, consumers vote with dollars for the products they like—and against those they dislike. They can do so because they have the power to allocate those dollars to whatever producers they prefer (except for a few monopolies like the telephone company). Since the income represented by consumers' dollars is vital to producers, consumer-spending choices tremendously influence producer behavior. Similarly, if competition is to have any meaningful impact upon big-city public school systems, the consumers must have control over at least some resources used in their operation.

Some control is already exercised by school consumers. As voters, they decide on bond issues and sometimes indirectly upon other tax increases affecting the total resources available to the system. When a family moves from one place to another to gain access to better schools, it shifts its taxable resources into the new area. This increases the tax base there, and perhaps decreases it in the original area. It also moves its children from one school to another, and children are significant educational resources in several ways. First, they influence the total attendance figures used by each school as part of its formula for obtaining state aid. Second, the quality of education in each school is markedly influenced by the nature of the students attending it. In general, students from middle-income, upper-income, or other homes with strong cultural environments represent an educational asset to any school. But students from culturally deprived homes may represent an educational liability —considered solely from this viewpoint. Thus when parents move a child from one school to another, they affect both the financial and nonfinancial resources available to the two schools concerned.

Naturally, they also affect the demands placed upon those schools by their student loads.

But what about parents who cannot afford to move in pursuit of better schools, or are prevented from doing so by racial prejudice or some other force? If they are offered true choices among alternative schools, they can at least shift their children from one school to another instead of shifting their homes. However, this might result in a marked disparity between the number of students asking to attend each school and its physical capacity to handle them, as mentioned earlier. If 500 students apply to a school with a capacity for 100 students because it provides unusually desirable educational opportunities, how can the available places be rationed among the applicants?

At present, this problem is solved by setting boundaries so that the situation does not arise. But at the same time this eliminates any true choice among alternatives. Private schools often handle this problem by raising their tuition. But such price rationing discriminates against poor families and hence is inappropriate for public schools. The simple rule of first come, first served may be used, but this tends to favor students from the most intelligent and culturally advanced families, since they are more likely to plan ahead. The only remaining methods of allocation I can think of are random selection and use of geographic quotas. The latter can be illustrated by a system that divides the total attendance area into five parts with equal student population; classifies all applicants by location into five groups corresponding with these zones; sets a quota of 20 percent of total enrollment for each zone; and fills that quota from the applicants for each zone through random selection among them. If the boundaries of the five areas are carefully drawn in relation to the socioeconomic and ethnic traits of the population, this system can result in a well-balanced student body providing both ethnic and social-class integration in combinations likely to remain stable (that is, parents of one group will not withdraw their children to avoid the resulting balance).

Nevertheless, as long as any such rationing system still allocates the same proportion of total resources to each school as an exclusive district system, consumer choices are not really affecting the distribution of resources in the system. The worst school would still get

20 percent of all students, state aid, and other resources. Furthermore, parents whose children were assigned to that school would not really be exercising the kind of free choice vital to a truly competitive system. Many would have preferred to send their children to some other school, but it was too crowded. This brings us to the final requirement for a truly competitive system.

FREEDOM FOR CONSUMER PREFERENCES TO
INFLUENCE RESOURCE ALLOCATION

A key long-run advantage of competitive markets is that they cause the production of those goods consumers like to expand and the production of those they dislike to contract or disappear. This same characteristic is essential to effective competition within big-city public school systems. Consumers must be able to use their power over resources to alter the long-range output of different types of education. At present, this is possible in theory when consumers move from one city to another. If most of the residents of city A were so repelled by its schools that they moved to much-preferred city B nearby, then the schools in city A would be forced to reduce their operations—and those in city B would expand.

Unfortunately, the economic ability to shift locations in search of better schools is unevenly distributed in society. Wealthier people can and do move to areas where the schools are reputed to be excellent. Those schools consequently expand. They can do so partly because the arrival of more middle-income or upper-income families within their attendance areas gives them the taxable resources they need for expansion. Furthermore, most students from such homes are positively oriented to education and benefit from relatively cultured home environments. Hence, their very presence in classrooms improves the quality of education. In contrast, poor students whose families cannot afford to move are left in the schools considered relatively undesirable. The departure of middle-income and upper-income students from those classrooms causes a higher concentration of students from relatively deprived homes, thereby lowering the quality of education. Moreover, rising concentration of poor families within the attendance areas of such schools reduces the per-student taxable resources available to support them. Thus, making alternative choices available to the wealthier families in society but not to the poorer—and to middle-income whites more than to middle-income nonwhites—tends to create long-run effects beneficial to the wealthier—especially whites—and detrimental to the poorer—especially nonwhites. What other tactics might help public school consumers gain the long-run advantages of competition without this undesirable result?

We have already described a system for allowing parents to express choices among five elementary schools all serving the same merged attendance area. But if all the parents who wanted to send their children to the best-liked school actually were allowed to do so, it might become extremely overcrowded. At the same time, the worst-liked school would be nearly empty. This would result in an inefficient use of invested capital, and might significantly reduce the quality of education in both schools. Yet adopting any system of student rationing that ultimately allocates 20 percent of all resources to each school does not result in any expansion of the most-preferred school or contraction of the least-preferred one. Expansion and contraction could be encouraged by either or both of the following tactics:

The first tactic is the use of a certain amount of flexible classroom and other school facilities that could be moved from one place to another. For example, if a school system consisted of 60 percent permanent buildings and 40 percent mobile classrooms, then the latter could be shifted around each year to accommodate parents' preferences for specific schools. Teachers and other resources would also be shifted correspondingly. This kind of arrangement could quickly be put into effect in cities with rapidly growing populations and school enrollments. A high proportion of the new physical capacity to be added each year could consist of portable facilities. In cities that already have fixed plants adequate for present and future enrollments, addition of such mobile capacity would represent a huge added expense and cause underutilization of existing capacity. However, in such cities, if some older facilities must be retired because of obsolescence, they could be replaced with portable units so as to arrive at the desired balance without added expense.

This tactic has two decided disadvantages. First, most parents—and many teachers—regard portable facilities as inferior per se and stigmatizing to the schools concerned. Second, moving such facilities—and other resources—each year would be expensive and might be administratively disruptive.

The second tactic is that of shifting control over the nature of education in accordance with the expressed votes of parents' attendance choices while still using the same buildings and classrooms. For example, assume there are five equal-sized schools in an attendance area containing 1,000 students. If 500 of these students apply to attend school X because its approach is so well liked (or for any other reasons), then the methods used in school X would be extended to at least one and perhaps one and a half other schools. This could be done either by expanding the administrative and curriculum jurisdiction of the principal of school X to these other schools or by putting pressure on the principals of the other schools to adopt the methods used in school X. Both of these tactics imply that some central agency exists within the system to perform these reallocations of resources or authority. They also imply that the methods used in school X can be extended almost instantaneously, or at least quite rapidly, to other schools without loss of quality. This is highly unrealistic, but it could be rendered more feasible if a longer period of adjustment were allowed.

Both of these tactics probably seem utterly impractical to the people who actually operate big-city school systems. Yet some version of them must be incorporated into those systems if competition is to have meaningful impact upon public education in large cities. Even now, there is an implicit assumption that each centralized school administration will somehow seek out and discover the most effective methods of education, and introduce them into the classrooms throughout its system. But it is precisely the failure to incorporate the most desired educational methods—and to reduce those least desired—that is one of the chief complaints against existing big-city systems. Moreover, a key response to this failure is the continuing migration of middle-class families with children from big cities to the suburbs. Consequently, even if big-city school administrators believe the responsiveness to consumer preferences indicated by the above tactics are impossible, many consumers clearly believe they are both desirable and possible—and act accordingly.

The Need for a Comprehensive Evaluation System

The preceding analysis emphasized the critical need for accurate and easily available information which evaluates both the educational performance of public schools and the methods of education used in them. Without such information, consumers cannot tell whether their children are really getting proper training or to what extent certain parts of that training are fine and others are terrible. Parents make such judgments now. But they do so only on the basis of personal impressions gained from comparing experiences in different schools with their friends and acquaintances or with the few national test scores that professionals release to them. Many parents in low-income neighborhoods do not even have these elements upon which to base accurate judgments. Therefore, it would be pointless to make the other institutional changes necessary to introduce competition into big-city public school systems without first creating an accurate and comprehensive educational evaluation system, putting it into operation throughout the school system, and making the results known to parents.

Such an evaluation system might also create pressures on individual schools, principals, local boards, and teachers to adopt those methods that have proved most effective in training various specific kinds of students. Knowledge of the success of certain approaches, and the failure of others, would generate both parental and professional pressure to expand the former and contract the latter. Hence, an accurate and widely publicized evaluation system could act as a substitute for the two tactics described in the previous section which seem both so necessary and so impractical.

Furthermore, an evaluation system of this type could greatly improve the efficiency of resource allocation within our enormous national education system. It is rather astounding that around $50 billion per year is spent on education in the United States and yet there is no systematic way of measuring the effectiveness of this giant expenditure. Few accurate measurements of relationships between costs and effectiveness are made anywhere in the system, and none are regularly applied, even to the larger parts, to measure comparative performance. As a result, widespread disparities in both effectiveness and efficiency appear and continue without any corrective action. It is widely believed that public schools in the South are generally inferior to those in the North. Many observers also believe that public schools in the East have higher academic standards than those in the West (especially in California). Yet even these conclusions are based mainly on a few national achievement tests in a narrow range of subjects, casual inspection of expenditure-per-pupil data, and personal observations. Admittedly, I am no expert on the nature of educational research, and I may be ill-informed about much pertinent analysis in this area. Yet I believe it is fair to conclude that existing methods of evaluating educational performance are grossly inadequate. They can neither identify nor encourage the adoption of many potentially huge gains in effectiveness from our current national spending on schools.

Accurate evaluation of educational effectiveness will be especially important if community schools become widespread in the United States. The shift of control over curricula to many decentralized school boards will probably lead to a wide variety of educational approaches in different cities, and even within each large city. Each school board will have a vested interest in claiming that its approach is successful. Unless there is some relatively objective way to evaluate these multiple approaches, neither parents, nor national educational policy makers, nor local taxpayers will know which methods are really working and which ones are failing. Admittedly, they do not know now either. Thus, the case for an accurate, comprehensively applied evaluation system will be no stronger under community schools than it is at present. But this case is already overwhelmingly persuasive.

Problems in Performance Evaluation Systems

One of the main reasons for which so few school systems have developed comprehensive and accurate means of evaluating their performance is the extreme difficulty of doing so. The need for good evaluation is desperate, but the need alone yields no clue as to how it can be met. In this section, I will identify some of the key problems involved, and suggest some potential approaches to solving them—or at least coping with them.

MULTIPLE ASPECTS OF EDUCATION

It is widely agreed that children who go to school should learn how to read, write, and perform certain basic mathematical skills with at least minimal proficiency. Their ability to do these things can be objectively measured by means of tests and compared with the abilities of other children of the same age and background. But schooling is also designed to have many other impacts on the children it affects. These include creating or bolstering self-confidence; inculcating certain basic democratic values; encouraging positive attitudes toward work; providing minimal skills and disciplinary habits relevant to work; and teaching basic skills of interpersonal relations. Measuring these things—indeed, just defining them—is extraordinarily difficult. In some cases, it may be impossible. Yet few educators believe that these nonacademic aspects of schooling are unimportant, and many believe they are more important than basic reading, writing, and arithmetic.

Therefore, no evaluation system should evade trying to measure the capabilities, and changes in capabilities, of students regarding these nonacademic aspects of education. Attempts should be made to develop clear definitions of the traits concerned, and descriptions of various states of proficiency concerning them. These will differ from place to place, especially if community schools become widespread. Nevertheless, the different participants in the education system—including teachers, students, parents, and counselors—should be asked to evaluate students using these criteria. Admittedly, subjective judgments may be prominent in such measurements, but trying to meet this problem head on will provide many significant insights, even if precise interpersonal or interschool comparisons prove elusive.

MULTIPLE DISTRIBUTION GOALS

Viewed as a whole, the nation's public school system (or that of any state, district, or city) expends certain resources in order to attain one or more of the following distributions of educational results:

1. *The minimum-citizenship goal*—there should be some basic minimum level of proficiency and capability for all students regarding the various aspects of education discussed above, especially those most relevant to democratic citizenship.

2. *The maximum-system-output goal*—the total capabilities of all students considered as a group (perhaps best measured by their total resulting productivity) should be made as large as possible within the constraints imposed by the total resources available to the system.

3. *The equal-opportunity goal*—all students emerging from the system (say, upon high school graduation) should have approximately the same capabilities for entering into the postschool portions of their lives.

4. *The maximum-individual-advancement goal*—each student should be given as much development of his individual potential as possible, within the constraints imposed by total available resources.

Undoubtedly, other worthy goals could also be identified. But I believe these four express the major system-wide objectives of education most commonly discussed in the United States.

These goals imply widely differing distributions of publicly supplied educational resources among various types of students and various geographic areas. This is true mainly because such resources are only one of the four basic inputs affecting the educational performance of particular students, as will be discussed later. The degree to which individual students possess the other three inputs varies widely in a rather systematic fashion. This variance is related to such factors as their parents' income and socioeconomic status, their geographic location in the nation and within metropolitan areas, and their ethnic nature. Consequently, pursuing each of the goals exclusively, without regard to the others, would result in very different allocations of publicly supplied educational inputs. At one extreme, the equal-opportunity goal would require a heavy concentration of resources among the poorest and most culturally deprived students. They would receive much higher per-student inputs than children from higher-income and more advantaged homes. The minimum-citizenship goal would also require concentrating more inputs per student among the most-deprived children. It might not result in quite as unequal a distribution, since the poorest-qualified children would not have to be brought up to the level of attainment with the best-qualified but only up to some minimum standard of basic achievement. In contrast, the maximum-system-output goal would concentrate publicly supplied inputs on the best-qualified students. This would result in the greatest total gain in technical proficiency per dollar invested.[1] The maximum-individ-

---

[1] Henry Levin argues that the highest marginal payoff would come from applying added resources to students from the most deprived backgrounds. He assumes that there are constantly declining marginal returns to investment in education. Since deprived

ual-advancement goal results in an indeterminate allocation pattern, since it really provides no precisely defined objective. If the goal is interpreted as equal advancement (in contrast to equal achievement), then this allocation would also probably favor the lowest-income and most-deprived students. It takes more dollars of publicly supplied inputs to advance such students a given amount in achievement than it does students from more advantaged homes.

At present, the allocation of such inputs greatly favors children from middle- and upper-income homes, especially whites, and penalizes those from poorer homes, especially nonwhites. This most closely resembles the allocation appropriate for the maximum-system-output goal. It is so unlike the allocation appropriate for the equal-opportunity goal that any major public emphasis upon that goal would call for radical revisions in the existing distribution of educational resources.

The existence of multiple goals and their call for such widely varying resource allocation patterns for publicly supplied inputs pose a difficult problem for anyone trying to design an educational evaluation system. Such a system should tell its users how well existing education methods achieve some set of goals concerning the performance of the educational system as a whole, as well as the performance of each district, school, or classroom. But which of these system-wide objectives should be used in making this assessment? Since any educational system should probably serve several goals simultaneously, the question really becomes what relative emphasis should be placed on each goal? Different groups of consumers would undoubtedly provide widely varying answers. Their answers would depend to a great extent on how each type of emphasis

---

children have had fewer total resources applied to their education (by their parents as well as by public school systems) than less-deprived children, the more-deprived children are not as "far out" on their marginal payoff curves as less-deprived children. However, I believe that the marginal returns from education are not constantly declining. Translating this jargon into English, it seems to me that children from affluent backgrounds who have already received considerable education can absorb a given additional amount of knowledge, or learn an additional amount of a skill, with less input from teachers or other publicly supplied resources than deprived children can. Admittedly, this is a purely subjective judgment on my part. See Henry M. Levin, "The Failure of the Public Schools and the Free Market Remedy," *Urban Review*, Vol. 2 (June 1968), pp. 32–37 (Brookings Reprint 148).

would affect the total share of publicly supplied inputs going to their children. Therefore, the evaluation system would probably have to be designed so that it could be used to assess the effectiveness of the system in attaining each of these four goals (and perhaps others) independently. This would allow each consumer group to arrive at its own conclusions concerning whether the system was allocating publicly supplied inputs properly.

MULTIPLE INPUTS AFFECTING EDUCATIONAL ACHIEVEMENT

Recent large-scale studies of educational performance in the nation's schools have dramatically shown that activities in those schools are only one of the basic factors influencing educational achievement.[2] In fact, it is useful to view the output of the educational process as resulting from at least four different inputs for each child: (1) genetically determined capabilities inherited from parents; (2) the child's home environment, both present and past (particularly during the first few years of life); (3) the school system and all its component parts (including teachers, buildings, other facilities, methods, systems of mixing students); and (4) the child's nonhome, nonschool environment, which will be referred to as the neighborhood environment. These causal factors could be broken down somewhat differently, but this classification is sufficient to illustrate the key points concerned here.

Educational achievement, however defined, is influenced by all four of these factors simultaneously. Thus, attributing it to only one factor is neither just nor accurate. For example, system-wide testing usually indicates that children in schools serving upper-income white neighborhoods score much better on most tests than those in schools serving low-income nonwhite neighborhoods. Yet it might be false to conclude that the former schools were doing a better job than the latter. The superior achievement of the higher-scoring students might be entirely attributable to the three nonschool factors. The schools serving the lower-scoring students could actually be doing a much better job than those serving the higher-scoring students, thereby causing the achievement gap between

[2] See James S. Coleman and others, *Equality of Educational Opportunity* (U.S. Office of Education, 1966), referred to as the Coleman Report. See also U.S. Commission on Civil Rights, *Racial Isolation in the Public Schools* (1967).

these two groups to be smaller than it would have been if both schools had performed with equal effectiveness.

Clearly, any useful educational evaluation system must be able to measure the impacts of the school system itself separately from the impacts of these other factors. Moreover, it should be able to measure the specific effects of various parts of the school system (such as training of teachers, quality of facilities, system of mixing students, attitudes of teachers, methods of instruction, and types of curricula). Only if it exhibits such sensitivity can an evaluation system enable those using it to make effective decisions on which publicly supplied inputs to alter and in what ways. But this kind of analytic separation of causal contributions to a single result is extremely difficult to build into any educational evaluation system. The widespread controversy among statisticians over the meaning of the Coleman Report perfectly illustrates this problem. To cope with this problem will require any workable evaluation system to have the following characteristics:

First, it must be used throughout a large part of the entire American school system simultaneously and in the same manner. Only in this way can a sufficiently large and varied sample be obtained so that the impact of a wide variety of individual factors can be isolated through standard statistical techniques. An evaluation system adopted by a single city might be large enough if that city was a big one. But if it is used only in one small suburban area, with a relatively homogeneous population in terms of socioeconomic and ethnic traits, then the evaluations it provides may not be measuring the performance of schools at all. This means that entire states would be much better units for the definition and administration of educational evaluation than individual school districts, and the entire nation would probably be the best base. However, it will be extremely difficult to get statewide or nationwide agreement on any specific method of measuring educational achievement—especially concerning those elements not easily subjected to written performance tests (such as success in building student self-confidence or imparting basic democratic values).

Second, a key part of the system should be comparing the performance of each group of children at different points in time. This would provide before and after results that would isolate the impact of the schools since—presumably—the other three factors will not have varied significantly between these testing points. In reality, children's capabilities change significantly merely because they get older and acquire better coordination and more general experience. But this could be largely offset by relatively frequent evaluation (at least once a year, and perhaps more), and by the next device described.

Third, major emphasis in evaluation should be placed upon comparisons among parts of the school system serving students from similar home and neighborhood environments. Thus, the performance of schools serving low-income neighborhoods should be compared with each other, rather than with the performances of schools serving upper-income areas. (This should not preclude the latter kinds of comparison, however, since they are necessary to certain system-wide effectiveness evaluations.) This would be analogous to dividing sailboats into specific categories or classes for comparing the performances of their crews. Such categorization should at least intellectually—though perhaps not emotionally—counteract some of the resistance to evaluation from teachers and administrators who fear that unfair comparisons will be made in criticism of their performances. (Unfortunately, many are equally afraid of fair comparisons.)

Fourth, the specific contents and procedures used in evaluation tests must be adapted to the particular experiences of students with tremendously varying backgrounds. Negro children reared in low-income urban slums do not have the same mental images, vocabularies, sense experiences, or even world outlooks as children growing up in wealthy all-white suburbs, on isolated Appalachian farms, or in borderline barrios where English is seldom spoken. Therefore, the techniques used to evaluate children's educational skills, and the impact of schools upon them, must be adapted to the particular experiences of the various types of children concerned. This implies that a wide variety of evaluation techniques and vehicles must be developed. It also seems inconsistent with the first characteristic for an effective evaluation system mentioned above: that it be used throughout a large part of the entire school system simultaneously and in the same manner. Admittedly, creating differently adapted evaluative techniques that still permit intergroup comparisons will not be easy. But reaching the moon was not easy either, yet sufficient national resources were applied to accomplish that task. And in my opinion the potential payoff for developing an effective educational evaluation system is vastly greater than the payoff for reaching the moon. Hence, an effort much greater than our present one should be devoted to this task.

DEFINING SYSTEM BOUNDARIES

Selecting the area to be included in any evaluation system will have a crucial impact upon the ways in which that system might be used to influence the allocation of publicly supplied educational inputs. At least two of the other three basic educational inputs are unevenly distributed through space. Thus, each school attendance area, or school district, contains a set of consumers quite different from the average composition of students in the nation or state as a whole. Families with home environments conducive to relatively high-level educational achievement tend to live in areas with other such families. Together they create neighborhood environments equally conducive to high-level achievement. Conversely, families with home environments that discourage high-level educational achievement also tend to cluster together. This produces neighborhood environments with similarly discouraging effects. Moreover, since most school systems use the neighborhood school principle to establish student mixtures, such spatial clustering means that students of each type tend to encounter similar type students in their classes. But classroom environment is a key ingredient in any school system. Hence the operation of the school system in such a residentially clustered society tends to further aggravate the inequalities of educational achievement resulting from home and neighborhood environments.

Insofar as the equal-opportunity objective is relevant to public education, it calls for an allocation that uses publicly supplied inputs to compensate for the inequalities resulting from the other inputs affecting educational achievement. But the practical implications of this conclusion for any given school vary sharply. They depend on whether that "system" is considered to be the schools in just one small community, an entire metropolitan area, a state, or the whole nation. At present, states provide a significant part of all publicly supplied inputs to local public schools. Most states do not allocate those resources to any well-defined and high priority goal (or set of goals). They largely leave the pursuit of such goals to individual school districts. The formula used to pass out state educational funds is based mainly (though not always exclusively) upon equal per-student distribution. Insofar as the sources of such state funds are regressive (as are property taxes and sales taxes), this approach aggravates income inequalities. But this aspect of the issue is too complex to explore here. However, it is clear that the basic duality of state funding for educational operations—collecting funds on a statewide basis but leaving the decision of their effects up to individual districts—has a profound impact upon the net inequalities of educational achievement in each state.

This result could be either reinforced or counteracted by future educational evaluation systems, depending upon what geographic areas they apply to. If a single evaluation system is used throughout an entire state, it will soon reveal profound inequalities in educational achievements. Experts know that these inequalities now exist. But there are few stark statistics that explicitly identify and measure them in the dramatic ways that a statewide evaluation system would. Political or legal pressure for much greater equality of results would be likely to emerge quickly from such a revelation. This might result in some effort to allocate state-supplied resources to compensate for the inequalities of distribution of the other causal factors described above. On the other hand, if all evaluation systems are strictly local in nature, they would use varying techniques that would obscure such statewide comparisons. The resulting pressures for greater equalization of educational opportunity would probably be much lower, as they are now.

In my opinion, every state should insist upon statewide evaluation of at least some key components of educational achievement. Since the state supplies a significant fraction of public school funds to all districts, it has the right—indeed, the obligation—to ask for some accounting of how effectively its funds are being used—not just whether they are being spent without fraud. Many states already require local schools to teach certain subjects or even use certain textbooks. Therefore, it is certainly reasonable for them to ask localities to appraise the effectiveness of their educational efforts by

COMPETITION AND COMMUNITY SCHOOLS 239

using certain standardized evaluation methods. As an added encouragement, the federal government should require every state that accepts any federal educational assistance to institute at least some statewide evaluation system on an annual basis, with results made public for each district and school.

LOCAL RESISTANCE

Most people do not like to have their activities scrutinized and evaluated by "outsiders." This seems especially repugnant if the results are to be made public and compared to similar examinations of other people engaged in the same activities. Such "auditing" of behavior may be both within the rights of the community that pays the auditors and highly beneficial to it, but these truths do not usually diminish community resistance. After all, any competent evaluation of an activity carried out on a large scale, like teaching in elementary and secondary schools, is bound to reveal that only a minority of those evaluated are superior in effectiveness. By definition, most will be rated as either average or below average. Thus, the majority have little to gain in terms of their own status and prestige, and perhaps quite a bit to lose. Even many parents, who stand to benefit most from evaluating the effectiveness of teachers, are often reluctant to subject the achievement levels of their own children to rigorous comparison with those of other children for fear of losing prestige or status.

This nearly universal resistance to evaluation occurs in many forms. The most obvious is opposing any evaluation scheme at all. More subtle is limiting the scope of such schemes. A third is insuring that control over the design and operation of the schemes is maintained by members of the organizations to be evaluated, so they can exclude the most threatening forms of evaluation. A fourth form of resistance is insisting that the results of any evaluation be kept confidential, or disclosing them to the public in such diluted forms that no individuals or schools can be pinpointed as incompetent or ineffective. The last form is demanding that no remedial actions be based upon the results of evaluation systems—particularly that salaries and other types of compensation be entirely divorced from effectiveness of performance.

In my opinion, the basic motive for all these forms of resistance is the dual fear of being revealed as ineffective, or being pressured to change in ways that might increase individual effort. However, this fear is rarely mentioned by those who support such resistance. Instead, they contend that the particular form of resistance they support is in the public interest. For example, it is commonly argued that outsiders should neither design nor control evaluation systems since they are not familiar with local problems, techniques, or educational objectives. Even more frequent is the contention that evaluation schemes cost far more money than the hard-pressed school systems can afford to spend.

It is these forms of defensive resistance, rather than any technical difficulties of designing or operating evaluation systems, that are now and will continue to be the major obstacles to widespread adoption of evaluation systems. Moreover, as teachers' unions become more widespread and more powerful, such resistance will greatly increase. Ironically, supporters of community schools are likely to be just as defensive about subjecting themselves to "impartial evaluations" as are the supporters of established school systems, who are now accused of ineffective performance—and for the same reasons.

How can such nearly universal—and intense—resistance to evaluation be overcome? I can only offer the following suggestions as possible tactics:

First, state and federal agencies responsible for providing funds to local school districts should insist upon use of evaluation systems with certain basic characteristics as a requirement for receiving aid. This would provide a strong incentive for adoption.

Second, evaluation systems should be designed and operated by persons outside the district public school administration, but that administration should have some voice in selecting the evaluators. They could perhaps come from local universities or consulting firms in which the administration has confidence, possibly because of previous experiences.

Third, the analogy of public auditing done by outside accountants should be used to persuade congressmen, other officials, citizens, and major public media that evaluation systems not only make sense but are necessary to protect the public's legitimate interest in using its money wisely. The growing understanding and support for planning, programming, and budgeting systems provides further intellectual underpinning for effective evaluation systems.

Fourth, proposed evaluation schemes should not be linked to

mechanisms that would translate evaluation results into changes in school behavior. Deciding what to do in response to such results should be left up to the parents, educators, and politicians in each district. Thus emphasizing only the provision of accurate data may reduce the threatening image of evaluation systems in the minds of those who fear any loss of local control over public education.

Finally, evaluation schemes could initially be restricted to community schools. The diversity of approaches likely to appear in these schools makes the need for some means of measuring their performance seem plausible. Also, their experimental character fits in well with the need for innovation in the design of evaluation systems. Even more important, the majority of existing educators will not be involved in running community schools; thus they would not feel threatened by evaluation systems aimed only at those schools. Using evaluation systems only in community schools could even have a vindictive appeal to those educators who believe that community schools cannot work. Even if community schools did fail to improve educational effectiveness directly, they would still be making an important contribution to overall educational effectiveness by opening the door to widespread employment of accurate evaluation systems.

SCARCITY OF RESOURCES

Most big-city public school systems are desperately short of financial resources. Therefore, they regard any diversion of available funds from educational programs to other activities as too wasteful or luxurious to contemplate. The argument that diversion of $\frac{1}{2}$ of 1 percent of all their funds into evaluation might result in a 10 percent or greater improvement in the effectiveness of the remaining 99.5 percent of all funds has so far failed to sway this resistance. However, I believe this is largely because there is so little evidence that effective evaluation systems can actually be designed. Once the possibility of creating and using such systems effectively has been demonstrated, school boards throughout the nation will be far more receptive to installing them. The initial, key task, then, is getting a few well-designed systems under way.

This is a "natural" situation for the use of foundation funding or federal experimental funding. Money for development of a large-scale evaluation system over a five-year period might be tied to money for some other kind of program which a big-city system especially desires. This would "sweeten" the package so as to make acceptance of an evaluation system more likely. One such program, which could also be used as a testing ground for the evaluation system, might be the development of prototype community schools on an experimental basis. Once an evaluation system was placed in operation, its success (or failure) at stimulating improvements in the schools concerned would greatly increase (or further reduce) the incentive of other school boards to launch similar programs.

Alternative Ways To Introduce Competition into Big-City Public School Systems

Assuming that greater competition in big-city public school systems is generally desirable, there are several specific ways to attain it. Some are mutually exclusive; but most could be used in combination.

WIDESPREAD AND WELL-PUBLICIZED USE OF EVALUATION SYSTEMS

The simplest way to create greater competition among public schools would be to design, install, and use educational effectiveness evaluation systems along the lines discussed earlier. Although such systems would probably encounter great initial resistance, their use would actually require no significant institutional or administrative changes in existing public school systems. They would generate greater competition solely by revealing to the consumers of education, and to all the professionals concerned, the relative effectiveness of each school, district, educational approach, or other element subject to measurement. Presumably, the persons in charge of those aspects that appeared to be least effective would receive heavy pressure from those they serve, from their own professional pride, and from other educational professionals to adopt elements revealed as more effective.

Competition through better information would be most furthered by evaluation systems that measured (1) the objective level of achievement of the students in each school (or even each classroom) related to analogous levels for all the other students in the system concerned, in the entire state, and in the whole nation, and particularly to other students in similar home and neighborhood environments; (2) the contribution to that achievement of the school itself, and of specific elements within the school (such as teachers, methods, student mixture); (3) the contribution of the school to the attainment of nonacademic goals of education; and (4) the effectiveness of various specific educational techniques in relation to their costs (not just in relation to their results, as is typical of existing educational evaluations).

As noted earlier, formidable technical and political obstacles inhibit immediate use of evaluation systems to stimulate competition in big-city school systems. Therefore, two types of compromises concerning evaluation systems appear necessary. First, any evaluation scheme that is at all sensible should be encouraged and initiated as soon as possible, even if it does not exhibit all or most of the desirable qualities described above. Second, there is no reason to wait until effective evaluation systems are designed before using the other forms of competition, as set forth below. It may be hard for parents to assess the quality of the alternative educational products offered them by competition without a good evaluation system. Nevertheless, any significant increase in competition is likely to produce desirable results and generate healthy pressures on present big-city school monopolies.

USE OF COMMUNITY SCHOOLS TO ENCOURAGE DIVERSITY

Community schools would also encourage a degree of competition within public school systems if they had at least two key characteristics. The first is a diversity of educational approaches. This would presumably arise if a wide variety of communities actually had control over significant portions of the curricula in schools serving them. The second is an evaluation system that would measure the effectiveness of these different approaches and promulgate the results throughout the system. Both of these attributes would generate some of the benefits of competition even if students are compelled to attend the school serving their area of the city rather than being given a choice of several schools. Again, knowledge of what worked and what failed should generate at least some pressure on schools that are failing to adopt the successful approaches used in those that are succeeding—or at least doing better.

USE OF OVERLAPPING ATTENDANCE AREAS

There are several ways that overlapping attendance areas, discussed earlier, could be used to create greater competition within an existing public school system.

Expansion of existing attendance areas. If attendance areas for several schools located close to each other were merged, then students anywhere in the enlarged area could attend any of the schools serving it. This would cause a concentration of applicants at the schools considered the best, and a shrinkage of applicants at those considered the worst. This approach would generate higher total transportation costs than the pure neighborhood school system. It might also require some form of student-rationing system other than geographic location. However, because simply merging attendance areas would not involve deliberately planned diversity, differences in quality within the system would mainly result from accidents of supervisory abilities. Most parents would probably continue to send their children to the school that was geographically most convenient, rather than encouraging them to go longer distances to find higher quality. Hence, the magnitude of the additional transportation costs involved, and the pressure to use nongeographic rationing, would probably not be great over the whole system; nor would the impact of the resulting competition become very significant.

Expansion of attendance areas plus creation of community schools. This plan is similar to the one above but would involve more deliberately planned diversity among schools. Hence, the ability of students to choose from among several reasonably proximate schools would represent a more meaningful choice. This might result in a greater convergence on certain schools regarded as superior, and more avoidance of those considered inferior. Consequently, the whole system would not be so dominated by sheer geographic convenience (though I believe that would probably remain the single most significant factor in parental choice of schools). Transportation costs would rise significantly, and the pressure to adopt some kind of nongeographic student-rationing system would also mount. Furthermore, the appearance of much greater diversity of educational approaches would create greater pressure to allow parents in any given area to send their children to schools located elsewhere, even though doing so would be less convenient. This would occur because some parents in each neighborhood would surely disagree with the particular educational approach or emphasis adopted by the community school serving that neighborhood. To insure proper freedom of choice, these parents would have to be allowed to send their children to some alternative schools. These alternatives could either be community schools elsewhere or schools still run by the centralized school administration, or both.

Community schools can either be entirely new structures (or at least structures newly used for schooling) added onto the existing system (in which case, the central authorities might still operate schools in almost every neighborhood), or conversions of existing schools into community-controlled schools (in which case, the central authorities would be running fewer schools). But in either case, use of enlarged attendance areas would be extremely important as a means of introducing and maintaining competition within the system.

Expansion of attendance areas plus creation of experimental schools. This approach is similar to the one just described except that the alternative schools would be run by innovation-oriented groups (such as private firms, universities, or local volunteers) rather than community-oriented groups—or perhaps in conjunction with the latter. For example, a community school board might select a basic approach to education, and then contract with a private firm to carry out that approach. This mixture of public control and private administration has already been endorsed by such educational experts as Theodore Sizer and Christopher Jencks.[3] It would provide many private firms interested in educational markets with a chance to show what they could do, thereby generating a new source of competition to existing public schools.

AWARDING PARENTS VOUCHERS TO BUY SCHOOLING

Milton Friedman has suggested that competition could be injected into public education by having educational services financed publicly but produced by a variety of private, profit-motivated

---

[3] See Christopher Jencks, "Is the Public School Obsolete?" *Public Interest*, No. 2 (Winter 1966), pp. 18-27, and Theodore Sizer, "Reform and the Control of Education" (processed; Harvard University, Graduate School of Education, 1967).

firms. The parents of every child would receive a publicly financed voucher of a fixed sum per child. They could then use this voucher to buy educational services from any approved supplier they wanted to patronize.[4] As Henry Levin pointed out in his excellent analysis of this proposal, it would undoubtedly increase the variety of educational services offered to parents, thereby enabling them to find more easily the kinds of educational services they wanted.[5]

But this scheme would also have two less desirable effects. First, it is vital for society as a whole to insure that all citizens receive a minimum quality education in certain skills and knowledge necessary for effective citizenship. Yet experience with other forms of private consumption shows that ignorant, low-income consumers can be exploited by unscrupulous producers who persuade the consumers to pay exorbitant prices for inferior-quality goods. To prevent this outcome from occurring in education, it would be necessary for public authorities to exercise some form of regulation over all private producers of educational services. Such regulation might become almost as extensive and standardized as existing public production of education.

Second, wealthier parents could add more funds to the voucher to buy better-quality services, but poor parents could not. Wealthier parents would evoke high-quality schools that would attract the best teachers and use the best facilities; poor parents would be compelled to give their children much lower-quality educations. Thus, direct price discrimination based on incomes would accomplish precisely the same result that geographic discrimination based on incomes now achieves. This might aggravate existing inequalities of educational opportunity rather than diminish them.

However, this second disadvantage could be offset by awarding a much larger voucher to low-income families than to high-income families, as Levin points out. He describes two methods: a sliding scale with payments varying inversely with income, and provision of such aid only to the lowest-income families. He rejects the first as politically unrealistic, but regards the second as politically possible —perhaps because it is essentially a novel version of the aid pro-

[4] Milton Friedman, "The Role of Government in Education," *Capitalism and Freedom* (University of Chicago Press, 1962), pp. 85–107.
[5] Levin, "The Failure of the Public Schools."

vided under Title I of the Elementary and Secondary Education Act of 1965.

For purposes of this analysis, I will assume that some form of providing either full vouchers or bonus payments to students from low-income households, and allowing them to choose where to apply such grants, could be used to inject a significant degree of competition into big-city public school systems. Every such voucher or bonus should be at least large enough to pay for the extra inputs needed to offset the disadvantages imposed on the child's education by deficiencies in his nonschool environment. In fact, any voucher or bonus should be made large enough to convert each low-income child from a liability into an asset, as seen from the viewpoints of the suppliers of education and of the parents of other children in the schools involved. Then, the voucher or bonus would create a surplus over and above the marginal cost of educating the low-income child. That surplus could then be applied to improving the quality of the entire school that accepted such a child. This would provide a positive incentive for schools to accept or even seek out such children. However, it is unlikely that society will presently pay the relatively large amounts needed to accomplish this outcome.

A voucher or bonus arrangement favoring low-income students could be used in any one of the three basic forms describing the use of overlapping attendance areas. That is, it could be employed in conjunction with an expansion of existing attendance areas into large and overlapping zones, or with a similar expansion plus the development of community schools, or with a similar expansion plus the development of experimental schools (which might be related to community control). In the last case, special schools catering only to students with vouchers or bonus payments might be developed. They would be able to use high levels of expenditure per student. In the first case, special schools with geographic quotas or bonus-student quotas could be developed. They could provide a socially integrated educational environment that would still take advantage of the added resources made possible by the bonus payments. But in all cases, the parents of low-income children would have to be allowed at least some discretion about where their children would use their bonuses if the benefits of true competition were to be generated.

Conclusion

Large bureaucratic organizations almost never make major changes in established behavior patterns unless strongly pressured by outside forces.[6] The most powerful form of such pressure is a direct threat to their continued existence, or to their current perquisites of office. This kind of threat can usually be created only by an alliance of all or most of the outside agents who support the bureaucracy. They must get together and demand that the bureaucracy change, or else they will remove or drastically reduce their support. But when the bureaucracy produces some vital service, they can reduce their support only by creating a competitive institution to provide that service. Competition has the advantage of generating sustained, almost automatic, pressure upon the organizations involved to keep adapting their production to consumers' wants, without constant vigilance by the consumers themselves.

Big-city public school systems are huge bureaucracies. Therefore, one of the potentially most effective ways of getting them to change their unsatisfactory behavior is to introduce significant elements of competition into their operation. It would be totally unrealistic to assume that most, or even any large fraction, of the existing school systems in large cities could soon be replaced by competitive systems created or run by outsiders. There are simply not enough qualified—or even unqualified—teachers to create truly parallel systems that could compete with existing public school systems across the board. Moreover, the additional capital investment required to build physical facilities for such an all-out system would be prohibitive.

Nevertheless, even a small dose of competition in certain forms could produce important—even radical—changes in the nature and quality of education in big-city public schools. The first and most crucial step is developing and using effective ways of evaluating the educational performance of public schools. Other devices may also be employed to generate the benefits of competition, with varying

---

[6] This definitive generalization is taken from a source in which I have an unusually high degree of confidence. See Anthony Downs, *Inside Bureaucracy* (Little, Brown, 1967), Chaps. II and XVI.

requirements concerning the amount of basic institutional change involved.

Community schools are currently being advanced almost as a panacea that will create the clearly needed changes in big-city public school systems. But unless community schools are designed and operated so as to increase competitive pressures within those systems, I do not believe they will have the desired effects. The pressure of competition is the crucial ingredient needed to force big-city school systems to adapt their outputs to what consumers want and need. Without such pressure, school systems will continue succumbing to the natural tendency of all monopolists: providing what is most convenient for them to produce regardless of its suitability to the needs of those who must consume it.

[5]
THE ECONOMICS OF NEW TOWNS

By Anthony Downs

Although many regard new cities as an exciting way to escape the persistent ills of urban life, few new-community advocates have confronted certain unromantic but vital questions about economic feasibility. Will new cities pay for themselves, or must they be subsidized? If subsidies are required, who will pay for them, and who will reap the benefits? Would building new cities really help solve existing urban problems? Or would it merely divert leadership and other scarce resources from decaying older urban areas to glorified, high-income suburbs?

Before examining these questions, some definitions are required. In order to be considered a new city, a community must 1) be initially developed under a single comprehensive plan; 2) contain multiple land uses — residential, commercial, office space, and recreational; and 3) be planned for a certain minimum population. I believe 15,000 people is a reasonable estimate for the smaller cities and 50,000 for the larger.

Several fundamentally different types of new cities must be distinguished on the basis of their geographic relation to existing settlements and size. Geographically, a new city can be *in-city* (within a heavily built-up area — such as the Welfare Island project in New York City), [52] *peripheral* (on the edge of an existing metropolitan area, such as Foster City near San Francisco), *satellite* (outside of but within commuting distance of a metropolitan center, such as Columbia between Washington and Baltimore), or *autonomous* (beyond commuting range of any existing metropolitan area, such as Lake Havasu City in Arizona).

As regards size, for convenience I will use only two categories. A *full city* contains a very broad spectrum of land uses, including industrial, and should provide nearly as many jobs within its boundaries as there are workers living there. A *mini-city* contains a much narrower spectrum of land uses, perhaps not including industrial, and relies mainly on surrounding communities to provide its residents with both jobs and key urban services and amenities.

The Economics of Land Development

From a strictly economic viewpoint, creating any new city is a special form of land development. The basic principle underlying all land development is to buy land cheaply, enhance its desirability, and sell it more expensively. The profit produced depends upon 1) the spread between the buying and selling prices, 2) the costs incurred by enhancing the land's desirability, and 3) the time required to complete the whole process.

The price spread is increased by making the buying prices as low and the selling prices as high as possible. Land prices generally decline with distance from already settled areas; so there is a strong pressure on developers of new cities to build satellite or autonomous projects. This pressure is especially powerful if they seek to create full cities, which require immense tracts of vacant land (6,000 acres or more). On the other hand, selling (or leasing) prices are maximized by the highest-density uses, which are usually found near the centers of large cities. In all new (and existing) cities, the highest land prices are generated by high-rise office buildings, shopping centers, and high-rise apartments, and the lowest by single-family home sites. That is why many new-city developers rapidly sell single-family home sites to housing developers, but retain major commercial, retail, industrial, and high-rise apartment locations. High land values and rents generated by such sites have been the economic salvation of British new cities.

A crucial economic aspect of new cities is their attempt to internalize the economic "spillovers" that occur in all land development. Whenever someone builds a major regional shopping center or other commercial project, the value of all the land around it rises. If the shopping center developer does not own that nearby land, someone else captures the "spillover effects" of his investment.

But a new-city developer initially controls enough land to capture almost all such spillovers within the community's boundaries. Furthermore, he deliberately plans all parts of the new city so their spillovers [53]

Dialogue

reinforce each other. This stimulates land values to rise even faster. For example, he designs local streets to maximize the convenience of his shopping center and then uses that convenience to convince both residents and retailers to move in. This ability to internalize and set up an "economic reverberation" among spillovers provides the greatest relative advantage of new-city development over traditional subdivision development. But this ability requires both a huge site and an excellent comprehensive plan, which add to development costs.

Environmental and Esthetic Values

A new city's comprehensive plan offers environmental and esthetic qualities lacking in typical competitive subdivisions. Therefore, a well-planned new city is able to both offset its more distant location and speed up the process of marketing its land. Traditional land developers enhance land values by installing mains and sewers, creating streets and lakes, providing open space, donating school sites, building structures, or some combination of these. But new-city developers seek to create a completely new, almost self-contained environment through the careful positioning of many land uses under a single plan. In this respect, they are catering to a rising desire among Americans to purchase an entire environment along with their home. Thus, creation of an esthetically, socially, and environmentally attractive comprehensive plan is critical to any new city's success.

The most critical factor of all, however, is speed of development. New cities require huge "front-end" investments of cash to acquire big sites and to install enough facilities and improvements before anyone moves in to convince potential residents that they will actually receive the wonderful environment promised by the developer. If the developer has borrowed this money, it costs him staggering interest payments daily. (In the early stages of building Columbia, the Rouse Company was paying $5,000-a-day interest on money borrowed to buy the land, even before there was any real assurance that a new city could be built on it.) Tying up the developer's cash means sacrificing interest it could be earning elsewhere. Therefore, economic success requires speeding up development to shorten the period before sizable revenues start to flow back to the investors. Even if a new city eventually becomes completely occupied and a great human success, it can be an economic disaster for its developers if too much time elapses from start to finish.

Locating as close as possible to an existing metropolitan area speeds up development by exposing the new city to a bigger potential market. But this drives up the initial purchase price of the land. Furthermore, creating an entire new city is an extremely complex process, involving three sources of delay not connected with traditional development: assembly of the entire site; development of a good comprehensive plan; and completion of intricate negotiations with a whole set of govern- [54]

mental bodies. These actions provide innumerable occasions for unforeseen delays.

Even in principle, therefore, creating new cities is an extraordinarily risky form of private investment — probably the riskiest of all. That is why the single most important ingredient in any new city is the principal developer himself. Only individuals with a rare combination of vision, persuasiveness, energy, financial acumen, inventiveness, promotional flair, and endless persistence have much chance of seeing a new-city investment through to profitable fruition.

A Variety of Developers

In light of these demanding conditions, what kinds of institutions or individuals have tried to create new cities and how successful have they been? Our catalogue includes the following types of developers:

• *Central governments* have created many new cities as a means of opening up underdeveloped areas, counteracting excessive urban centralization, or achieving other national objectives. Economic feasibility has been neither an objective for nor a constraint on such attempts, which include Washington, Canberra, Brasilia, Oak Ridge, Ciudad Guayana in Venezuela, and Chandrigar in India.

• *Public corporations* have been created expressly to develop new cities in most nations that have adopted explicit new-city policies, such as Great Britain, France, and Sweden. These corporations have pursued economic feasibility, and in some cases have produced discounted rates of return on investment of around 8 percent. Although this is satisfactory for a public body, it would be unacceptably low for private capital.

• *Owners of large land parcels* have sometimes chosen to create new cities rather than to sell or develop their land piecemeal. Such developers have the tremendous advantage of not having to assemble or make a huge cash investment in a big site. Examples are most common in California, where remnants of Spanish land grants provided the basis for the giant Irvine project. The development of Miami Lakes (with a projected population of 50,000 residents), about ten miles northeast of Miami, by the Graham family is another illustration. Computing the initial land value is extremely difficult in such cases; hence no one really knows what rate of return on investment these new cities have produced.

• *Developers who create sites through land-fills or clearance and drainage of swamps* also minimize land-assembly and initial-cost obstacles. Examples are Redwood Shore (municipally owned) and Foster City in the San Francisco Bay area, and many new communities in Florida.

• *Combinations of individual entrepreneurs in partnership with large lenders or corporate investors* — with the former supplying the ideas, skill, and energy, and the latter putting up most of the money — have produced apparent successes in Columbia (Maryland) and Rancho

Dialogue

California, but initial financial failures in Reston (Virginia) and Clear Lake City (Texas).

The Problem of Capital Outlay

This list includes most new-city developers. It strongly implies that creating new cities is a task suitable only to very large organizations — whether public or private — possessing lots of cash and staying power. Most other new-city developers have enjoyed some hard-to-duplicate initial advantages, such as inheritance of a giant estate. Individual entrepreneurs operating on their own are notably scarce in this business. The few who try it have usually become partners with some source of money, instead of following the mortgage route typical of other developments, in order to meet the large front-end cash requirement.

The size of this requirement is illustrated in part by land acquisition costs of $25-million at Columbia (an average of $1,700 per acre), $13.2-million at Reston ($1,780 per acre), $32-million at Westlake Village, California ($2,700 per acre), and $40-million at Park Forest South, Illinois ($5,000 per acre). Moreover, costs of infrastructure and buildings are much greater. In our recent preliminary analysis of a new community of 75,000 persons proposed for a suburban location near Detroit, we estimated total capital outlay requirements (public and private) would be $663-million over a twenty-year period (in constant dollars) — of which only $7.2-million (1.1 percent) would be for land acquisition. [56]

Another strong implication of this analysis is that mini-cities are far more likely to prove feasible for private investors than full cities. Mini-cities require smaller initial cash outlays for land and improvements, can be located closer to existing markets, need less complex plans and negotiations with governmental bodies, and take less time to carry out. Yet they can still be large enough (say, from 800 to 3,000 acres) to allow internalization of the most significant economic spillovers and creation of an unusually attractive environment through comprehensive planning. Chicago's privately owned Urban Investment and Development Company has proposed a series of suburban mini-cities, each to be built around a major regional shopping center — the key tenants of which are partners in the venture. Several of the projects proposed by New York's publicly owned Urban Development Corporation are new mini-cities either within or on the edges of existing metropolitan areas.

A Federal Role

The Urban Growth and New Community Development Act (passed by the U.S. Congress in 1970) seeks to help both public and private new-city developers overcome some key obstacles. The most important forms of assistance it provides are:

The Economics of New Towns

- Federal guarantees backing debt obligations issued by developers to pay for acquiring land, conducting initial development, and installing utilities. Such guarantees can be made up to $50-million for any one project for 100 percent of these costs for public developers and about 85 percent for private developers.
- Federal loans to cover the interest payments on money borrowed by developers for financing the specific front-end costs mentioned above, even when no federally guaranteed obligations are involved. No repayments on these federal loans need be made during the first few years of the project.
- Public service grants to local government bodies to help them pay for essential public services required in a new city before it has an adequate tax base.
- Planning grants to pay up to two-thirds of all planning costs for public developers, or two-thirds of special costs for private developers in excess of normal planning and feasibility studies.
- Special supplements added on to 13 existing federal programs (such as sewer and water aid) when they are used in approved new cities.

In theory, these programs could provide major reductions in the front-end cash requirements of both public and private developers. But Congress has not yet appropriated funds for most of these programs, and budget restraints may hold down the amounts the Department of Housing and Urban Development (HUD) has requested. HUD has already received hundreds of inquires about such assistance, but past experience proves that genuinely worthwhile applications amount to only a small fraction of initial inquiries.

These funds would not help new-city developers pay for initial planning costs. Nor do they help either public or private developers assemble large sites, pay for housing and other structures, or market their products. Furthermore, using federal aid poses three added problems for new-city developers: more red tape; required inclusion of new low-and moderate-income housing (which is desirable socially but is a potential drain on profitability); and the need to tie up the site through purchase or options before applying for federal aid, without knowing whether funds will be provided. Consequently, I believe there are still formidable financial obstacles to the successful development of new cities, especially by private enterprise.

[57]

Suggested Policies

If new cities are to represent much of the nation's future urban growth, creating them must be made still more profitable and less risky for private developers. However, Congress may be reluctant to adopt policies that would generate sufficient profits to attract large numbers of top-quality private developers into this field, or to lead to large-scale public development of new cities. Among such policies would have

Dialogue

to be the following:
- Creation of state or federal public development corporations (like New York's Urban Development Corporation) with powers to condemn land, override local zoning and building codes, float their own financing, and actually build utilities and structures.
- Provision of special land-assembly powers usable by either public development corporations or private developers. The latter would first have to assemble some large fraction of a proposed new-city site, formulate an acceptable plan, and provide sound financial backing.
- Actual appropriation and expenditure of vastly greater funds for all the federal financial aids passed in the 1970 act. Congress and the administration usually allow far less spending than the amounts legally authorized. For example, HUD only requested new-city supplemental grants of $5 million in fiscal 1971, as compared to an authorization of $63.5 million.
- Priority allocation of existing federal planning, housing subsidy, sewer and water, and transportation program funds to proposed new cities meeting certain standards.

A possible alternative to larger federal assistance might be provision of a powerful private financing mechanism such as the National Urban Development Bank recently proposed by David Rockefeller. It would make land-development loans to new-city builders with funds from special security issues or pooled bank loans.

The suggestions outlined above assume that both public and private efforts to build new cities should be encouraged simultaneously in order to maximize effective results. In addition, the following *more experimental suggestions* might be considered:
- Designation of certain new-city zones by individual states, within which no new urban development could occur at less than mini-city scale. This would encourage land owners in such zones to aggregate their holdings.
- Provision of highly accelerated depreciation write-offs for all private structures built in designated new cities.
- Construction of one or two experimental new cities built around new federal installations, or existing installations in relatively remote locations, with special incentives for private firms to move there. Emphasis could be upon ecological-system innovation and improvement.

Unless many of these policies are forcefully carried out by key states and the federal government, there is little chance that any new cities will play a really important role in our future urban growth.

Experimenting with Urban Forms

Full-sized autonomous new cities offer our best chance to try out alternative urban forms that might reduce key problems (such as de-

[58]

signing a city mainly for public transit to cut air pollution and traffic congestion). However, truly radical innovations would be extremely expensive as compared to continuing urban sprawl around existing urban areas. This is partly because new cities must contain *all* new structures, even though more than half the nation's households (and many firms) cannot afford to occupy new quarters without subsidies. Yet these people and activities are needed to make any city work economically. In existing areas, they can occupy older structures; but in autonomous new cities, they must be heavily subsidized because there are no older structures nearby. Moreover, radically designed new cities might be politically threatening to the chief beneficiaries of existing urban forms (such as the giant automobile industry). Therefore, I believe it highly improbable that we will build many such innovative autonomous new cities in the near future, though I support trying one or two.

Satellite and peripheral new cities — particularly mini-cities — could improve the neighborhood texture and quality of life in urban areas without generating enormous costs beyond those associated with normal urban development. They could also provide some planned economic-class mixture (if sufficient subsidies are granted to allow low- and moderate-income households to live in new units) and planned racial integration.

A Balanced Program

But satellite and peripheral new cities would not reduce traffic congestion, air pollution, the solid waste problem, or other problems arising from the sheer size of metropolitan areas. Only a general urban growth policy that forbids or controls expansion of our largest areas could do that. This in turn would require stronger public controls over private land use.

No form of new city will significantly reduce the problems of older existing urban cores unless the "two urban frontiers" of core decay and suburban growth are explicitly linked together for their mutual benefit. This has recently been proposed in the "paired new city" concept of Detroit's Metropolitan Fund. Without some such linkage, there is a strong probability that society will concentrate most future resource investments in suburban areas and continue to let central cities decay physically and go bankrupt fiscally.

Thus, new cities are not a panacea for existing urban problems. Yet they offer definite opportunities for improving the quality of growth. But any policies supporting them should be part of a balanced program that also recognizes the need to improve older core areas and to upgrade traditional forms of urban growth, which are still likely to dominate the future.

[6]
The Automotive Population Explosion

ANTHONY DOWNS

Dr. Anthony Downs is a Senior Fellow at the Brookings Institution in Washington D.C. He received his B.A. in political theory from Carleton College, and his M.A. and Ph.D. in economics from Stanford University. For 18 years, he was a private consultant on real estate and urban affairs with Real Estate Research Corporation. Dr. Downs is the author of six books and over 100 articles, including "An Economic Theory of Democracy," "Inside Bureaucracy," "Urban Problems and Prospects," and "Opening Up the Suburbs." He is currently working on a large-scale study of urban decline and the future of American cities.

THE United States is experiencing an amazing yet almost unnoticed "population explosion"—not of people, but of automotive vehicles. The nation's total population of passenger cars, trucks, and buses in use is still much smaller than its total human population—129 million vehicles versus 217 million people as of 1977. The vehicle population in the United States is growing 2.5 times as fast in absolute numbers, and 4.9 times as fast in percentage terms.

This ever-escalating use of cars and trucks is not confined to the United States. It is a worldwide phenomenon wherever consumers have free choice, and it has profound impacts on the societies concerned. Most of those effects are already evident in U.S. life, and many are rapidly emerging in other nations. There is no evidence as yet that this worldwide trend is slowing down because of recent increases in gasoline prices. In fact, world production of motor vehicles set an all-time record of 41.0 million units in 1977. Hence the automotive vehicle "population explosion" may continue to be one of the major social and economic forces of this era.

RECENT CHANGES IN U.S. VEHICLE POPULATION

In every year since 1945, the vehicle population of the United States has grown substantially. Table I sets forth estimates of the nation's population of automobiles, trucks, and buses *in use* for

347

TABLE I—U.S. MOTOR VEHICLES IN USE, 1945 TO 1977
(IN THOUSANDS)

Year	Automobiles	Trucks	Buses	Total Vehicles
1945	25,201	4,149	162	29,512
1950	35,992	7,567	224	43,783
1951	38,516	8,065	230	46,811
1952	39,770	8,420	236	48,426
1953	42,202	8,693	243	51,138
1954	44,387	8,800	249	53,436
1955	47,378	9,162	255	56,795
1956	49,804	9,544	258	59,606
1957	51,432	9,776	262	61,470
1958	52,493	10,056	265	62,814
1959	55,085	10,532	269	65,886
1960	57,103	10,803	272	68,178
1961	58,854	11,044	280	70,178
1962	60,920	11,464	285	72,669
1963	63,384	11,899	298	75,581
1964	66,051	12,445	305	78,801
1965	68,940	13,127	314	82,381
1966	71,264	14,357	322	85,943
1967	72,968	14,988	338	88,294
1968	75,358	15,685	352	91,395
1969	78,495	16,586	364	95,445
1970	80,449	17,686	378	98,513
1971	83,138	18,465	397	102,000
1972	86,439	19,773	407	106,619
1973	89,805	21,412	426	111,643
1974	92,608	23,312	466	116,386
1975	95,241	24,813	470	120,497
1976	97,818	26,560	480	124,858
1977	99,904	28,222	490	128,616

Source: Motor Vehicle Manufacturers Association, *Automobile Facts & Figures*—various annual editions.

selected years from 1945 through 1977.[1] In that 32-year period, the nation's total vehicle population rose from 29.5 million to 128.6 million—an enormous increase of 99.1 million, or 336 percent. In contrast, the human population of the United States increased by 76.1 million, or 54.2 percent in the same period.

Moreover, increases in the U.S. vehicle population have been accelerating during the 1970's in spite of the "energy crisis" and

1. Vehicles *in use* in any year is about 91 percent of the total number registered in that year. Total vehicle registration includes all vehicles legally registered by every state during each year. Some vehicles, however, are registered in two states for part of every year. Vehicles in use, therefore, is a more accurate measure of vehicles actually available to the population each year.

THE AUTOMOTIVE POPULATION EXPLOSION

increases in prices of both gasoline and vehicles. The sharpest increase has been in the truck population. It shot up an average of 1.425 million units per year in the early 1970's—56 percent faster than the next-fastest period (the late 1960s) This is partly the result of the use of more and more light trucks and vans by households as second or third cars. By way of comparison, the automobile population went up only 25 percent faster in the early 1970s than in the early 1960s—the period of its previous highest growth rate.

The pattern of automotive vehicle population growth-rates for more than a decade has been just the opposite of that for human beings. After 1962 the vehicle growth rate exceeded that for population in every year and by increasing amounts. By the early 1970s, the vehicle growth rate was twice that for total population.

This explosive growth in vehicle population cannot be fully explained by the rising growth rate of households. Increased household formation in the early 1970s undoubtedly raised the number of households requiring vehicles. But the growth rate of automobiles in the early 1970s was almost twice that of total households.

Multivehicle Ownership in the United States

One reason the population of vehicles has risen so fast is a rapid increase in multicar ownership, as shown in Table II. In 1955 about one-fourth of all households owned no cars at all, and only about

TABLE II—MULTI-CAR OWNERSHIP BY HOUSEHOLD, 1955-1974

Year	Total Households (thousands)	No Cars Number (thousands)	Percent	One Car Number (thousands)	Percent	Two or More Cars Number (thousands)	Percent
1955	47,874	12,974	27.1[b]	29,299	61.2	5,601	11.7[b]
1960	52,799	13,517	25.6[c]	29,831	56.5	9,451	17.9[c]
1965	57,436	13,153	22.9[c]	30,728	53.5	13,555	23.6[c]
1970	63,401	12,934	20.4[d]	31,891	50.3	18,576	29.3[d]
1974	69,859	12,925	18.5[e]	34,091	48.8	22,843	32.7[e]
			Total change 1955-1974				
Number	21,985	−49	−0.2	4,792	21.8	17,242	78.4
Percent	+45.9	−0.4	—	16.4	—	307.8	—

[a]Household data source: U.S. Department of Commerce, Bureau of the Census.
[b]Statistical Abstract of the United States, 1977, 98th Annual Edition, p. 41, Chart #56.
[c]and *1968 Automobile Facts and Figures*, p. 45.
[d]Motor Vehicle Manufacturers Association, *Automobile Facts & Figures*, 1971, p. 46.
[e]Motor Vehicles Manufacturers Association, *Motor Vehicle Facts & Figures, 1977*, p. 38.

one-tenth owned two or more cars. But in 1974 less than one-fifth of all households owned no cars, and about one-third owned two or more. In fact, when trucks are taken into account, only 18.5 percent of all households did not own any vehicles in 1974 and a 45.1 percent owned two or more.[2] At the end of 1978, it is reasonable to assume that approximately one-half of all U.S. households owned two or more vehicles.

This immense increase in multicar ownership was only partly caused by rising real incomes. Within each income group surveyed in a 1967 study, the percentage of multicar ownership at least doubled from 1950 through 1965; it tripled in the lower income groups.[3]

U.S. Vehicle Production and Vehicle Population Growth

There is surprisingly little relationship between annual vehicle production in the United States and annual retail sales of vehicles on the one hand, and annual changes in total vehicle population on the other hand. This can be seen from Figure 1. One reason is that annual changes in total vehicle population are *not* equal to either total production or total sales minus total vehicles removed from use. That is because imports are a part of total sales not included in annual production. Inventory changes also intervene between production and sales, and nonretail sales influence the total vehicle population.

These relationships indicate that annual vehicle production and sales can fluctuate widely without producing corresponding large fluctuations in annual additions to the total vehicle population. Consequently, the total vehicle population of the United States will keep rising steadily even if there are wide annual swings in both production and retail sales—and if no further long-range upward trend occurs in either of them.

On the other hand, continued high-level production and sales of vehicles will almost certainly cause further rapid increases in total vehicle population. In theory, greater removals from the inventory (vehicle scrappage) could offset continued high-level sales and production. But this seems unlikely. Whenever the U.S. automotive industry has achieved total sales of 10.7 million or more cars and trucks in recent years, there has been a net addition to the total vehicle population of at least 3 million vehicles.

2. Motor Vehicle Manufacturers Association, *Motor Vehicle Facts & Figures, 1977* (Detroit, Michigan: Motor Vehicle Manufacturers Association), p. 38.
3. John B. Lansing and Gary Hendricks, *Automobile Ownership and Residential Density* (Ann Arbor: University of Michigan Survey Research Center, 1967), pp. 4, 6.

THE AUTOMOTIVE POPULATION EXPLOSION

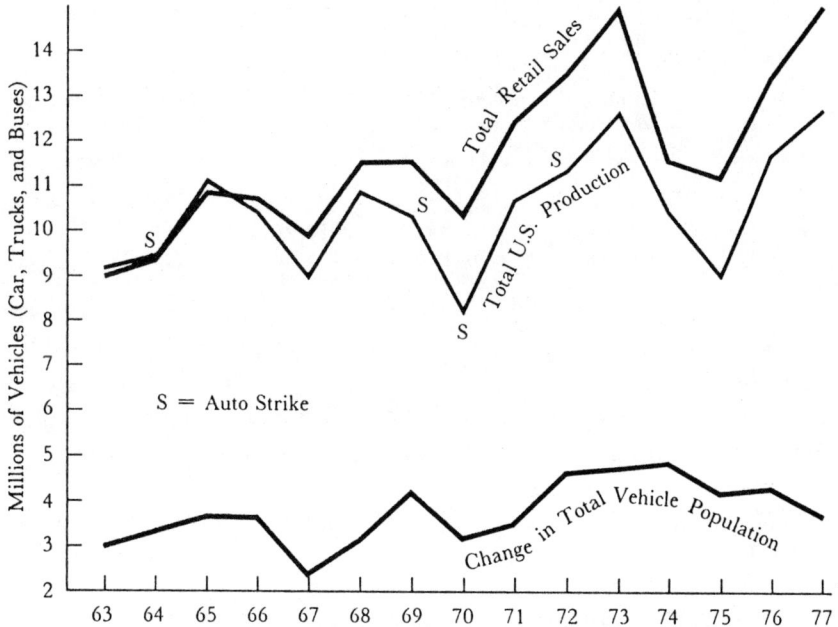

Figure 1. Annual total vehicle retail sales, U.S. production, and changes in vehicle population, 1963–1977

Since 1965 automobile sales have failed to reach 9 million only in 1967, 1970, 1974, and 1975. The last three of these were recession years in which the industry endured low profits and high levels of unemployment. Truck sales have been above 1.8 million ever since 1968. Hence maintaining prosperity in the vital automotive industry requires total sales and production levels that will continue to cause rapid increases in total vehicle population. Only some remarkable acceleration of obsolescence would seem able to raise the removal percentage enough to halt the upward march of total vehicle population. If there were a severe gasoline shortage accompanied by stringent rationing, owners of automobiles with poor fuel economy might trade those vehicles in more swiftly. A heavy license tax on such cars might accomplish the same thing. But such drastic changes seem unlikely at present.

FUTURE U.S. AUTOMOTIVE POPULATION GROWTH

How fast will the nation's automotive vehicle population grow in the future? A "base case" projection can be built on assuming no major changes in existing trends. Then the implications of any major policy or trend changes can be examined separately.

TABLE III—PROJECTED TOTAL VEHICLE POPULATION IN USE
(IN THOUSANDS)

Year	1945-1976 Regression	1969-1976 Regression	1945-1976 Exponential Curve	4 Percent Annual Growth Rate Compounded
1976 (actual)	124,858	124,858	124,858	124,858
1980	129,814	142,002	140,046	146,066
1985	144,649	163,672	163,053	177,712
1990	159,484	185,343	188,197	216,214
1995	174,319	207,013	215,539	263,057
2000	189,154	228,683	245,142	320,049

Several different projections can be derived from the data in Table I on the past growth of the U.S. vehicle population. Literature concerning previous attempts to forecast automotive vehicle population does not impart much confidence that complex methods of forecasting can improve accuracy or reliability.[4]

Four projection methods were used initially, with results shown in Table III.

Projected 1985 Households and Car Ownership

Projections of automotive vehicle populations can vary widely. One way to check their reliability is to project future households and car ownership among households, thereby deriving an estimated total vehicle population. Vehicle population can be estimated for 1985, for instance, if the following assumptions are made.

1. Households will increase in number in accordance with the Census Bureau's Series C projection. It indicates 14,796,000 more households in 1985 than in 1974, the latest year for which detailed car ownership data are available.

2. The increased number of households can be allocated among car ownership categories in about the same proportion as the increase in households from 1955 to 1974 was distributed among such categories: 22 percent in the one-car category, and 78 percent in the multicar category.

3. Multicar households will own an average of 2.2 cars in 1985 (compared to about 2.1 in the 1960s).

4. The number of cars owned by businesses, governments, and

---

4. L. L. Liston, *Projections of Motor Vehicle Registrations, Driver Licenses, and Motor-Fuel Consumption to 1990* (Washington, D.C.: U.S. Department of Transportation, Federal Highway Administration; and U.S. Department of Transportation, Federal Highway Administration, Urban Planning Division, *Trip Generation Analysis* (Washington, D.C.: Government Printing Office, August 1975).

THE AUTOMOTIVE POPULATION EXPLOSION

TABLE IV—NUMBER OF HOUSEHOLDS (IN THOUSANDS) AND PERCENTAGE OF HOUSEHOLDS IN EACH CATEGORY OF CAR OWNERSHIP

Year	Total Households	No Car Number	No Car Percent	One Car Number	One Car Percent	Multi-Car Number	Multi-Car Percent
1974	69,858	12,924	18.5	34,091	48.8	22,843	32.7
1985	84,653	12,924	15.3	37,345	44.1	34,384	40.6

other fleet operators will grow from about 9.9 million in 1969 to 10.4 million in 1975 to about 11.0 million in 1985. This is equivalent to a straight-line projection.

Under these assumptions Table IV gives the distribution of households by car ownership categories in 1985, compared to 1974. All households combined will own 112,990,000 cars in 1985. Another 11 million will be owned by nonhouseholds, for a total of 123,990,000 cars in use. This estimate almost exactly corresponds to the linear regression projection of cars in use from 1969 through 1976, which produces an estimated total car population of 123,862,000 in 1985.

"Base Case" 1985 Vehicle Projection

Moreover, if that linear regression estimate is combined with the one cited earlier for all vehicles, there is an indicated truck and bus population of about 39.8 million in 1985, or 12,760,000 more than in 1976. This implies average annual truck and bus population growth of 1,420,000 from 1976 to 1985—about 1.5 percent lower than the actual average of such growth from 1969 to 1976. From these calculations it can be concluded that the linear regression projection based on the period 1969 to 1976 is reasonably reliable, assuming no major shifts in present conditions. Therefore in 1985, the "base case" projection is for a total automotive vehicle population of 163,700,000, consisting of 123,000,000 cars, 40,000,000 trucks, and 700,000 buses.

Implications for Future Vehicle Sales

If annual removals of all vehicles average about 8.0 percent of each year's inventory in this period as they did from 1963 through 1975, then total sales would have to average 15,700,000 per year to arrive at this vehicle population in use by 1985. That is 28 percent higher than average retail sales from 1970 through 1975. It implies relatively high levels of U.S. automotive production in the near future, unless imports greatly expand their share of retail sales. If owners keep their vehicles longer than they have in the past, the indicated levels of sales and production will be somewhat less.

Thus if present vehicle production, importation, demolition, and use trends continue over the next decade, the nation can expect to experience almost another one-third increase in its 1976 total vehicle population by 1985. This is a lower rate of growth, both absolutely and relatively, than occurred from 1970 through 1976, when the total vehicle population rose 31.8 percent. Nevertheless, if this "base case" projection actually occurs, it will have profound impacts on life in the United States.

WORLDWIDE EXTENT OF VEHICLE POPULATION EXPLOSION

The current rapid growth of automotive vehicle population is a worldwide phenomenon. Table V compares changes for the period 1970 to 1975 in total vehicles registered and total human population in 17 nations around the world.

TABLE V—CHANGES IN VEHICLE AND HUMAN POPULATION IN VARIOUS NATIONS, 1970-1975

Nation	Rise in Total Registered Vehicle Population 1970–1975		Vehicle Population Rise/Human Population Rise, 1970–1975	Number of Persons per Vehicle, 1975
	Number (thousands)	Percent Rise		
United States	24,543	22.6	2.17	1.62
Canada	2,945	36.4	1.85	2.09
West Germany	3,848	24.7	1.69	3.18
Great Britain	2,293	16.7	8.82	3.50
France	3,527	24.5	1.87	2.94
Netherlands	919	32.4	1.29	3.66
Japan	10,509	59.8	1.42	3.94
Sweden	485	19.8	2.98	2.81
Switzerland	444	29.0	Human population declined	3.24
Denmark	200	15.0	0.87	3.36
Austria	551	41.6	5.51	4.01
Brazil	3,161	89.3	0.26	16.07
Turkey	348	110.1	0.09	59.01
Mexico	1,548	86.4	0.16	18.01
U.S.S.R.	3,595	57.5	0.28	25.84
Poland	783	101.4	0.65	21.88
Iran	596	163.3	0.14	34.36
Entire world outside U.S.	56,988	41.3	0.16	18.98
Entire world	81,531	33.1	0.22	11.94

Source: Motor Vehicle Manufacturers Association, *Motor Vehicle Facts & Figures,* 1972 and 1977 editions.

THE AUTOMOTIVE POPULATION EXPLOSION

Growth in Vehicle Ownership Outside the United States

The United States is clearly the most "vehicle saturated" nation, with 1.62 persons per vehicle, as compared to 2.09 in Canada—the second most "vehicle saturated" nation. Japan and most highly developed Western European nations average between 2.8 and 4.0 persons per vehicle, whereas less automobile dependent nations have much higher ratios, such as 25.84 in the Soviet Union and 59.01 in Turkey. Many of these nations, however, have recently been experiencing very rapid percentage increases in vehicle populations—including more than 100 percent increases for the 1970 through 1975 period in Turkey, Poland, and Iran. Moreover, since 1970, most developed nations (except Great Britain, Sweden, and Denmark) have had greater percentage increases in their vehicle populations than the United States. Japan's vehicle population has grown especially fast, rising almost 60 percent in 5 years. In fact, Japan had about 75 percent of all the motor vehicles in Asia in 1975, although it included only 5 percent of Asia's total population.

The world's vehicle population has been rising at a compounded rate of 5.9 percent per year—and outside the United States, at 7.2 percent per year compounded (the rate needed to double the automotive population in one decade). In percentage terms, this is much faster growth than that of the world's human population. In absolute terms, however, the human population of the entire world is still growing about 4.5 times as fast as the automotive population.

Growth in Foreign Vehicle Production

One reason vehicle populations outside the United States are growing so fast is the astounding increase in vehicle production rates throughout the world, as shown in Table VI. From 1950 through

TABLE VI—TOTAL MOTOR VEHICLE PRODUCTION (IN THOUSANDS)

Year	Worldwide	Outside the United States	In the United States	Percent Outside the United States
1950	10,577	2,571	8,006	24.3
1960	16,488	8,583	7,905	52.1
1970	29,304	21,020	8,284	71.7
1977	40,958	28,255	12,703	69.0
		Increase		
1950–1977	30,381	25,684	4,697	84.5

Source: Motor Vehicle Manufactures Association, *Motor Vehicle Facts & Figures,* 1978, p. 16.

1977 motor vehicle production outside the United States soared by 999 percent, compared to 59 percent within the United States. Automotive manufacturers are now pumping immense numbers of additional vehicles onto the world's roads each year in both developed and less-developed nations.

Clearly, many other nations are now, or soon will be, experiencing many of the impacts of vehicle saturation that the United States has been living with in recent years, unless higher petroleum prices cause radical changes in these worldwide trends.

SOME IMPACTS OF THE AUTOMOTIVE "POPULATION EXPLOSION"

What impacts will these massive increases in vehicle population have on the societies involved? These impacts are clearest in the United States, which has had the highest degree of vehicle saturation over the longest period. The effects in other nations, however, may be quite different from those in the United States because (1) most nations have more centralized government control over urban land development than in the United States, (2) many have far lower levels of real income, and (3) none have yet approached the U.S.'s degree of vehicle saturation. Therefore, the summary descriptions of both beneficial and harmful effects set forth below have been divided into those in the United States and those in other nations.

Increased Fuel Consumption

In the United States, gasoline used in motor vehicles accounts for about 18 percent of all energy consumption and 39 percent of all petroleum consumption.[5] Consumption rose even faster from 1950 to 1975 than the number of vehicles, mainly because the truck portion of total vehicles in use increased and overall gasoline mileage per vehicle declined.[6] This has aggravated the U.S. balance of payments by increasing the demand for oil and helping to increase the reliance on imported oil supplies. Whether the 31 percent growth of vehicle population from 1976 to 1985, projected earlier, will expand oil consumption still further depends on how fast older, less fuel-efficient automobiles are replaced with lighter, more fuel-efficient vehicles. Automotive engineers say vehicle-miles per gallon can rise about 15

---

5. Herman Enzer, Walter Dupree, and Stanley Miller, *Energy Perspectives: A Presentation of Major Energy and Energy-Related Data* (Washington, D.C.: Government Printing Office, February 1975), U.S. Department of Interior, Stock No. 024-000-00812-6, pp. 36, 91, 93.

6. Motor Vehicle Manufacturers Association, *Motor Vehicle Facts & Figures*, p. 62.

percent very quickly, and by another 30 to 40 percent by 1985.[7] Because of the time lag in replacing present vehicles, however, a slight increase in motor fuel consumption seems likely in 1985 over 1976—possibly meaning about a 6 percent growth in total U.S. petroleum consumption if all other uses of oil do not rise.

In other nations, most motorists are already using smaller and lighter cars that consume far less fuel per mile than the U.S. automobile fleet. Hence, offsetting their future increases in vehicle population by shifting to more efficient engines is likely to be less dramatic than in the United States. Moreover, they have raised the price of gasoline through taxes to much higher levels than in the United States, without halting their rapid vehicle population growth. So a continuation of such growth may directly aggravate their balance of payments if they are oil-importing nations, as are Japan and most Western European nations with high vehicle ownership.

Air Pollution Effects

Thanks to soaring motor vehicle usage, smog has become an urban phenomenon. Recent mandatory use of automotive exhaust pollution control devices, plus more stringent industrial pollution controls, have reduced levels of man-made air pollution in most U.S. cities. Whether future vehicle populations adversely affect air quality depends in part on how well pollution control laws are enforced.

In other nations, vehicle-caused air pollution is often worse than in the United States. Air quality in cities like Hong Kong, Bangkok, Teheran, and Mexico City has already deteriorated to lung-choking, eye-searing levels. Centuries-old monuments in Athens, Greece, and elsewhere are being seriously eroded by air impurities reacting with sunlight. Statistical linkages between motor vehicle-caused air pollution and respiratory diseases are not clear, but it seems likely that the world-wide deterioration of urban air quality associated with increasing vehicle use has some detrimental health effects.

Increased Mobility

No citizenry in human history ever enjoyed the personal mobility that the U.S. public does every day in its gigantic fleet of vehicles. The average U.S. automobile is driven around 9,400 miles (15,125 km) per year. About 78 percent of all workers commute by car every day;

---

7. General Motors Corporation, *1974 General Motors Report on Programs of Public Interest* (Detroit, Michigan: General Motors Corporation).

85 percent of intercity travel is by car; U.S. residents average 2.2 trips per day per person; and the average number of miles driven per household per year rose about 26 percent between 1955 and 1975.[8]

In other nations public transit systems generally play far greater roles in people movement than in the United States. Whether people in other nations who depend mainly on public transit, bicycles, or walking for their mobility enjoy a lower quality of transportation than in the automobile-oriented United States is impossible to determine conclusively. Many of them, however, clearly want to emulate U.S. trends in vehicle ownership as rapidly as possible.

Spreading Out of Urban Development

For several decades, U.S. metropolitan areas have been spreading out through both growth and decentralization. Because of the pervasive use of cars and trucks, plus many other factors, urban settlement patterns have shifted toward lower densities than in the pre-automobile era. This has undermined the economic viability of many high-density core areas by attracting both households and jobs to lower-density suburbs. Consequently, 94 of the 153 U.S. cities with over 100,000 persons in 1970 lost population from 1970 to 1975, as compared with only 56 from 1960 to 1970.[9] If the U.S. vehicle population explosion continues as projected, further decentralization seems likely in spite of rising energy costs. This escalating vehicle use is intimately related to such urban problems as inner-city unemployment and housing abandonment.

In other developed nations, such urban spreading-out has been constrained by government control of land-use patterns, scarcities of available land, and higher resource costs affecting vehicle ownership and operation. Nevertheless, core areas of many large cities in Canada and Europe, for instance, have recently been losing both population and jobs, and various forms of "urban sprawl" are cropping up more widely.

Major cities in lesser-developed nations are still experiencing massive in-flows of rural poor, and vehicle usage there is far below the levels in more developed nations. Such cities have not yet entered a

---

8. Transportation Association of America, *Transportation Facts and Trends—Thirteenth Edition* (Washington, D.C.: Transportation Association of America, July 1977), pp. 18–20.

9. Anthony Downs, "Urban Policy," *Setting National Priorities: The 1979 Budget*, Joseph A. Pechman, ed. (Washington, D.C.: The Brookings Institution, 1978), p. 163.

THE AUTOMOTIVE POPULATION EXPLOSION

declining-density stage. They are spreading out through continued growth rather than decentralization.

Impacts On National Economies

The U.S. automotive vehicle industry is one of the most important components in the nation's economy. Eight of the ten largest manufacturing companies in the *Fortune 500* are engaged in either building vehicles or supplying them with fuel.[10] More than 13 million U.S. citizens make their living producing, distributing, selling, maintaining, repairing, fueling, junking, driving, and creating parts for motor vehicles.[11] Consumers devote around 13 percent of their total spending to transportation—mostly for motor vehicles.[12] The nation's goods distribution system is built around trucks. The automotive vehicle population explosion has obviously been a major stimulus to U.S. economic growth and prosperity.

Cars and trucks are similarly beneficial to the economies of other developed nations—especially those that produce and export vehicles, such as West Germany and Japan. Nations that must use scarce foreign exchange to import motor vehicles and petroleum, however, have suffered heavy costs from the expansion of vehicle use. Further escalation of motor vehicle use is likely to expand both of these economic impacts, while making nearly all transportation systems more dependent on cars and trucks.

Congestion Effects

In spite of the immense growth in U.S. vehicle use, there is little evidence that U.S. traffic congestion has grown worse in the last two decades. For one thing, large-scale road construction—especially the Interstate Highway System—expanded traffic capacity tremendously. Also, jobs and retail trade centers have become more decentralized so people do not have to congregate together as much as formerly. It is true that rush-hour congestion on many major expressways seems horrendous—but that is because peak-hour use of commuter roads always rises to surpass the designed capacity of those roads, no matter

---

10. *Fortune*, May 8, 1978: 240.
11. U.S. Bureau of the Census, *Statistical Abstract of the United States: 1977*, 98th edition (Washington, D.C.: U.S. Bureau of the Census, 1977), p. 431.
12. Motor Vehicle Manufactures Association, *Motor Vehicle Facts & Figures*, p. 68.

how large they are.[13] But a U.S. Census Bureau study of 1975 work-trip travel in 21 metropolitan areas shows that, except for a few weekday hours in a few metropolitan areas, traffic moves freely.[14] Among persons who use vehicles for work-trip travel, 86 percent use automobiles or light trucks. The median travel time to work ranged from 16 to 23 minutes in the 21 metropolitan areas surveyed.

There is little doubt, however, that traffic congestion in many other nations is becoming worse. It is particularly frustrating in cities like Paris that have many narrow streets but have not tried to accommodate their soaring vehicle flows by building urban expressways. Such cities experience monumental traffic jams and intensive competition for downtown parking space. Congestion has become so bad that some cities prohibit vehicles in certain shopping districts (as in several German cities) or charge high fees for rush-hour downtown entry (as in Singapore). Some city planners have mistakenly concluded they could reduce surface congestion by building subways or other costly off-street transit systems. Any space these systems initially free up on surface streets, however, soon fills with more cars and trucks as ownership and use expand.[15] Urban traffic congestion is an inescapable accompaniment to economic development wherever consumers are allowed to choose private vehicle ownership.

Accidents and Their Effects

In 1976 there were 25.4 million traffic accidents in the United States, in which 5.2 million persons were injured, 47,100 were killed, and economic losses amounted to $41 billion.[16] Although automobile accidents cause only 2.4 percent of all deaths every year, they are the leading cause of death among persons 15 to 24 years old. The numbers of both accidents and fatalities have actually declined since reaching peaks in the early 1970s, and the U.S. traffic death rate per 100 million vehicle-miles has been falling steadily since the 1920s.[17]

---

13. Anthony Downs, "The Law of Peak-Hour Expressway Congestion," *Urban Problems and Prospects: Second Edition* (Chicago, Illinois: Rand McNally Publishing Company, 1976) pp. 185–199.

14. U.S. Bureau of the Census, "Selected Characteristics of Travel to Work in 21 Metropolitan Areas," *Current Population Reports*, Series P-23, no. 68 (Washington, D.C.: U.S. Bureau of the Census, February 1978).

15. See Wilfred Owen, *The Accessible City* (Washington, D.C.: The Brookings Institution, 1972), pp 15–21.

16. U.S. Bureau of the Census, *Statistical Abstract*, p. 56.

17. Motor Vehicle Manufacturers Association, *1978 Motor Vehicle Facts & Figures* (Detroit, Michigan: Motor Vehicle Manufacturers Association, 1978), p. 56.

THE AUTOMOTIVE POPULATION EXPLOSION

Traffic accidents also have the effect of tying up the nation's court system with loss settlement and tort litigation, thereby detracting from its ability to deal more effectively with criminal cases. In California, only 3 percent of all automobile-related claims are ever filed in court, but they constituted two-thirds of all tort cases in 1976. Their continuing growth absorbs a large portion of additional resources available for improving the U.S. system of justice.[18]

The U.S. traffic death rate per 100 million vehicle-miles is the lowest of any nation—3.5 in 1975, dropping to 3.3 for 1977. This compares with a 1975 rate of 5.6 for Canada, 5.9 for Australia, 8.0 for Japan, and 12.6 for Belgium.[19] In the less-developed nations, fatality rates are much higher than these.

Whatever the reasons for the higher traffic fatality rates outside the United States—whether due to less advanced road systems, less experience of the driving and nondriving population in dealing with traffic conflicts, or greater numbers of small cars that give less protection to occupants during collisions—it seems likely that traffic deaths will increase in the rest of the world as the number of cars in use increases.

CONCLUSION

The automotive "population explosion" has already had profound effects on life in the United States and in many other nations. It has had both benefits and drawbacks. On the plus side, use of motor trucks has vastly widened the geographical distribution of both agricultural and manufactured products and lowered their cost. Similarly, the flexibility provided by personal transportation vehicles gives their users greater access to educational, employment, medical, shopping, and recreational opportunities.

On the negative side must be listed the rising costs of vehicles and motor fuels, air pollution, loss of population and jobs in central cities of developed nations, increasing traffic congestion in foreign countries, and direct and indirect costs of traffic accidents.

Recent huge increases in energy costs make it uncertain whether growth in automotive use will continue unabated in the future. Nevertheless, automotive use will continue to expand in size and

---

18. California Citizens' Commission on Tort Reform, *Righting the Liability Balance* (Los Angeles, California: California Citizens' Commission on Tort Reform, September 1977), p. 53.

19. Motor Vehicle Manufacturers Association, *1978 Motor Vehicle Facts & Figures*, p. 59.

impact, to at least some degree, everywhere consumers can make free choices about how to spend their incomes. So the vehicle population explosion is literally shaping the world's urban development, bringing a mixture of benefits and drawbacks.

Author's Note

This article was written before recent events in the Middle East greatly increased the probability of severe and prolonged shortages of gasoline in the United States before 1985. Hence the projections of future automotive population herein are subject to certain qualifications. If gasoline prices rise to around $1.00 per gallon or more, but supplies are still readily available, I do not believe Americans will greatly alter vehicle usage trends, except in compensation for somewhat slower growth in their real incomes. They will react to higher gasoline prices by switching to smaller, more efficient cars, rather than by substantially reducing miles driven. It should be remembered that as of 1978, the average price of regular gasoline in the U.S. (including taxes) in 1967 dollars was 9.5 percent *below* what it was in 1950. Even if this price doubles from 1978 to 1985 to $1.31 per gallon, if inflation continues at 6.7 percent per year (its average in the 1970s), the price in 1967 dollars will have risen to only 15 percent above its 1950 level. If, however, serious absolute shortages develop and remain in existence for long periods, total miles driven will have to be cut back greatly. This would be accomplished through more use of carpooling, vanpools, and careful trip planning, rather than by any massive switch to public transit (though bus ridership would rise somewhat). In that case, total vehicle population will increase more slowly than indicated in the article because fewer additional households will attain multi-vehicle ownership.

The views expressed in this article are solely those of the author and do not necessarily express those of the Brookings Institution, its trustees, or its other staff members.

[7]
Living with Advanced Telecommunications

Rapid ongoing innovations in telecommunications will affect both real estate development and the future location of economic activities. Just what these effects will be has been uncertain. The swift pace of technical change in this field has produced a bewildering variety of telecommunication modes and facilities—from satellites and microwave relays to privately-owned local cable networks. There is confusion among federal, state, and local regulatory authorities about how to react to these constant innovations. Real estate developers have also been groping for an appropriate strategy for designing telecommunications into their new buildings. Urban planners have made wildly varying predictions about whether telecommunications would centralize or decentralize economic activities.

These uncertainties have been greatly reduced by experts on telecommunications, regulation, real estate development, urban planning, and the effects of technical change on our patterns of thinking. In this article I summarize some important findings and evaluate their most crucial implications for future real estate and urban development. Certain elements of an overall perspective about the effects of telecommunications emerge from this exploration.

Emerging technological trends in telecommunications push toward greater integration of diverse elements into larger and larger unified systems. This permits both economies of scale within each mode and more efficient linkages among modes. From a purely technological viewpoint, the eventual outcome might be a single, unified, worldwide network linking all types of modes and all users together. Yet the dynamics of relatively deregulated telecommunications markets push toward greater diversity of choices and more competition among providers. There is now a bewildering variety of communication modes from which users can choose. There are dozens of providers for each mode, each claiming to offer some unique amenities. A chaotic jungle of options faces users.

That is one reason many tenants will welcome the opportunity to rent space from a developer who has already explored the options and made preliminary choices that the tenants can use if they desire. Such confusing diversity is typical of markets in which tremendous competition and rapid innovation exist simultaneously—each reinforcing the other. This is probably an inescapable price of the resulting rapid increases in long-run productivity.

Recent studies of what actually happens inside structures have been made in both the United Kingdom and the United States. Many more varied activities are occurring within each type of structure than did in the past, because more diverse types of firms are occupying such space and the life-cycle of each firm involves more marked changes in what its members do. As a result, there appear to be greater space needs for equipment, professional workers, individual offices, training and support areas, and other ancillary services. There also appear to be lesser space needs for clerical workers and high ceilings.

Telecommunications technology is only one of many forces influencing developers' behavior, regulatory behavior, and the location of economic activities. Many other forces exert at least as much, sometimes far more, influence on those areas. Forces influencing developers' behavior include interest rates, tax regulations, population growth and migration, material and labor costs, and local government zoning and other regulations. Forces affecting regulatory behavior include the fiscal health of local governments, competition among cities for jobs, federal court decisions, and federal budgetary policies concerning aid to state and local governments. Urban development patterns are also influenced by many additional factors. In view of the power of these other forces, the net impact of telecommunications technology upon future conditions must be considered marginal, especially in the short run. (An exception is telecommunications regulation, which is centrally focused upon such technology.) This cautious conclusion is much more realistic than often repeated exaggerations of telecommunications enthusiasts about how drastically their field will "revolutionize" future real estate development and urban spatial patterns.

Telecommunications developments can have either a centralizing or a decentralizing impact upon specific activities—sometimes both simultaneously. Mitchell Moss put it profoundly when he said, "Telecommunications exert a permissive impact upon the location of activity, rather than a determinative impact." People employing these technologies can do so in many ways with quite different effects; their selection of specific uses and modes will depend upon the goals they are pursuing. Those goals will in turn be influenced by all the other causal forces in their environments. If those forces indicate that greater decentralization is desirable, as in moving back-office workers out of downtown into less expensive space, telecommunications technology will help achieve it. If those forces show that more centralization is desirable, as in extending the administrative control of a firm's top executives over more outlying activities, the same technology will help achieve that too. Telecommunications technology will have highly diverse effects both among similar types of activities and among different urban areas across the nation. [26]

No present or future telecommunications innovations are likely to affect the nature and location of economic activities as much as the introduction of telephone service has already. The difference between not having telephones and having them is much greater than analogous differences concerning television, cable TV, satellites, microwave systems, teleconferencing, and so on. We can learn something about the likely future impacts of these newer technologies by examining the effects of using telephones during the past 100 years. Effects of their use have included:

- Activities of all types have become much more widely dispersed in space—within and among urban areas and around the world—than would otherwise have been possible with the same degree of efficient coordination. A lot of administrative centralization has been made possible by telephones, but their net impact upon all activities taken together has been decentralizing.
- The total volume of communications among any set of persons or organizations who normally interact has immensely increased over what it would have been without telephones. The total number of persons likely to become involved in any one decision—epecially a public-sector decision—has expanded greatly because of the ease of contacting more people. The percentage share of communications accomplished electronically

rather than by traveling to meet other people face-to-face has increased enormously.
- The total amount of travel permitting face-to-face meetings has grown rapidly in absolute terms, much faster than the population as a whole. This outcome has been partly stimulated by the larger number of interpersonal contacts made possible by the telephone.

Telephones have had a permissive rather than a determinative impact upon the locations of most activities. Yet the other forces strongly influencing such locations during the past century have overall been far more decentralizing than centralizing. Telephones have furthered the net dispersive thrust of these forces.

As Joseph Haring declared, the human desire to communicate is virtually unlimited. That is because communications is the most important function in the management of all types of economic and other activities. Communicating with others is the essence of human culture itself; therefore, the volume of communications of all types—measured either per person or in total—will continue to rise in the future, as it has steadily for at least the past two hundred years. Even sex is to a great extent a form of communication. Clearly, not all human communications can be effectively accomplished electronically. Some require direct face-to-face contact—even though one futurist has implied that "holographic experiences" might someday replace sex as we know it.

For real estate developers, the most important recent innovation in telecommunications consists of shared telecommunications services (STS) that a developer can create and offer to tenants within a single building or a single multibuilding project. STS cannot be precisely defined, since the basic concept is relatively open-ended. The idea as applied to a single building is that the developer or a firm he or she hires would install a high-capacity private branch telephone exchange (PBX) in the basement or somewhere else when constructing the building, extend its wiring throughout the building, and offer all tenants the use of these facilities and services available through them. The services would include (1) the purchase or rental of equipment, such as telephones; (2) access to the local Bell Operating Telephone Company for local calls; (3) access to various long-distance telephone providers; and (4) one or more optional additional enhancements that might be provided. Optional enhancements could include satellite link-ups, minimum-cost routing of long-distance calls, teleconferencing, direct microwave link-ups, and cable television. These services could vary greatly from project to project, depending upon what the developer wants to provide. The developer would charge tenants fees for providing the facilities and for resale of the basic services, where such resale was not prohibited by local or state regulations.

STS could achieve economies of scale that would reduce per-unit costs to its users. For example, by aggregating long-distance calls of many tenants within a single STS system, its operator could obtain volume discounts from providers such as AT&T or MCI. Similar economies might be possible for use of satellite relays, microwave systems, teleconferencing, etc. In really large projects, such as Olympia and York's huge lower Manhattan development containing millions of square feet of offices and residences, such aggregation can reach truly impressive volumes. Communications within such projects would not have to use the local telephone company's lines, so they could be provided at a lower cost. STS systems are not true telephone companies; they rely upon either local or long-distance telephone companies to provide the dial tones they use.

The technology for providing extensive STS systems is already available, although additional innovations will expand enhancement services in the future. Use of STS [27] need not wait on further technical developments. Many specialized firms have already been formed to install and manage STS systems. These firms include all but one of the Bell Operating Companies—the local telephone companies surviving after the AT&T divestiture. Bell Operating Companies are prohibited from providing long-distance services directly, but they can team up with other firms permitted to do so.

The firms offering STS to developers generated super-optimistic publicity about what so-called smart buildings can already do or will be able to do soon. Some of these buildings have been upgraded from merely "smart" to "intelligent," which seems even smarter. I expect to encounter promotions of even wiser "brilliant buildings" at any moment. The goal of all this hype is to shame developers into abandoning traditional "dumb" buildings by installing various controls and telecommunications at the outset. How effective will this publicity be?

Many developers of new office, industrial, research and

development, retail, and even residential projects will soon offer some type of STS to their tenants as an additional amenity. Prudent developers will rarely provide STS themselves; instead, each will use an existing firm that performs such services as either a subcontractor or a coventurer. This relieves developers of both technical and legal responsibility for systems about which most of them have little knowledge. Specialized installation firms will often put up the capital required to install STS systems in return for a share of the profits.

Prudent developers should also never include STS as part of their basic leases for space; STS should be covered by entirely separate contracts. Failure to install STS on time because of technical delays might block scheduled occupancy of a tenant's entire space, even if the space was ready in all other respects. That could postpone the developer's receipt of vitally needed rent for months, resulting in much lower overall profits. Also, developer liability for STS malfunctions or difficulties is not yet clear. The potential profits to developers from STS are far too small to risk jeopardizing the basic profitability of the entire project.

Developers who offer STS systems should not try to require tenants to accept such services, especially in today's highly competitive office and industrial-space markets. STS should be used primarily as an added amenity to help attract tenants. This means developers must be able to offer tenants the alternative of direct links to local Bell Operating Companies and major long-distance carriers. That will require some duplication of wiring within each structure.

How fast will developers adopt STS systems? This issue is controversial among the developers and other experts. One obstacle to installing STS systems is uncertainty about what regulations will be applied to them. Moreover, not all tenants need or will want STS. Developers who build new projects without STS will still have a market, but their potential market will be smaller than it would be if they offered STS. Few developers can afford to ignore any potential market segments under today's extraordinarily competitive conditions.

Developers of nearly all new first-class office, industrial, and research and development buildings will soon be driven by competition to offer some type of STS as an option to all of their tenants. The mere availability of STS will increase the attractiveness of a building or project to many potential occupants. That includes some who will not use STS initially, but who will want to have it readily accessible in case their needs change or STS enhancements become more attractive. Such universality of STS among new projects has already happened in the Dallas office-space market and will soon spread to others. Retrofitting of existing buildings will take longer, since it is much costlier than installing STS systems during construction. Competition will eventually force many owners of existing buildings to equip them with STS too. At a minimum, developers of all new buildings must install the capacity to relatively easily add various types of new wiring serving all spaces in those buildings. This requires running large-sized piping for wires throughout each structure, which will provide fexibility for relatively low-cost future installation of whatever technologies emerge as most desired by tenants.

Starting with telephone service, telecommunications have long been subject to government regulation at federal, state, and local levels. This reflected (1) the belief that they were "natural monopolies," so consumers had to be protected from possible exploitation by such monopolists; and (2) the need to construct facilities crossing publicly-owned streets and other rights-of-way. There has recently been a dramatic proliferation of alternative means of communication with widely differing characteristics. This technological explosion challenges both the usual rationales for public regulation. How will the regulatory arrangements that eventually emerge from this situation influence the behavior of real estate developers and the location of economic activities? The answers depend in the long run upon which governments will regulate which services and what the objectives of each regulator will be.

Motives other than protection of consumer interests greatly influence regulatory behavior. The most important is the desire of local governments to capture revenue from firms providing telecommunications services, including both telephone companies and cable television companies. Many local governments have claimed the authority to award exclusive franchises to both types of companies and to regulate their rates and other behavior. Local governments seek both to charge large franchise fees (concerning cable TV) or taxes (concerning telephone service) and to compel cable TV firms to furnish certain services to the public at no or low cost. A local

[28]

government can capture more revenues if each firm it franchises has a local monopoly than if many such firms compete with each other, since competition would erode each firm's profits. Local governments have strong incentives to create or protect monopoly market positions among suppliers of telecommunications services within their borders.

Local governments have almost no incentives to maximize the speed with which their constituents can enjoy the latest technology. No one rewards local officials for permitting extensive competition among telecommunications suppliers (except in the bidding for an exclusive franchise), even though that might stimulate suppliers to offer better services; nor does each local government have any motivation to decide quickly who should provide new telecommunications services within its boundaries. As a result, many city governments have delayed such decisions for years while local politicians jockeyed to have exclusive franchises awarded to suppliers whom they sponsored or who sponsored them.

Telecommunications suppliers can come under any or all of three different levels of government regulations. The broadest is that of the Federal Comunications Commission (FCC), based upon legislation going back to 1934. The FCC's principal goal in recent years seems to have been encouraging as great a diversity of different services as possible to be offered to consumers. The second level of regulation comes from state government public utility commissions (PUCs) or their equivalent. They have long governed rates that utility companies could charge for intrastate services. A third layer of regulation has come from local governments. The agencies at these three levels have not always exhibited mutually consistent goals or policies. For example, one city government compelled the cable TV firm that it had franchised to install two-way communications facilities able to transmit data in competition with services offered by the local telephone company. But the public utility commission with jurisdiction over that area prohibited the cable TV firm from offering such service in order to protect the telephone company's monopoly.

Current regulatory confusion is aggravated by two other factors. First, the regulatory scene is dominated by bureaucrats, elected politicians, and lawyers—probably the three most obstructionist groups in society when it comes to facilitating innovation. These same groups, along with the press, are also our key protectors of consumer and other human rights. That is precisely why they have responsibility for offsetting possible harmful effects of "pure" free-market operation by creating and enforcing various nonmarket regulations. Another source of confusion has been the speed and complexity of recent telecommunications innovation. Even the swiftest-moving, most efficient regulators imaginable would have a hard time keeping up with the amazing proliferation of new telecommunications technology. Here is a list of new telecommunications services I hardly knew existed before this year. This list is by no means a complete set of such services, since new ones are constantly being developed. These services are in addition to traditional television, cable TV, and telephone services:

- SMATV: satellite master antenna television, which delivers TV programs from a master satellite to individual households over cables wholly on private land.
- MDS: multipoint distribution service, which transmits TV or other signals directly by microwave.
- STV: subscription, over-the-air television, which sends scrambled signals over normal TV channels, receivable through normal TV sets with unscramblers.
- LPTV: low power television, which sends TV signals to households like traditional television, but covers only a small geographic area near each station.
- Teletext: transmission of textual information over unused parts of a normal TV signal, receivable by anyone with a normal TV set plus some supplementary equipment.
- Videotex: transmission of textual information over cable or telephone wires.
- LAN: local area networks, which link computers and related equipment to each other directly by wires not passing over public rights-of-way.
- DTS: digital termination systems, which handle WATS (Wide Area Telephone Service) line connections to local telephone users.

There are now many different ways to transmit the same information. Because these ways have different technical characteristics, they often fall under different regulatory bodies and/or do not fit past regulatory categories.

Up to now, there has been immense confusion, controversy, and uncertainty about who should regulate whom and for what purposes. Experience in other nations shows that similar, essentially political factors can thwart the introduction of new technologies for long periods. A current example is the unwillingness of Italian authorities to allow any telecommunications competition to the state-run telephone company once signals pass beyond a firm's own offices. Closer to home are long delays in introducing cable television into many large cities in the United States.

In our democratic society, two underlying pressures are moving most telecommunications services toward what will ultimately be a relatively unregulated, highly competitive state. The first consists of the power of innovation plus the entrepreneurial initiative inherent in our free enterprise system. So many new and different means of sending similar messages are being invented and promoted that regulators will have a hard time inhibiting [29] their use in the long run. Even if some types are blocked by a few local or state regulators for a while, other competitive types not under their jurisdiction will forge ahead and other communities will not block the first types. In our federal system, cities and states compete vigorously with each other to attract or retain jobs; each must strive to be as technically advanced as any others. The resulting pressure to make the latest technology available to resident firms and individuals will eventually cause regulators in every community to abandon highly restrictive telecommunications regulations.

The second major pressure for deregulation will come from the Federal Communications Commission. It has been vigorously pursuing its mandate to promote the widest possible diversity of services and freedom of access to them. The FCC has been given the power by both Congress and the courts to preempt or abolish local and state regulations in many situations. It has usually used that power to further innovation and permit adoption of new technologies.

One exception involves local telephone service, for which strong monopoly elements still remain. Since most potential competitors are highly market-oriented, they might not use the cross-subsidies that traditionally have benefited rural and low-income consumers and helped maintain a virtually universal telephone network in the United States. True, ending such cross-subsidies would increase "pure market efficiency." Their demise has also been accelerated because many users who were formerly discriminated against have shifted their business to other carriers or modes. This process is pejoratively labeled "bypassing" by the telephone companies, but really stands for "competition," according to Frank Lloyd. If it goes far enough, governments may be compelled to provide assistance to low-income, rural, and other high-cost telephone users to keep them in the network. Nearly all governments would rather use cross-subsidies hidden within the private sector than have to overtly raise taxes in the public sector. Some element of cross-subsidization concerning local telephone service will probably remain in the long run.

In spite of current regulatory confusion over telecommunications, regulation is not likely to impede the introduction and widespread use of new technologies in the long run. Whatever impacts those technologies would have had upon real estate and urban development because of other factors will eventually come to pass.

Recent innovations in telecommunications technology form only one of many forces that affect the location of economic activities—and it is not one of the most powerful. More important are changes in real household incomes, expanding use of automotive vehicles, federal policies concerning aid to highway and housing finance, farm technology and migration patterns, spatial concentrations of minority populations, desires among certain groups (such as the middle class) to segregate themselves spatially from others (such as the poor), household formation trends, interest rates, and even the international value of the U.S. dollar.

The net result of these forces over the past twenty years has been decentralization of most economic activities outward from big cities to suburbs, smaller cities, nonmetropolitan areas, and even other parts of the world. Many causal forces have been exerting strongly dispersive influences for much longer. I mention a twenty-year period because it was around 1965 when the massive post-1930s migration from rural to urban areas stopped. After that, decentralizing forces were no longer counteracted by the heavy flow of people—especially the poor—from farms into cities.

The dominance of decentralizing over centralizing forces is reflected in U.S. population trends. Many of the largest U.S. cities have been steadily losing both population and jobs for three decades or more. From 1970-80, the total population of the United States grew 11.4 percent. In the 318 largest metropolitan areas, all central cities combined grew only 0.2 percent. In contrast, all suburbs combined grew 18.2 percent, and all nonmetropolitan areas combined grew 15.1 percent. Suburbs captured about two-thirds of the nation's total population growth in the 1970s—almost exactly the same share as in the two preceding decades. Among the 170 cities with over 100,000 inhabitants in 1980 (which include many large suburbs), 77 lost population during the 1970s, as did 14 of the 25 largest cities. There is no evidence of any overall big-city resurgence, at least insofar as population is concerned.

Some forces have generated centralizing movements at the same time. Use of computers and improved telecommunications has enabled many large organizations to bring more administrative control back to their home offices than ever before. The same developments have also permitted large firms to disperse many activities not requiring face-to-face interactions to less expensive office space outside of central business districts. This illustrates the principle that, concerning location, telecommunications are permissive rather than determinative. Recent changes in telecommunications technology are not likely to change this situation in the foreseeable future.

A huge downtown office-space construction boom occurred in the 1970s and 1980s. This boom partly reflects a current bias in the nation's capital markets toward investing funds in real estate. This bias has been especially evident in the past few years as a result of both financial deregulation and changes in tax laws. In 1983, federal ceilings were removed from interest rates that banks and savings and loans institutions could pay to savers. That enabled them to use the full power of the attraction to savers of their federal deposit insurance against competing financial institutions that did not have such insurance. As a result, banks and savings and loan associations were flooded with money they had to invest somewhere. So were real estate syndicators, whose tax-shelter benefits were sweetened by 1981 legislation. These institutions all put most of their long-term funds into real estate (banks mainly involuntarily by making poor-quality construction loans). When nominal interest rates are high, a lower fraction of such funds can flow into housing than when rates are low, since fewer households can afford to borrow to buy homes; more money is available for investment in nonresidential properties such as office build-

[30]

ings. Pension funds were also investing heavily in real estate in the early 1980s.

The resulting flood of funds into office-space markets stimulated massive overbuilding, the extent of which became evident in the mid-1980s. The Coldwell Banker office vacancy index for thirty urban areas was below 5 percent in 1981, but has steadily risen since then. In June 1985, that index reached over 16 percent for downtowns and over 19 percent for suburbs. Yet some developers will build new structures regardless of current market conditions, as long as they can arrange more financing than their projects will cost. The surplus of investment money has enabled many to do just that. So developers continued to erect more and more new buildings in the face of high and increasing vacancy rates. This constellation of financial forces has been a more important cause of the downtown office-construction boom than any recent telecommunications innovations. Adoption of the income tax reforms recently proposed by the U.S. Treasury would curtail the contribution of real estate syndicators to this process; but it would not stop savings and loans or pension funds from continuing to invest in real estate.

There has been an extraordinary increase in high-rise office-building construction in most large central business districts since 1970. Some have cited this boom as evidence of a big-city renaissance—"a new urbanism." Closer examination reveals a different picture. Nearly all the new office space in big-city downtowns has been occupied by organizations already located there before the boom. Their economic expansion has supplied the demand for more space, and capital markets have supplied the resources to create it. Why have these organizations expanded downtown, where rents in each urban area are the highest, instead of in less costly outlying space? Why have downtowns not experienced the strong decentralization that has affected residences?

To some extent such decentralization has taken place. In many large metropolitan areas, total suburban office-space growth has been just as large, and often much larger, than downtown growth. Because outlying offices are scattered in many locations, and often are in low-rise structures, they do not create such highly-visible impressions as clusters of downtown skyscrapers (with a few exceptions such as Las Colinas in Dallas, the Galleria area in Houston, or Century City in Los Angeles). Even though office vacancy rates are typically higher in the suburbs than downtown, that does not mean occupancy growth is lower in outlying areas. Additions to supply are much easier to accomplish there, so that overbuilding is more endemic.

The concentration of new office space downtown is still impressive. Why has it occurred? Many top-level executives in both private and public sectors have recognized the crucial importance of engaging in face-to-face interactions with people outside their own organizations. Such direct contacts protect confidentiality, stimulate innovation and creative thinking, and permit rapid and flexible decision-making involving outside parties. Also, downtown locations provide fast, efficient access to specialized services that cluster in and around central business districts. Top executives like to work in downtowns, where they are close to others like themselves as well as to lawyers, accountants, and key government officials.

Downtowns have other attractions that sustain their vitality in spite of decentralizing forces. These include the largest agglomerations of all types of services and facilities in each metropolitan area, the easiest access to a large labor pool, and proximity to major government offices. Telecommunications services that make it easier for executives to communicate with distant subordinates have encouraged the former to keep their offices where they can take advantage of these amenities.

The boom in new downtown office space has not produced a commensurate rise in total downtown employment—particularly for city residents. Downtowns in our largest cities have lost many manufacturing, distribution, and mass-retailing jobs while they were gaining office and boutique-retailing jobs. Even in downtowns where spectacular new "festival retailing" centers have prospered, such as in Baltimore and Boston, traditional department stores have gone out of business, with a net loss of retail jobs and space. Many new downtown office jobs are held by suburban commuters. As a result, there is a continued mismatch in many large cities between the type of residents unemployed and ready for work, and the type of jobs accessible to them. Our big cities contain thousands of poor, unskilled, badly educated, unemployed residents, [31] many of whom are minorities. Most new jobs they might be able to fill are being created in the suburbs or outside of metropolitan areas altogether. Up to now, there is no sign that changes in the location of either workers or jobs induced by telecommunications technology—or anything else—will notably reduce this mismatch.

In a few of the nation's largest cities, further downtown office-space growth may be inhibited by rising traffic congestion. This possibility can be illustrated by considering the future of downtown Los Angeles. William Fain has indicated that plans are underway for adding another 18 million square feet of office space to downtown Los Angeles within the next decade. Existing streets and freeways do not have enough capacity to handle the additional 60-70,000 daily commuters who would work in the new offices. This huge increment of office space could only be accommodated by construction of an extensive network of offstreet public transit lines converging on downtown, similar to those in New York and Chicago. In view of this situation, Fain concludes that the automobile is "basically obsolete" as the key means of urban commuting in Los Angeles.

What is truly obsolete is thinking that downtowns can grow indefinitely large in big cities that are not already supplied with fixed-rail transit systems. Architects and city planners have been arguing for decades that automobile use should be drastically restricted and people either persuaded or compelled to use public transit instead; but the citizenry has blithely ignored all such advice. The public has continued to buy and use more and more automotive vehicles. In the 1970s, the population of cars, trucks, and buses in use in the United States grew about 4.2 million per year—1.8 times as fast as the human population. Although growth of the vehicle population has slowed somewhat in the 1980s, it still exceeds that of the human population. Americans in general, and Californians in particular, continue to love their vehicles far more than they love advice from urban planners.

Downtown Los Angeles might be able to grow much larger if it constructed an extensive off-street fixed-rail system. Who will pay the many billions of dollars needed to build such a system? Los Angeles citizens do not appear willing to bear the full cost of even the proposed subway, which would run from downtown westward through Hollywood to the San Fernando Valley. Advocates of a new full-scale public transit system for Los Angeles are trying to get most of the required funds from the federal government; however, the current federal administration has proposed eliminating all construction subsidies for public transit systems. No one appears willing to bear the cost of making the proposed downtown office-space expansion feasible.

Why should federal taxpayers from all over the nation pay for a costly improvement that would benefit only some residents of Los Angeles? I do not believe they should. If California—the richest state—wants to enjoy subways, let its residents pay for them, rather than foisting most of the bill off on the rest of us. The same principle should hold true for residents of every other big city. In this instance, I believe the policy of the present federal administration is correct.

Some argue that Californians have already sent billions of dollars to Washington as federal gasoline taxes and should now get "their fair share" back for a subway system. This argument does not impress me one iota. The federal government already spends vastly more in California than it collects in taxes there. The mere fact that we have unwisely spent federal funds elsewhere building too-costly fixed-rail systems—as in Washington, Baltimore, San Francisco, and Miami—hardly justifies continued engagement in such folly. Unless Californians are willing to pay for their own transit system, or the federal government changes its mind, downtown Los Angeles will be unable to efficiently grow as large as its advocates currently believe it can, no matter what telecommunications innovations are adopted there. That probably will not stop developers from continuing to add office space downtown beyond the point of "efficient" commuting. Each developer has no incentive to recognize the total costs to society of the added congestion his or her new building generates. Each is motivated to create that building on the optimistic assumptions that (1) some commuting solution will be provided by others, and (2) any vacancies caused by traffic congestion will appear in someone else's buildings. Developers as a whole will probably overshoot the total amount of office space that is theoretically optimal for downtown Los Angeles. That will lead to even more rush-hour traffic congestion, which will in turn cause some tenants to move out. Eventually, downtown as a whole will return to some equilibrium balance between traffic congestion and space occupancy. At that point, the average downtown office vacancy rate will be higher than it is now.

Such limitations on downtown office-space growth apply only to those very few other huge cities that do not already have big fixed-rail transit systems (such as Houston), or that have such systems but may lose much of their current federal subsidies (such as New York and Chicago). Without federal subsidies, public transit fares— or state-local taxes to replace the subsidies—would become so high in the latter cities that they might be unable to keep their existing downtown office space fully occupied. Most U.S. cities do not suffer from severe enough traffic congestion to limit their future downtown office-space growth in this way. [32]

Some have predicted that mobile telephones would help offset the ill effects of downtown commuting congestion. People phoning each other from their cars would regard the time they spend trapped in traffic jams as quite productive. I fear this reflects parochial, upper-class thinking. The vast majority of commuters will be unable to afford mobile telephones. Even if they could, most would have little to say to each other from their slowly-creeping cars from seven to nine in the morning and four to six at night. Many people repeatedly stuck in such congestion would decide they were better off working somewhere outside of downtown.

One more effective tactic will be for more people to work at home, at least part of the time, communicating with their offices electronically. Many people agree that such "telecommuting" would increase and that most people doing it would still want to work at the office part of the time. Only by doing so can they gain the benefits of socialization, spontaneous contacts stimulating creativity, and "staying close to the throne" for promotion. Enough telecommuting will be done to reduce the total demand for office space by a small but noticeable fraction, but not enough to help resolve downtown commuting congestion.

Telecommunications innovations will have extremely diverse impacts upon the future location of economic activities. In a few large cities that are already communications hubs (especially New York), greater centralization of many administrative and other activities will occur. The basic thrust of all those forces influencing the location of economic activities combined will remain essentially decentralizing, as it has been for at least two decades. Fast economic growth will not be restricted to those cities that serve as communications hubs. Some mid-sized cities and metropolitan areas will continue to expand rapidly for reasons unrelated to their communications qualities—as have Phoenix, Orlando, Raleigh-Durham, and Riverside-San Bernardino during the past fifteen years.

Most of the people who read this article will benefit

from future telecommunications and computer developments. They have the knowledge, sophistication, and other resources to take advantage of them. But these same developments will produce at least two quite negative results. First, they will further isolate the big-city poor from expanding economic opportunities. The quality of most big-city public schools is far below that of suburban public schools in nearly every metropolitan area. Yet nearly all public school systems in our largest cities have majorities of minority-group students, and a high fraction of all minority-group students attend city schools. (In 1980, 58 percent of all U.S. black residents and 45 percent of all U.S. Asian residents lived in central cities, compared to 25 percent of all U.S. whites.) This disparity in school quality reflects big differences in how well students are trained to use computers and other sophisticated techniques, as well as how well they learn the basic skills of reading, writing, and mathematics. The lower quality of most big-city schools perpetuates the relatively disadvantaged position of poor big-city residents.

America's continued neglect of the education of its poor and minority-group children is the greatest scandal of U.S. public policy today. Most Americans do not realize that about 24 percent of all U.S. children under fifteen years of age are either black or Hispanic. The future abilities of these children are of vital importance to the entire nation, as well as to themselves. Unfortunately, neither the current federal administration nor most of the interests represented in the area of telecommunications consider this problem important enough to pay it serious attention.

A second negative impact involves a bias in our thinking about issues likely to arise from more widespread use of computers and telecommunications. It is the tendency to confuse manipulating data on a computer screen with actually being in contact with, and understanding, the real world. A similar confusion has long existed in academic circles between knowing about some subject abstractly, from a distance, and knowing about it concretely, from direct experience and observation. Some realities—such as gross national product or geopolitics—can only be grasped abstractly. In many fields, true understanding of reality requires at least occasionally getting up from one's desk and going out to see, taste, hear, feel, and be affected by it. For example, I know from personal experience that I could never remain the world's leading authority on U.S. real estate and urban affairs solely by sitting at the Brookings Institution in Washington, reading books and reports, and conducting computerized analyses. Knowing what is really happening in this field, and many others, requires traveling around the nation and the world, talking to the practitioners involved on their home territories, and seeing their diverse situations directly.

An extreme example of the error I am describing was embodied in the futuristic home projected by one specialist. The dwelling he visualized had no windows through which one could directly view the world outside. It had huge computer-driven view-screens on which the residents could project either live or previously-recorded scenes from whatever region gripped their fancy. He claimed that residents of this home could easily manage almost any type of enterprise, from an interviewing firm to a trucking company, without ever leaving the place, as long as they had the right computer hardware and the relevant data inputs. This view reflects what I believe is an arrogant fallacy: that human beings can totally control their environments abstractly or electronically without ever getting their hands dirty by grappling directly with the real world. It becomes tempting to engage in this fallacy to at least some degree when we spend much of our time in front of a CRT screen. Viewing the world from there is so much more comfortable, convenient, and neater than confronting it directly. Yet I do not believe anyone could run a successful trucking company without occasionally talking face-to-face to a few drivers and customers and without kicking a few tires. [33]

The desire to replace nature, society, and other people with a purely computerized rendering of those realities is a new form of hubris. Indulging in it is bound to generate massive errors in both perception and behavior. We human beings did not create ourselves, and we cannot fully control our own destinies. Believing that reality can be wholly grasped through computer screens or statistical analyses is a denial of our creatureliness that will surely do us in. No one fully succumbs to this delusion; but it is increasingly tempting to spend more and more time sitting in front of some computer console, trying to manipulate reality electronically rather than going out to meet it on its own ground. This temptation reinforces an already strong tendency for the more affluent, sophisticated members of our society to continue ignoring the problems, even the very existence, of the poorest members.

Most middle-income and especially upper-income Americans have neatly separated themselves from the poor by living and working in economically segregated communities, riding around in their own luxurious private vehicles, viewing mass events from afar on television, and interacting only with other people like themselves. It makes the poor and their problems virtually invisible to most of us nearly all the time, regardless of how acute those problems become.

Most of us need far more opportunities for confronting the full spectrum of our nation's life directly. Technical developments in telecommunications and computers are removing us ever farther from these opportunities. Many Americans are totally engaged in enjoying and profiting from the new technologies and the myriad other opportunities that confront us. We are too busy to really give a damn about our widening separation from those at the bottom of society, whose prospects are very different from ours.

The impact of telecommunications innovations within individual real estate developments will be far less than meets the eye compared to the hyped-up expectations their promotors have been broadcasting. "Smart" buildings—even "brilliant" ones—cannot replace intelligent judgment and risk-taking by developers, or solve any of society's real problems. Nevertheless, those innovations will soon affect how nearly every developer constructs first-class office, industrial, and research and development buildings, and perhaps even retail and residential projects. Competition will make inclusion of some type of shared telecommunications services nearly universal in the first three types of structures, even though not all tenants will use those services.

All the authorities now regulating telecommunications services will come under rising pressure to permit more competition among providers and more widespread accessibility among potential users. Current regulatory inhibitions on both competition and accessibility have been caused by a lag of administrative and legal practices behind swift-moving technologies and by power struggles among competing regulators. Those inhibitions will gradually weaken or disappear. In the interim, a period of continued confusion is likely.

The larger-scale impacts of telecommunications upon the future location of economic activities will primarily confirm and strengthen already on-going trends caused by other forces. That is because telecommunications exercise essentially permissive, rather than determinative, influences upon location. As a result, there will be:

- Further spreading out of most activities within each urban area, across the nation and even around the world. This will cause continued faster growth of most suburban areas, many smaller metropolitan areas, many smaller cities, and some nonmetropolitan areas, rather than of big cities.
- More diversity of activities within each commercial or industrial building.
- More centralization of administrative control within many large organizations, but fewer people at the headquarters of each.
- A blurring of distinctions among different types of work locations, such as home vs. the office, the car vs. the office, downtown vs. the suburbs, and the United States vs. the rest of the world.
- A reinforcement of the importance of those few, very large central business districts that act as major communications nodes, especially New York City.

The most important implication of telecommunications innovations is the continued expansion of individual choices available to the upper and middle echelons of American society. As telecommunications options increase, we have more choices concerning where to live and work, what type of work to do, how much time to spend working at home, with whom to interact, how to do it, and how to arrange almost every other aspect of our lives. These same developments may provide the lower echelons of our society with fewer choices concerning many of these matters. The political and moral climate currently dominating American society focuses economic opportunities and government policies upon serving those who are already strong, with little regard for those who are weak. For the strong, innovations in telecommunications will further enhance their individual choices and freedom. □ [34]

[8]

A strategy for designing a national housing policy for the federal government of the United States

Introduction and summary

Purpose of the paper
This paper presents an overview of key issues relevant to formulating a comprehensive national housing policy for the federal government of the United States. It is designed to serve as a background resource to persons developing a proposed Housing Act of 1988, which would embody, or at least be based upon, such a comprehensive national housing policy. Related papers are also being prepared by other authors concerning more detailed aspects of this same general subject.

This paper seeks to be broad enough to serve as a unifying background to those more detailed papers, but specific enough to deal clearly and directly with the key issues involved. It adopts as factual and objective a perspective as possible. But it also discusses certain issues that are inherently value-laden, and therefore cannot be dealt with in a purely scientific manner. In those cases, the paper either describes alternative viewpoints reflecting different underlying values, or describes a single viewpoint clearly labelled as that of the author. In fact, I have deliberately built great flexibility into this whole approach to creating a comprehensive national housing policy. Hence anyone can use it to define such a policy in conformity to his or her own values and policy judgments.

The paper has been prepared by Anthony Downs at the request of the staff of the Senate Housing Committee. Anthony Downs is a Senior Fellow at the Brookings Institution in Washington DC. However, this paper reflects his views only, and not necessarily those of the Brookings Institution, its Trustees, or any of its other staff members.

Summary of findings

Housing goals These are the ultimate objectives concerning housing conditions in the United States that federal housing-related policies are designed to achieve. Analysis of past Congressional statements about housing policy objectives reveals the following as *primary target goals*[1]:

- 'Realization as soon as feasible of ... a decent home and a suitable living environment for every American family.'[2]
  This is the central housing goal of national housing policy, as set forth by Congress in the Housing Act of 1949, and cited repeatedly in later legislation.

- Providing housing assistance to low-income households by:
  Enabling those now living in physically adequate units but paying 'excessive' fractions of their incomes for housing to reduce those fractions to desirable levels.
  Enabling those now living in physically inadequate units to occupy 'decent' quality units.
  Enabling those now living in overcrowded units to occupy units that are not overcrowded.

- Providing similar housing assistance to numerous specific groups, including the elderly, Indians, disabled veterans, persons displaced by government actions, etc.

- Encouraging homeownership among households, regardless of their incomes.

- Increasing the total available supply of decent-quality housing units of all types and at all price levels.

- Eliminating racial and ethnic discrimination in housing markets.

- Stimulating the economy by increasing construction activity in the housing industry.

- Improving the quality of deteriorated neighborhoods.

- Reducing the concentration of low-income households in poverty areas.

Housing problems The major housing problems currently prevalent in the United States can be divided into two main groups: *consumer-oriented* (viewed from the perspective of housing occupants) and *industry-oriented* (viewed from the perspective of the housing industry). These problems are set forth below. Most data are from 1983 because that was the latest year for which detailed calculations concerning the extent of housing problems are available.

- *Consumer-oriented housing problems*

  1 *Low-income housing problems* are those suffered primarily by households with incomes below 80% of their area median incomes, mainly because of their relative poverty. In 1983, about 45% of all US households, or 38.3 million, had low incomes. They included 27% with *very low incomes* (under 50% of their area median incomes) and 18% with *moderately-low incomes* (50% to 80% of their area median incomes).

  Affordability problems Many households have such low money incomes they cannot occupy decent quality units without paying 'excessive' fractions of their incomes for housing (that is, more than about 30%). Most of these households are already living in decent-quality housing. Hence what they need most is either higher incomes or lower prices for the same housing, rather than physically-improved housing units.

Physical inadequacy Many low-income households live in units that are deteriorated below decent quality levels, or lack facilities considered essential for decent housing, such as adequate plumbing.

Overcrowding Some low-income households live in units that have too many persons per room for decent quality living. Units with more than 1.0 persons per room or 2.0 persons per bedroom are usually considered overcrowded.

Poor-quality neighborhoods Many low-income households live in neighborhoods that are unsafe, inadequately provided with public services and facilities, or otherwise undesirable.

Homelessness Thousands of very poor persons across the nation do not have any permanent dwellings at all, but reside in streets, parks or other outdoor locations. They are especially concentrated in large cities.

Desubsidization Thousands of now-subsidized housing units occupied by low-income households may cease being subsidized because their owners are eligible to remove them from such status, or they are in dire financial straits. In either case, their removal from subsidized status threatens to sharply raise housing costs for the low-income households now occupying them.

2 *Racial and ethnic discrimination* in housing markets is much more common than most people think; hence it was a key obstacle to the effective use of housing vouchers by black households in many cities. Its most common form is 'steering' of white households seeking dwellings into all-white neighborhoods, and black or minority households seeking dwellings into mostly black or minority neighborhoods.

3 *First-time buyer affordability problems* arise when households seeking homeownership for the first time cannot afford to purchase homes without spending excessive fractions of their incomes to do so. These are similar to affordability problems among low-income households, but first-time buyer households normally do not have low incomes.

4 *Excessively costly local government regulations* raise the cost of building new housing units far above both (1) what is necessary to provide decent, safe, and sanitary dwellings and (2) what many moderate-income and nearly all low-income households can afford to pay without spending excessive fractions of their incomes for housing, if then.

5 *Regional or sub-regional housing exclusion* occurs when large portions of a metropolitan area have such high housing costs that many moderate-income and nearly all low-income households cannot afford to live there without spending inordinately high fractions of their incomes for housing, if then. Such exclusion results from a combination of excessively costly local government regulations and high land costs caused by strong demands for land in economically-growing areas.

- *Industry-oriented housing problems*

  1 Insolvency and financial instability in the thrift industry threaten that industry's ability to continue financing home ownership. Several hundred of the nation's 3,200 savings and loan associations are bankrupt and losing net worth through their continuing operations. Yet the Federal Savings and Loan Insurance Corporation is also virtually bankrupt. Therefore, it cannot afford to shut down these defunct thrifts, as it is supposed to do. This situation is so serious that the continued separate existence of the entire thrift industry is threatened. Yet savings and loans hold over $800 billion in home mortgages, and are the still largest single source of home mortgage funds.

  2 Volatility of overall housing demand raises housing costs and causes great instability within the homebuilding industry. Housing construction has always been a highly cyclical activity because of the dependence of housing demand upon interest rates, which move up and down during the general business cycle. The resulting instability of total housing demand causes periodic shrinkage in the number of firms engaged in housing construction during housing 'slumps', followed by rapid expansion during housing 'booms'. This cyclicality raises the average cost of new housing above what it would be if demand were much more stable over time.[3]

  3 Volatility of home mortgage interest rates affects the ability of potential homebuyers to borrow the money necessary for such purchases. This volatility results from the linkage of interest rates to the general business cycle. When interest rates in general are relatively high, so are mortgage interest rates. Hence the number of households who can afford to borrow to buy homes falls. Conversely, that number rises when interest rates are low. This volatility affects not only new home construction, but the sales of existing homes. The number of such sales made each year is usually several times greater than the number of new homes built, so this volatility affects a great many households, as well as the home-sale and resale industries.

  4 Regional shortages of trained construction workers have arisen in some areas because of a decline in new housing construction during periods of high interest rates, especially the early 1980s. Skilled workers moved out of regions where housing production was depressed for prolonged periods, especially in the Midwest, to more dynamic areas. When demand revived in the former areas, shortages of skilled workers emerged there. Yet few skilled construction workers were willing to move back to these areas because they did not believe housing demand would remain strong there.

It should be noted that the above list of major housing problems is a tentative one drawn up by the author without extensive consultation with other members of the real estate industry. Suggestions for modifying this list would be welcomed by the author.

The relative magnitude of those consumer-oriented housing problems that can be quantified can be judged from the percentages of *all* households affected by each such problem *each year*. They are shown below, in descending order of their relative extent, based upon 1983 data:

Specific housing problem	% of all households experiencing that problem
Affordability	24.3%
Physically inadequate units	8.9%
Overcrowding	3.5%
Racial discrimination	2.0%[4]
First-time homebuying affordability	1.5%
Desubsidization	1.0%[5]
Homelessness	0.14%

Clearly, *housing affordability problems are by far the most widespread*. In 1983, they affected 24.3% of all households, or 20.6 million – almost one out of every four US households. These included 34% of low-income households. That is almost three times as many households as are affected by the second most prevalent housing problem – physically inadequate units. All the other consumer-oriented housing problems directly affected relatively small fractions of the US population. However, the affected fractions are much higher than average among certain groups, especially blacks, Hispanics and female-headed households.

Some households experience more than one of these problems. Taking that into account, in 1983 about 28.5% of all households in the US experienced at least one of the first three housing problems listed above. That means over one-fourth of all US households suffer from housing problems. But it also means that almost three-fourths do not. That may help explain why Congress has never funded any housing programs at sufficient levels to come close to serving all those eligible for assistance under them.

No attempt has been made to quantify the extent of industry-oriented housing problems. This is partly because they only indirectly affect most households, and partly because they are far more difficult to quantify.

Key housing issues These are policy questions that require choosing among alternative courses of action in order to pursue housing goals effectively. Most such choices inherently require subjective value judgments; hence they are very likely to be controversial. However, the issues themselves constitute a relatively objective set of choices that must be resolved in order to form a truly comprehensive national housing policy.

These issues have been divided into four groups, and are set forth at the end of this summary chapter. The same issues are also presented below along with recommended policy choices concerning each. It should be emphasized again that some policy choice must be made concerning every key housing issue in order to formulate a comprehensive national housing policy. This is especially important because many issues are highly interdependent; hence failure to make an explicit choice concerning one will make it impossible to make effective choices concerning the others.

Specific housing policy recommendations Below are set forth all the key housing issues identified as vital to formulation of a comprehensive national housing policy, along with the specific policy recommendations made herein to resolve each of these issues. These recommendations are based upon my own subjective value judgements, made in light of the facts and other objective considerations presented in this paper or otherwise available to me. Hence many of the policies recommended below are likely to be controversial. The purpose of making them is not to impose my views upon anyone else, but to offer a sample set of resolutions to key housing issues. Readers are encouraged to substitute their own policy recommendations as resolutions to these issues, thereby formulating their own versions of a comprehensive national housing policy.

- **Issue Number 1:** What housing-related roles is it appropriate for the federal government to perform?

  Financing housing subsidies for low-income households The federal government should finance a major portion of all resource-redistributive housing and other aids to low-income households. This includes various forms of housing and income subsidies that are considered appropriate, including housing vouchers and subsidies for the construction of new housing units.

  Maintaining a general economic climate favorable to high levels of housing transactions Through appropriate monetary and fiscal policies, the federal government should help create and maintain a general economic climate conducive to (1) high-level construction and sales of new housing units, (2) high-level financing and sales of existing housing units, and (3) adequate job opportunities and income levels for households.

  Regulating and supporting housing finance institutions The federal government should regulate and support existing institutions engaged in both *primary* and *secondary* financing of home mortgages so they can make adequate funds available to households who want to buy or refinance homes, and so they remain economically strong and viable.

  Encouraging maximum feasible private-sector actions regarding housing The federal government should encourage efficient use of resources in housing by maximizing the roles performed in housing markets by private firms as opposed to public agencies. Specifically, it should (1) encourage homeownership among all types of households and (2) encourage maximum use of private firms to plan, finance, build, and operate subsidized housing.

  Attacking racial discrimination in housing The federal government should vigorously enforce all federal laws against racial and other ethnic discrimination in housing markets. It should take an active role in such enforcement, and should encourage state and local governments to increase their enforcement efforts.

Setting general housing quality standards The federal government should set *general* standards of acceptable housing quality for units subsidized with federal funds. But it should leave *detailed* standards for such quality to be determined by local authorities (possibly subject to periodic federal review).

Developing a comprehensive national housing policy The federal government should develop a comprehensive national housing policy from combinations of specific tactics that effectively reduce low-income and other housing problems, but also constrain total federal spending on housing assistance within limits related to reducing current high levels of federal budget deficits.

- **Issue Number 2:** What housing-related roles is it appropriate for other key actors to perform?

Setting their own agendas The federal government should not attempt to limit the actions of states, localities, and private actors concerning housing. Rather, it should encourage them to undertake any and all housing-related roles that will help the nation meet its housing goals, when combined with responsible performance by the federal government of the federal roles described above.

- **Issue Number 3:** What public or private actors should be primarily responsible for funding the following:

Housing-oriented assistance for low-income households? The federal government should have primary responsibility for funding such assistance.

Housing-oriented assistance for non-low-income households? State governments and private actors – especially the households themselves – should have primary responsibility for funding such assistance. The federal government should finance as little such assistance as possible.

Creation, repair, and maintenance of housing-related infrastructures State and local governments should have primary responsibility for funding such activities, with two exceptions. The federal government should have primary responsibility for building and maintaining the Interstate Highway System and for financing facilities to meet environmental quality standards which federal legislation has mandated.

Credit-cost reduction programs designed to make housing finance easier Recommendations for who should have primary responsibility for such cost reductions should be contained in legislation dealing mainly with financial institutions, rather than in legislation dealing mainly with housing.

- **Issue Number 4:** How much money should the federal government spend on housing-oriented assistance?

Moderate federal funding The federal government should have as a spending 'target' enough annual outlays and budgetary authority to add 200,000 households per year to the total number being assisted. That is about one-half the number added during the years of maximum additions. However, because of the stringent budgetary situation that exists when federal deficits are large, it may be desirable for federal housing-oriented expenditures to rise gradually over time from their 1987 level to this higher 'target' level.[6]

- **Issue Number 5**: How much money should state and local governments and key private actors spend on housing-oriented assistance?

Setting their own spending levels The federal government should not attempt to determine the spending levels appropriate to state governments, local governments and private actors concerning housing. Rather, it should encourage them to undertake any and all housing-related roles that will help the nation meet its housing goals, when combined with responsible performance by the federal government of the federal roles described above. Such encouragement could take the form of providing matching grants for funds from state and local governments and even from private actors.

- **Issue Number 6**: How should federally-funded housing assistance programs be related to other forms of federally-funded assistance to low-income households, such as welfare and food stamps?

Relating federal housing-oriented assistance to welfare reform The level and forms of federally-funded housing assistance should depend in part upon the forms and levels of other types of federally-funded assistance to low-income households. Specifically, the following alternatives should be considered:

IF WELFARE REFORM AND EXPANSION ARE ADOPTED The federal government may adopt significant welfare spending reforms that result in non-housing-oriented assistance providing a much higher level of income support to poor households than was the case in 1987. In that case, federal emphasis upon housing-oriented assistance should be relatively restrained. The housing affordability problems of many low-income households would then be remedied by higher welfare spending or income derived from welfare-related jobs.
In that case, federal housing assistance should emphasize new-construction-oriented housing subsidies, since the income-support function of housing vouchers would be taken care of by higher levels of welfare spending.

IF WELFARE REFORM AND EXPANSION ARE NOT ADOPTED The federal government may not adopt welfare spending reforms like those described above. In that case, federal emphasis upon housing-oriented assistance should reach the levels of spending described in the discussion of Issue Number 4 above.
In that case, federal housing assistance should emphasize both housing vouchers and new-construction-oriented housing subsidies, but primarily the former, since vouchers are more effective at remedying housing affordability problems.

- **Issue Number 7**: What proportions of all the federal government resources used for *direct* housing aid (that is, excluding tax benefits) should be spent for (1) income supplementation (as with housing vouchers), (2) constructing new housing units for low-income occupancy, (3) rehabilitating existing privately-owned units, (4) rehabilitating existing public housing, and (5) maintaining now-subsidized units in subsidized status?

Dependence upon welfare reform To some extent, the proper policy concerning this issue depends upon whether welfare reform and higher levels of welfare spending are adopted, as discussed concerning Issue Number 6 above. However, *the remaining discussion of this issue set forth below assumes that no major welfare reform or higher levels of welfare spending will be adopted in the near future.*

Dependence upon desubsidization research To some extent, the proper policy concerning this issue also depends upon further research about the magnitude and nature of potential desubsidization – that is, the removal of now-subsidized units from subsidy status.

(1) If that research indicates that many thousands of now-subsidized units are likely to be desubsidized in the near future, *and* that this could be avoided by federal spending *per unit* similar to that required for a housing voucher program, then using federal funds to avoid such desubsidization should have very high priority among the five forms listed above.

(2) If that research indicates that many thousands of now-subsidized units are likely to be desubsidized in the near future, *but* that avoiding this result would require spending *more per unit than housing vouchers, but less than new construction*, then using federal funds to avoid such desubsidization should have only moderate priority among the five forms listed above – lower priority than housing vouchers, but higher than new construction subsidies.

(3) If that research indicates that not many now-subsidized units will be desubsidized in the near future, *or* that preventing such units from becoming desubsidized would be more costly *per unit* than building new units, then using federal funds to avoid desubsidization should have very low priority among the five forms listed above.

Transferring resolution of this allocation issue to lower levels of government Ideally, decisions about which of these specific forms federally-funded housing-oriented assistance should take should be made at the metropolitan-area level in urbanized areas, and the regional housing market level in rural areas. Then different mixtures of forms could be designed to suit particular conditions in each metropolitan or regional area. In order for this to occur, however, two other issues would have to be resolved with appropriate policies.

Federal funding for housing assistance would have to take the form of some type of block grant made to each state or each metropolitan area or rural regional area. The funds in each grant would be used within that state or area as the decision-making authorities there thought best.

In addition, the federal government would have to designate some public agency at the appropriate geographic level as the legal allocator of federally-funded housing assistance. There are very few metropolitan areas, and virtually no rural regions, where such public agencies capable of making these allocation decisions effectively now exist. That might require the federal government to allocate the funds to state governments and let those governments decide who should allocate these funds within each metropolitan area or rural region.

Thus, resolution of this issue is closely interrelated to resolution of the 'appropriate administrative arrangements' issue.

If it is possible to transfer decisions about how to allocate federally-funded housing aid among the above forms to lower levels of government, and still be confident that those lower levels would pursue federal housing goals, such a shift would be desirable.

If it is *not* possible to transfer such allocation decisions to lower levels of government, then the considerations set forth below should be determining.

Resolving this allocation issue at the federal level If resolution of this allocation issue cannot be transferred to lower levels of government, it will have to be done at the federal government level. How it should be resolved there depends heavily upon the total amount of resources available for all these forms of housing assistance, as follows:

(1) If only relatively small amounts of federal funds are available for housing assistance, nearly all those funds should be used in the form of housing vouchers for very-low-income households. Housing vouchers address housing affordability problems more effectively than any of the other forms (except perhaps reducing desubsidization, if that costs no more per unit than housing vouchers). Moreover, housing vouchers cost about one-half as much per year per household aided as new construction subsidies or major rehabilitation subsidies.
In this case, it would be necessary to use a *demand-side subsidy strategy*, because not enough funds would be available to permit using many of them to augment existing housing supplies.

(2) If moderately-large amounts of federal funds are available for housing assistance (though much more than in 1987), a mixture of different forms should be used, though vouchers should receive considerably more than all other forms combined. All forms used should predominantly aid low-income households, with emphasis upon very-low-income households.
In this case, it might be possible to use a *deep-subsidy supply-side strategy*, which concentrates new construction subsidies on units for immediate occupancy by very-low-income households.

(3) If very large amounts of federal funds are available for housing assistance, those funds should be more evenly divided between housing vouchers and all

other forms of assistance, although vouchers should receive no less funding than all other forms combined. This allocation would permit using new-construction-oriented subsidies to achieve at least some locational objectives. *In this case*, it might be possible to employ a *shallow-subsidy supply-side strategy* or a *two-sided subsidy strategy*. In those strategies, shallow new construction subsidies would be used to maximize the total number of new units built per dollar of federal aid. That number would be large enough to affect the market prices of nearby non-subsidized rental units, thereby aiding non-subsidized low-income households. Housing vouchers would be used to insure that an appropriate share of those new units were occupied by very-low-income households.

- **Issue Number 8**: What proportion of all the federal government resources used for housing aid should be spent directly to aid low-income households, as compared to aiding moderate-, middle-, or upper-income households?

Concentration upon low-income households The federal government should confine its direct housing assistance funding as much as possible to aiding low-income households.

Taking homeownership tax benefits into account In deciding how to allocate federal funds for housing assistance among different income groups, Congress should take account of homeownership tax benefits and how they are distributed among income groups. Such taking account could assume two forms. *In all cases*, Congress should recognize that (1) homeownership tax benefits cause much larger net costs to the federal government than the outlay costs of all direct forms of housing subsidies combined, and (2) middle- and upper-income groups receive the vast majority of all homeownership tax benefits. These facts provide a solid moral basis for concentrating all direct federal housing assistance upon aiding low-income households.

If the Congress wishes to increase housing aid to low-income households without raising federal spending, it should consider a partial reduction of homeownership tax benefits – especially those now going to upper-income households. This could be done while still preserving most existing homeownership tax benefits, and therefore without attacking the basically sound policy of encouraging homeownership.

Making aid to non-low-income households dependent upon the total amount of federal housing assistance funds available The federal government should *not* provide significant housing assistance to non-low-income households – including first-time homebuyers – unless large amounts of federal funds are available for housing assistance of all types.

- **Issue Number 9**: Where in the 'trickle-down' process – that is, at what income level – should federal funds for housing aid be used to insert additional new housing units into the existing inventory?

Interdependence of this issue with others Proper policies concerning this issue are closely interrelated with policies adopted concerning other issues, especially Issues Number 4, 7, and 8 discussed above and Issues 11 and 12 discussed below. Hence no separate discussion of this policy is presented here.

- **Issue Number 10:** How should federal housing assistance be related to needs among occupants of federally-assisted housing units for receiving other social services, such as home health care, personal counselling and job training?

Non-treatment of this issue in this paper This issue is not analyzed in this paper; hence no policy recommendations are presented about it.

- **Issue Number 11:** How should federal funds for low-income housing be administered? At what governmental level should detailed fund allocation decisions be made? What specific mechanisms should be used to make such administration effective?

Locating resolution of the form-of-aid-allocation issue at lower levels of government As discussed above, in order to best adapt federal housing policies to local housing market conditions, decisions about which specific forms of federally-funded housing-oriented assistance should be used in each major market should be made at the metropolitan-area level in urbanized areas, and the regional housing market level in rural areas. In order for this to occur, however, two other issues would have to be resolved with appropriate policies, as pointed out earlier.

First, federal funding for housing assistance would have to take the form of some type of block grant made to each state or each metropolitan area or rural regional area. Second, the federal government would have to designate some public agency at the appropriate geographic level as the legal allocator of federally-funded housing assistance. Or it could allocate the funds to state governments and let those governments decide who should allocate these funds within each metropolitan area or rural region.

- **Issue Number 12:** Should federal housing assistance be used to further specific locational objectives (such as avoiding further concentration of poor households in deteriorated neighborhoods)? If so, which ones, and to what extent?

Shifting pursuit of locational objectives to lower administrative levels The federal government should declare the desirability of using federal housing assistance funds to achieve the following locational objectives: (1) generally avoiding further concentration of low-income households in poor neighborhoods, (2) up-grading such neighborhoods physically in a few cases, and (3) locating subsidized housing for low-income households in areas that both lack such housing and are experiencing rapid job growth.

However, the federal government should neither directly pursue those location objectives through use of federal housing assistance funding, nor mandate their pursuit by lower-level agencies to which it delegates administration of those funds. Rather, it should encourage those lower-level agencies to pursue these locational objectives to the maximum extent feasible, periodically review their efforts to do so, and use their success in doing so as one criterion for deciding what agencies will receive future federal housing assistance funds.

- **Issue Number 13**: What housing quality standards should be required in federally-assisted housing? Should federally-funded housing assistance programs aim at reducing construction costs required by local government regulations that seem excessive?

Housing quality standards in federally-assisted programs The federal government should usually require that all housing units its funds assist meet prevailing local minimum quality standards concerning health and safety wherever that housing is situated. It should not impose additional quality standards upon such units under normal conditions. Such reliance upon local standards may help avoid the excessive development and construction costs typical of federally-financed housing in the past.

Attempting to reduce 'excessive' quality standards set by local governments The federal government should establish *maximum* housing quality standards for health and safety, and initially require that no locality impose quality standards beyond those maximum standards on federally-assisted units. At least this should be its initial posture until some experience with this approach can be gained and evaluated. If this approach results in very few federally-assisted housing units being located outside low-income neighborhoods, it should be modified to avoid that outcome.

- **Issue Number 14**: To what extent, and how, should the federal government counteract current financial weaknesses in the savings and loan industry, including in the Federal Savings and Loan Insurance Corporation?

- **Issue Number 15**: To what extent should housing funds be raised through federally-linked credit agencies, as compared to non-linked sources that must pay higher interest rates for capital?

Deferring resolution of these issues to financial institution legislation Although resolving these issues would be necessary for formulating a truly comprehensive national housing policy, this paper does not present any specific policies for such resolution. It omits suggesting resolutions of these issues because dealing with them is more appropriate for *financial institution legislation* than for *housing legislation*. Yet this paper is intended as a background for the design of appropriate housing legislation.

Applying criteria of desirability to the recommended policies The set of recommended policies set forth above constitutes a tentative version of a comprehensive national housing policy. Several *criteria of desirability* have been defined to be used in evaluating the soundness of any proposed comprehensive national housing policy *when considered as a whole*. These criteria are as follows:

- Internal Consistency
- Completeness
- Minimal Contents (no unnecessary policies)
- Affordability
- Realistic Role-Assignment
- Consistency with Other Federal Policies

Application of these criteria to the set of policies recommended above shows that this set reasonably meets the criteria of internal consistency, minimal contents, affordability, and realistic role-assignment. No conclusion can be made within this paper about whether it meets the criterion of consistency with other federal policies because too many other policies would have to be analysed in detail.

However, this set of recommended policies clearly fails to meet the criterion of completeness for three reasons. First, it does not offer policies aimed directly at attaining two of the housing goals Congress has adopted in the past: stimulating the economy through housing activity, and improving the quality of deteriorated neighborhoods. These goals are pursued only indirectly. Second, it defers resolution of several issues to papers concerned with non-housing legislation – specifically, legislation on financial institutions. Third, it does not deal directly with any industry-oriented housing problems.

Nevertheless, this set of policy recommendations is as close to a comprehensive national housing policy as the author can produce at this time. Readers are encouraged to alter or supplement these recommendations in accordance with their own views, and to communicate those changes to the author.

Key housing issues that need to be resolved in formulating a comprehensive national housing policy

Issues concerning housing-related roles and responsibilities

- *Definition of appropriate housing-related roles.* What social functions or roles concerning housing should the following actors perform:

    The federal government
    State governments
    Local governments
    Private firms

Low-income households
Non-low-income households?

- *Responsibility for funding housing assistance.* What public or private actors should be responsible for funding the following:

    Housing-oriented assistance for low-income households
    Housing-oriented assistance for non-low-income households
    Creation, repair, or maintenance of housing-related infrastructure, such as highways, streets, water systems, sewer systems and environmental quality control systems
    Credit-cost-reduction programs designed to make housing finance easier for households of any income?

- *Appropriate funding levels.* How much money should the following actors spend on providing housing assistance each year during the next few years?

    The federal government
    State governments
    Local governments
    Private sector actors?

Issues concerning the allocation of federal resources WITHIN an overall policy

- *Relationship to other federal assistance programs.* How should federally-funded housing assistance programs be related to other forms of federally-funded assistance, such as welfare, food stamps and health care?

- *Relative emphasis on specific forms of housing aid.* What proportions of all the federal government resources used for *direct* housing aid (that is, excluding tax benefits) should be spent in the following ways:

    Increasing the incomes of low-income households in whatever units they choose to occupy, as through housing vouchers
    Constructing new housing units for occupancy by low-income households
    Rehabilitating existing privately-owned housing units
    Rehabilitating existing public housing units
    Maintaining now-subsidized units in a subsidized status, rather than having them shifted to non-subsidized status by their owners?

- *Relative emphasis on aiding low-income households.* What proportion of all federal government resources used for housing aid should be spent directly to aid low-income households, as compared to aiding moderate-, middle- or upper-income households?

    To what extent should tax benefits received by homeowners be taken into account in calculating such emphasis?

How much federal assistance should be used to encourage homeownership among non-low-income households? What forms should such aid take?

- *Where to insert new subsidized housing units into the existing supply.* Where in the 'trickle-down' process – that is, at what income level or levels – should federal funds for housing aid be used to insert additional new housing units into the existing inventory?

- *Relationship to occupant needs for social services.* How should federal housing assistance be related to needs among occupants of federally-assisted housing units for receiving other social services, such as home health care, personal counselling, and job training?

Issues of inter-governmental relationships in housing policy implementation

- *Appropriate administrative arrangements.* How should federal funds for low-income housing be administered? At what governmental level should detailed fund allocation decisions be made? What specific mechanisms should be used to make such administration effective?

- *Locational objectives.* Should federal housing assistance be used to further specific locational objectives (such as avoiding further concentration of poor households in deteriorated neighborhoods)? If so, which ones, and to what extent?

- *Level of quality standards and local regulations.* What housing quality standards should be required in federally-assisted housing? Should federally-funded housing assistance programs aim at reducing construction costs required by local government regulations that seem excessive?

Issues concerning housing credit institutions

- *Support of private housing finance institutions.* To what extent, and how, should the federal government counteract current financial weaknesses in the savings and loan industry, including in the Federal Savings and Loan Insurance Corporation?

- *Use of federally-linked credit.* To what extent should housing funds be raised through federally-linked credit agencies, as compared to non-linked sources that must pay higher interest rates for capital?

Notes

1. This list of Congressionally-defined objectives is taken from Anthony Downs, *Federal Housing Subsidies: How Are They Working?* (Lexington, Massachusetts: Lexington Books, 1973), pp. 1–2. Another set of *secondary target goals* taken from past legislation is also presented there. One of those secondary goals has been elevated to primary status here, because Congress officially adopted it in 1974. It is: 'Reducing the concentration of low-income households in poverty areas'. The

primary target goals stated here are virtually identical with the eight major housing goals cited by Henry Aaron in 'Policy Implications: A Progress Report', in Katharine L. Bradbury and Anthony Downs (eds), *Do Housing Allowances Work?* (Washington DC: The Brookings Institution, 1981), pp. 70–6.
2. From Section 2 of the National Housing Act of 1949. Taken from Committee on Banking, Currency, and Housing of the House of Representatives, *Basic Laws and Authorities on Housing and Community Development, Revised through July 31, 1975* (Washington DC: 94th Congress, 1st Session, July 31, 1975), p. 1.
3. This situation causes a serious problem *from the viewpoint of the housing construction industry*, but may not be a problem *from the viewpoint of the welfare of the nation as a whole*. The nation's economy benefits from having a large industry capable of both rapid expansion and rapid contraction in total output, without serious diminution of its long-run productive capacity. This is an advantage because, whenever the overall economy approaches its capacity output, it is desirable to slow down production in sectors in which increases in consumption can be relatively easily postponed, so as to continue production in other sectors where that is not so easy. Conversely, whenever the overall economy enters a slack period, it is desirable to increase production in sectors where deferred demand can be readily activated to help stimulate overall economic activity. Housing construction is such a flexible sector. Hence what is a problem of *cyclical instability* from the viewpoint of the housing construction industry, is an advantage of *counter-cyclical activity* from the viewpoint of the nation as a whole.
4. This estimate includes only those households who are actively affected by racial discrimination *while looking for housing in a given year*. It does not include households affected over long periods by the long-run impacts of racial discrimination on housing prices, locational choices or neighborhood quality.
5. This estimate of the percentage of households that might experience desubsidization problems assumes that one-half of the 1.7 million subsidized units eligible for desubsidization in the near future would actually be desubsidized. However, that process would take many years. Hence the 1.0% estimate shown here greatly exaggerates the extent of this problem likely to occur each year over the next few years, *in relation to all households*. But since the proportion of all households in subsidized units is small, this problem would be much larger *in relation to all now-subsidized households*.
6. This recommendation is proposed more as a basis of discussion than as a result of any careful consideration of all the implications of this level of federal spending on housing assistance.

[9]

The Fundamental Shift in Real Estate Finance: From a Capital Surplus in the 1980s to a Capital Shortage in the 1990s

by
Anthony Downs

Introduction

The "credit crunch" that is currently depressing real estate markets is not just a short-run phenomenon caused by an overzealous Comptroller of the Currency. Rather it is part of a fundamental, long-run shift in the world's basic monetary climate. In the 1980s, several unrelated developments in U.S. and foreign capital markets combined to produce an unprecedented flood of money seeking real estate investments — both equity and debt. That capital flood generated the greatest boom in new real property development in U.S. history. It also caused massive overbuilding in most real estate markets. Another series of events in the late 1980s and early 1990s has profoundly altered the world's financial climate. We are now in a period of acute capital shortage.[1] This drought is likely to be most severe through much of 1991: New commercial property development will plunge to rock-bottom levels, many properties will be foreclosed and change hands, and everyone's main goal will be sheer survival. Although this liquidity squeeze will ease somewhat after 1991, the lush oversupply of money typical of the 1980s will not reappear in the 1990s. During the coming decade, this major change in financial conditions will be accompanied by slower growth in the population, the labor-force and the overall economy. These factors will depress the rate at which the demand for additional space expands, further aggravating the negative impacts of the liquidity squeeze and the immense surplus of available space created in the recent development boom. Altogether, this constellation of factors heralds a basic change in all aspects of real estate markets in the 1990s relative to the prior decade. This study explores the nature of this shift and analyzes its major implications.

Financial Causes of the Surplus of Real Estate Capital in the 1980s

Several factors combined to produce an immense and unprecedented flood of investible funds into U.S. real estate markets in the 1980s. Five were mainly financial in nature: (1) the deregulation of U.S. savings and loan associations; (2) the absence of bank investment alternatives; (3) tax-shelter-driven syndications; (4) domestic pension funds; and (5) foreign investors.

(1) The deregulation of U.S. savings and loan associations. The deregulation of U.S. savings and loans and banks was begun in the late 1970s but not completed until 1983. Early in that year, thrifts — that is, savings and loans and mutual savings banks considered together — and banks were allowed to remove long-prevailing ceilings on the interest rates they paid to depositors. That change permitted these institutions to offer depositors rates competitive with money market funds and Treasury bills, with the added attraction of Federal deposit insurance. As a result, both types of institutions were engulfed in funds transferred from money market funds and other sources. Savings and loans alone experienced an average annual net savings inflow of $32.6 billion in 1979-82. In both 1983 and 1984, this inflow shot up to more than $110 billion per year.[2]

---
[1] See *Prospects for Financial Markets: Structural Change in a Capital-Short World*, David Shulman et al., Salomon Brothers Inc, December 1990.
[2] See *Statistical Abstract of the United States*, U.S. Department of Commerce, 1987, p. 486.

In a second aspect of thrift deregulation, the stringent limits on thrifts' ability to make commercial real estate loans and other nonresidential investments were removed. These limits were eased to encourage thrifts to better match the maturities of their assets and liabilities so that they would feel less pressure on earnings when short-term interest rates rose higher than long-term rates.

What regulators did not realize was that this easing of limits on how savings and loans could invest, combined with the presence of Federal deposit insurance, created a major "moral hazard": Many thrift executives were tempted to engage in a basic strategy of super-fast growth that was extremely risky — not to them or their depositors but ultimately to U.S. taxpayers. Founders of a small stock-based savings and loan could initially put up only a few million dollars and then launch a program of super-fast growth. Because depositors were insured by the Federal Government up to $100,000 *per account*, they did not have to worry about how prudently their money was being invested. Instead, depositors were free to pursue the highest rates offered by any insured institution, regardless of its managerial competence or integrity. So speculative thrift owners could attract immense additional deposits by offering above-average savings rates.

This super-fast growth strategy was designed to permit an initially small thrift to expand quickly. Then, as long as the yields earned on assets were even slightly above the high deposit rates, the thrift's huge leverage would produce an enormous rate of return on the investors' small initial stake. Moreover, if the strategy failed, the depositors would not lose anything, because their accounts were Federally insured, and the speculators themselves would lose only their small initial investment. The big potential loser was the Federal Savings and Loan Insurance Corporation (FSLIC), which would have to bail out any institutions in trouble.

This strategy suffered from five flaws — each fatal in itself. First, it required the thrifts involved to make high-risk investments, because only those promised yields greater than the high interest rates they were paying depositors to attain rapid growth. Second, the strategy assumed that rapid inflation would raise property values. Third, it did not anticipate the collapse in oil prices in the mid-1980s that devastated the economies of Texas, Oklahoma, Louisiana, Colorado, Alaska, and several other states. Fourth, the flood of funds created a reckless atmosphere of financial extravagance that in turn generated huge excesses of spending by thrift executives and downplayed the need for prudent loan underwriting. Finally, no one realized that even if only a few dozen reckless thrift operators pursued this strategy vigorously, their massive excesses could pile up many billions of dollars in losses that would exhaust the FSLIC's limited resources.

Ultimately, these flaws combined to cost U.S. taxpayers hundreds of billions of dollars. But while the extravaganza lasted, it contributed mightily to the flooding of commercial real estate markets with imprudent investment money. From 1980 to 1989, commercial mortgages held by all thrifts rose from $61.6 billion to $136.3 billion. While such mortgages comprised only 10.2% of thrifts' entire mortgage portfolio in 1980, that proportion had risen to 17.5% by 1987. In both 1986 and 1987, additional commercial mortgages accounted for at least one third of the entire increase in thrift mortgages outstanding. In addition, thrifts invested billions of dollars in joint commercial real estate ventures with developers.

(2) The absence of bank investment alternatives. U.S. banks were also deregulated in 1983, along with thrifts. Traditionally, banks had avoided long-term real estate mortgages, because the maturities of such loans did not match the short-term durations of their main liabilities: demand and savings deposits. Hence, banks concentrated their real estate investment in construction lending, which also had relatively short terms.

Unfortunately, in the mid-1980s, just when deregulation had flooded them with investible funds, banks lost some of their main alternative uses for that money. Loans to foreign governments had proved disastrous, because many of those governments could not repay either principal or interest. In addition, a virtual depression in U.S. agriculture in the early 1980s cut back on agricultural lending. Strong business firms — major past customers of banks — bypassed banks by selling commercial paper on Wall Street. And finally, the collapse of oil prices removed still more potential borrowers.

These adverse developments left real estate — along with consumer credit and the purchase of "junk" bonds to finance mergers and acquisitions — as one of the few apparently attractive ways for banks to deploy their deposits in the last half of the 1980s. Consequently, banks poured billions of dollars into construction loans for commercial and industrial property. They competed with each other so fiercely that many slashed borrower requirements for information and collateral to make deals with the best developers, strongly eroding underwriting standards in the process. For example, banks had traditionally refused to make a construction loan on a new project unless the borrower proved it had a long-term mortgage commitment that would take the bank out of the deal when construction was completed. In their eagerness to get business, however, banks began making construction loans without such "take-outs" in place. They also began extending the durations of their construction loans into the periods normally associated with long-term mortgages, creating new instruments called "mini-perms." As we will discuss later, this practice proved a major blunder.

(3) Tax-shelter-driven syndications. Tax-shelter-driven syndications, which had long existed at relatively low volumes, received a gigantic stimulus from the Tax Act of 1981 and became another major source of real estate capital in the 1980s. That act permitted wealthy individuals to offset their wage, salary and bonus income against accounting losses generated by the theoretical depreciation of real estate improvements. And a shortening of the depreciation period for commercial properties from 40 years to 15 years caused the annual depreciation allowances to balloon.

Consequently, syndicators were able to raise billions of dollars from high-income individuals motivated by the opportunity to reduce their income taxes, rather than by any true desire to own real property. Moreover, the syndicators themselves reaped huge front-end fees from these deals. Hence, they received most of their compensation from the organization of syndications, not from successfully creating and managing the properties concerned. As a result, those properties became simply vehicles around which syndications could be organized. This situation divorced the true social purpose of building real properties — providing space to end users — from the developers' and investors' motivation for doing so. Hence, syndicators eagerly funded new properties as long as money could be raised.

(4) Domestic pension funds. A somewhat more prudent set of investors — U.S. pension funds — also provided substantial funds to the real estate market. Their total assets were growing enormously: From 1980 to 1989, those assets increased by $1.842 *trillion* to a total of $2.741 trillion, an average annual increase of $205 billion or a compound growth rate of 13.19% per year.[3]

Pension fund managers had seen the real value of their asset portfolios eroded by inflation in the late 1970s and early 1980s, partly because they did not own much real estate equity at that time, and real estate equity was the only major asset class that sustained high total yields during that high-inflation period. To protect themselves from a possible repetition of that situation, pension fund managers decided to diversify their portfolios by buying real estate equities in the 1980s. However, they had a hard time getting their total holdings of such equities up to any significant percentage of their portfolios, because the market values of the stock and bond portions of those portfolios were rising so fast. Hence, these managers were pressured to keep spending more and more on real estate.

(5) Foreign investors. Another primarily financial factor generating capital flows into U.S. real estate was the deregulation of foreign banks, insurance companies and pension funds by their home governments, especially in Japan. These institutions became legally able to invest large sums of money in U.S. real property and were motivated to do so by three factors. First, like U.S. pension funds, they wanted to diversify out of stocks and bonds. Second, most foreign investors considered the United States to be the best nondomestic real estate market because of its huge size, political stability and great diversity of property types and markets. Third, U.S. real estate provided much higher current yields (excluding currency value changes) than either Japanese or European real estate.

The precipitous decline in the exchange value of the U.S. dollar also encouraged foreign investment in U.S. real estate during the last half of the 1980s. As the dollar fell in value, the prices of U.S. real properties plunged in terms of Japanese and European currencies, making such properties seem like bargains. As a result, foreign investors poured billions of dollars into U.S. real estate markets. The Japanese alone spent more than $48 billion in those markets in the 1980s.

Nonfinancial Factors Encouraging Real Estate Investment in the 1980s

Several nonfinancial factors also encouraged real estate investment during the 1980s. The following trends created a pressing need for additional office and other commercial space in the United States in the early 1980s. This need provided a real underpinning on the demand side of the market for the immense expansion on the supply side of the market that was fueled by the financial factors described earlier.

• **The growth of office-based employment.** Salomon Brothers estimates that the number of people employed in offices rose by an average of about 768,000 per year in 1983-86. The rate of increase then declined steadily to about 500,000 in 1989 and 230,000 in 1990.[4]

• **The increasing employment of women outside the home.** The growth in office employment was related to a remarkable increase in the proportion of women over the age of 16 working outside their homes.

---

[3] Data from the *1990 Life Insurance Fact Book*, American Council of Life Insurance, Washington, D.C., 1990, p. 55. Data cited in the text include pension funds held by life insurance companies but exclude Old-Age, Survivors and Disability Insurance funds. If pension assets held by life insurance companies are also excluded, pension funds gained $1.366 trillion from 1980-89, rising to $2.099 trillion in 1989.

[4] See *Real Estate Market Review: Annual Review and Outlook*, Salomon Brothers Inc, December 1990, p. 14.

Most such women workers are employed in offices. In 1970, 49% of all women over the age of 16 were in the formal labor force. By 1980, this fraction had risen to 59.5%, and by 1988, it had reached 67.1%.

- **The growth of office space per worker.** Another major factor expanding the demand for office space in the 1980s was growth in the amount of space used for each office worker. Sherman Maisel estimated that this amount rose from about 166 square feet in 1972 to 194 square feet in 1979 and 229 square feet in 1986 — an increase of 38% in 14 years.[5] The expansion in space per worker reflected the more extensive use of computer terminals and other office machinery, an increased proportion of high-paid workers with more "status" requirements, and greater corporate profits per worker, which created a more expansive attitude by managements. The great surplus of office space in the late 1980s also enabled firms to rent more space per worker relatively cheaply.

- **An initially low vacancy rate.** At the beginning of the 1980s, the vacancy rate in U.S. office space was typically below 5% in most major markets, according to data from Coldwell Banker. Hence, as office employment expanded rapidly, a genuine need for additional office space emerged.

- **The oil price boom and bust cycle.** Real estate markets in the Southwest and other energy-producing areas were significantly influenced by the boom and bust cycle in oil prices in the 1980s. The market price of oil shot up tenfold in 1973 and then doubled again in 1979. This raised the price high enough to stimulate a colossal boom in the oil exploration and drilling businesses throughout the world. Areas specializing in either the production of oil itself (such as Louisiana with its offshore deposits) or the manufacture of oil-drilling equipment (especially Houston) experienced a tremendous surge in the demand for offices and other real estate. Furthermore, their population soared, and the incomes earned there increased even faster. This stimulated massive production of new office buildings and other real estate in such cities as Houston, Dallas, Denver, Tulsa, Oklahoma City, and New Orleans.

  Then an unexpected world glut of oil in the mid-1980s cut the price by more than half. Suddenly areas that had been gearing up for enormous long-range growth found themselves in a deep recession. In Houston alone, total employment fell by more than 200,000 in a single year. Energy-related companies that had rented huge amounts of space disappeared altogether. Office vacancy rates soared to more than 30% in Houston, Denver, New Orleans, and other energy-based communities. Similar oversupplies occurred in both the single-family and apartment sectors of the residential market, as well.

- **Explosive population growth in certain regions.** Although the rate of population growth in the United States as a whole slowed in the 1980s, that rate varied significantly among different regions. A few metropolitan areas experienced explosive population growth, especially in their suburbs. The most amazing growth undoubtedly occurred in Southern California. In 1980-89, California as a whole gained 5.247 million people — an average of 583,000 per year. The increases exceeded 635,000 per year in each of the last four years, peaking at 734,000 in 1989. Just six *counties* in Southern California — Los Angeles, San Diego, San Bernardino, Orange, Riverside, and Ventura — together had a larger population gain than all 21 *states* in the Northeast and Midwest combined!

---

[5] See *Demand for Office Space*, Sherman J. Maisel, Salomon Brothers Inc, May 1989, p. 6.

Florida experienced a similar skyrocketing in growth in the 1980s: The state gained 2.599 million residents in 1980-88, an increase of 325,000 per year. Texas posted slightly larger absolute growth, but smaller percentage growth, than Florida in that same period. Its population rose by 2.612 million people, but most of that gain was concentrated in the first half of the decade, when the oil industry was booming.

California, Texas and Florida together accounted for 51.2% of total U.S. population growth in 1980-88, even though they contained only 23.4% of the nation's total population in 1988. Hence, many metropolitan areas in these states experienced growth rates far above the national average of 1.03% per year compounded. This concentration of growth in a few areas attracted real estate developers seeking to meet the resulting local space needs and financial institutions seeking outlets for their investible funds. The need to serve these rapidly growing areas justified a larger increase in supply in the nation as a whole than would have been necessary if growth had been spread evenly across the landscape.

The Effects of the Capital Surplus

Developers' access to immense amounts of money in 1983-89 had seven major effects on nearly all aspects of real estate markets in that period: (1) the disappearance of true ownership equity; (2) upward pressure on property prices; (3) overbuilding; (4) falling effective rents; (5) lax underwriting standards; (6) the immense expansion of the development and financing industries; and (7) the dominance of large financial institutions.

(1) The disappearance of true ownership equity. Developers have never liked to put their own money into their projects. With multiple sources of capital competing eagerly to finance new projects in the 1980s, developers were able to minimize their own capital contributions. In particular, the biggest developers with the best-established reputations were flooded with opportunities to use nothing but other people's money in their projects. In many cases, they borrowed more than 100% of the cost of the project and retained 100% equity, resulting in highly leveraged properties.

The purchase of finished projects by financial institutions seeking 100% equity positions also contributed to the disappearance of developer equity. Many pension funds, insurance companies running equity pools and tax-shelter-driven syndicators wanted complete ownership of the finished projects for their investment vehicles. But these institutions did not have a traditional "true ownership" view of their resulting 100% equity positions. In all cases, the individuals managing these institutions were investing other people's money, not their own. Hence, they did not stand to gain personally from the profitable operation and eventual sale of the properties involved.

(2) Upward pressure on property prices. The disappearance of true ownership equity led to the second major effect of the capital flood: upward pressure on the market prices of properties, especially the highest-quality properties built by developers with the soundest reputations. Rather than developers' competing to borrow funds from investors, investors were competing to invest in projects with developers. In essence, too much money was chasing too few good properties. The resulting price competition among domestic fund sources was intensified by the sudden entry into U.S. property markets of many foreign buyers in the late 1980s. Freed by deregulation in their home nations, these foreigners — especially the Japanese — began paying what seemed to Americans extraordinarily high prices for "trophy" properties.

The upward movement of property prices generated several other key consequences. More developers began to build properties not to retain ownership, as they had traditionally done, but strictly to sell them. They could sell properties at prices so much higher than the cost of creating them that many became multimillionaires from completing a single project. As the "build to sell" mentality became more prevalent, some developers forgot that the true social function of creating more space is to serve the needs of potential occupants. Rather their purpose was to sell such new space to investors eager to get rid of the funds they had to "put out" to meet their annual investment quotas.

(3) Overbuilding. The inevitable result of these trends was massive overbuilding. The overall office vacancy rate in major U.S. cities reported by Coldwell Banker was less than 5% in 1981, but it rose steadily after that. By December 1985, it had reached 20.1%, and it stayed above 19.5% continuously for the next five years.[6] Yet despite that clear signal of overbuilding, investors continued to pour money into financing additional office projects.

The degree of overbuilding was even worse in hotels than in office space, especially luxury-priced hotels. Retail overbuilding appeared somewhat later but soon became pervasive: For small- and intermediate-sized strip shopping centers, for example, vacancy rates exceeded 12% in 1989.

(4) Falling effective rents. This overbuilding became evident in the trend of effective rents (actual rents, taking concessions into account) relative to contract rents (those formally stated in the lease). Plagued by empty space, developers vying for tenants began offering long periods of "free rent," massive tenant improvement allowances and the buying-out of tenants' existing leases. For example, a five-year lease with a contract rent of $25 per square foot might include an initial two-year free rent period — which immediately cut the effective rent by 40% to $15 per square foot over the entire five years.

Effective rents' failure to rise after about 1985 had three major consequences. First, owning real estate equity was no longer an effective hedge against inflation — at least not based on the property's earning power from renting. The Consumer Price Index rose by 25.7% in 1984-90, whereas effective office rents in most markets did not rise at all and often fell drastically.

Second, many developers became saddled with negative cash flows from their properties. While they had anticipated that both rents and operating costs would increase by about 5% per year, rents did not rise at all, but operating costs did. With high vacancy rates, many developers could not even realize enough net income to cover debt service — especially since many had borrowed more than 100% of the cost of creating these buildings. Negative cash flows often existed even on buildings that were 100% occupied! Their owners had set rents so low to attract tenants that they could not cover both operating costs and debt service.

The third impact of falling effective rents was a decline in the yields achieved by institutional investors in real estate equities, especially office buildings. The Russell-NCREIF Property Index showed steady declines in real estate equity yields from high levels in the late 1970s to less than Treasury Bill rates by 1987. While this national index was depressed by heavy losses on Texas properties, and investments in certain other regions continued to do well, institutional investors in real estate equities generally

---

[6] See *Office Vacancy Index of the United States*, Coldwell Banker Torto Wheaton Services, Boston, Massachusetts, December 1989, p. 16.

became very disillusioned by their depressed yields. This undoubtedly will affect their attitude toward real estate investment during the 1990s.

(5) Lax underwriting standards. All this overbuilding raises an obvious question: Why did financial institutions continue to provide money for new projects long after it became clear that property markets were swamped with excess space? Three main factors contributed to incredibly lax underwriting standards among both banks and savings and loans, all of which were related to the surplus of investible funds.

First and by far the most important, underwriting standards became lax because of the competitive pressure to invest money. In the mid-1980s, the head of a well-known syndication firm said to me, "We believe we could prudently invest about $400 million in real estate next year. But we actually have $1 billion we must invest." In other words, he admitted that he was going to invest $600 million imprudently! Why did he "have to" invest the entire amount? His investors had given him money that they wanted sheltered from income taxes, and that could be done only by creating or buying real property. Moreover, his firm made fees from investing funds, not from wisely putting those funds into Treasury bonds — even if the latter would yield more than the investments he was making in real estate. The more money he could put into real property, the greater his fees and total profits. And those profits came "up front" — when the investment was made — not when the property had proven successful over time.

Similarly, a top official in one of the nation's biggest banks recently admitted that his bank had made many real estate loans without adequate documentation concerning who was borrowing the money and for what purposes. When asked why this happened, he declared that his staff could not have imposed more stringent information requirements on borrowers because of competition from other banks that were not doing so either. As my father used to say, "A loan officer who has a lot of money must make deals. If he cannot make good deals, he will make bad ones; if he cannot find bad ones, he will make terrible ones; if he cannot even find terrible deals, he will make horrible ones — but *he will make deals!*"

This pressure itself is related to a second factor previously discussed: the replacement of "true equity money" — funds provided by the actual owners of the property — with other people's money. If some or all of those funds are lost, the investment managers' reputations will be hurt but not their own capital positions. Moreover, they are paid in relation to the levels of activity they generate or the amount of assets they manage. Hence, they have powerful incentives to maximize both transactions and total asset levels.

The third major factor contributing to continued financing in spite of overbuilding is the long lead time required by many commercial real estate projects. In this era of complex local government permission processes for new projects, it often takes many years from the moment a project is conceived until the building actually opens its doors. The bank putting up the construction loan must commit to it relatively early in this long process. Hence, the bank may not realize that its project is in trouble until long after it has committed the funds involved — when it is too late to withdraw.

(6) The immense expansion of the development and financing industries. In a free enterprise economy, if one sector of activity prospers mightily, additional resources soon flow into it. Thus, when the real estate development industry experienced its all-time greatest boom in 1978-89, it expanded dramatically as more firms entered all phases of this industry. This is reflected by membership in the Urban Land Institute (ULI) — the premier leadership and information-exchanging organization of the real estate development industry. In 1980, ULI had 5,774 full and associate members; by 1990, that number had soared by 185% to 16,500. This tendency to expand also affected the major financial institutions providing funds for real estate. Every major insurance company increased its real estate staff, and many established separate real estate investment subsidiaries. Banks added to their real estate lending departments, and a whole new industry of pension fund investment advisers and consultants sprang into being.

The clinching sign of the industry's growth — and probably of its gross overexpansion — was the appearance of real estate departments, centers and courses in many of the nation's major universities and business schools. These new sources of trained real estate professionals hit their maximum output of graduates just as the industry plunged into its current recession.

(7) The dominance of large financial institutions. The final impact of the flood of money into real estate in the 1980s was the increasingly dominant role of large institutions in real estate finance. These institutions included both domestic and foreign pension funds, banks and insurance companies. Of course, a great many small-scale commercial real estate projects, such as local office buildings and strip retail stores, are still financed and developed by small-scale local firms and individuals. But the vast majority of large-scale projects of all types became increasingly influenced by money from major financial institutions. Not only were they putting up the funds for such projects, but they also retained the ultimate equity ownership of many, taking over the role traditionally played by developers.

Why the Capital Surplus of the 1980s has Changed to a Capital Shortage in the 1990s

A series of both financial and nonfinancial developments in the late 1980s and early 1990s has radically changed the economic climate in real estate markets. These developments ended the flood of financial capital into those markets described earlier and have ushered in an era of capital shortage. The major causes of this sea change are set forth below.

• **The collapse of savings and loans.** As the 1990s begin, the thrift industry is in its death throes. While not all individual thrifts will disappear, those that survive will no longer function as part of an institutionally separate set of financial organizations specifically designed to provide housing finance. It is not possible to analyze in detail here all the complex causes of the savings and loan debacle of the 1980s. However, the following are among its net results: (1) the disappearance of about half of the thrift institutions existing at the start of the 1980s; (2) massive consolidation among the remaining thrifts; (3) the shift of most such survivors into the legal form of banks or other nonthrift entities; and (4) the withdrawal of almost all surviving thrifts from investing equity or loan funds in commercial or industrial real estate projects. This final result will be a major cause of smaller capital flows into commercial real estate markets in the 1990s. In fact, thrifts had almost completely stopped making commercial real estate loans by 1988.

- **The demise of tax-shelter-drive syndication.** A second major source of capital for commercial property development in the 1980s — tax-shelter-driven syndicates — also has vanished. After flourishing for five years, tax-shelter-driven investments were dealt a fatal blow by the Tax Reform Act of 1986. Most of the major syndication firms active during the 1980s have either gone bankrupt, ceased operations or converted themselves into investment counselors and property managers. Hence, this source of funds will not be active during the 1990s, unless Congress again revives tax benefits for real estate. That seems highly unlikely, except possibly for investments in the creation of low-income housing.

- **The regulatory crackdown on bank real estate lending.** When the oil price collapse caused the failure of major banks in the oil-producing states, bank regulators began to worry about a repetition of the savings and loan disaster. Then the economic slowdown in the Northeast in 1988 and 1989 caused a rash of real estate loan delinquencies among banks there, too. Alarmed, the Comptroller of the Currency in February 1990 issued stringent orders to examiners to compel banks to tighten their real estate underwriting standards.[7] The policy was intended to force banks to stop making bad loans. In reality, however, the much tighter examination standards being imposed by regulators upon commercial banks, not only in the Northeast, but all over the United States have prevented them from making any real estate loans whatsoever.

By pressing bankers either to foreclose on nondelinquent real estate loans or to demand more equity from borrowers, the regulators are creating a partly self-fulfilling prophecy of lower property values. The shortage of available credit in real estate markets has dried up demand for both new and existing properties. As a result, owners who must sell are forced to accept much lower prices than would normally prevail. But the banks that foreclose are also forced to sell, since they are supposed to get rid of any real estate they own as fast as possible. When they sell, they realize lower prices than they would if credit were not so scarce. Hence, banks' behavior is putting downward pressure on the market values of some of their own assets.

This situation has contributed mightily to the reduction of capital available for financing real estate transactions, especially in 1990, and it is likely to last as long as the Comptroller keeps the lid on, possibly well into 1991. The longer it lasts, the greater the risk that this liquidity squeeze will undermine the value of billions of dollars of bank assets that otherwise would retain their initial values reasonably well.

- **The rise of greater capital requirements abroad.** The liberation of Eastern European nations from communism has generated demands for Western investment capital to restructure their economies. Rebuilding the former East German economy undoubtedly will absorb all of the surplus investment capital that Germany can generate during most of the 1990s. Other Eastern European nations — including the Soviet Union — have no such strong "big brothers" politically committed to financing their revival. Yet they do offer significant, though risky, investment opportunities to many Western firms and entrepreneurs. The pursuit of such opportunities surely will absorb some of the Western European investment capital that flowed into U.S. real estate markets in the 1980s.

Another expanding foreign source of capital demand involves entrepreneurial opportunities in the European Economic Community. Many European investors who formerly put funds into U.S. real estate will be investing such funds in Western Europe instead.

---

[7] See *Blame Avoidance, Overreactions and the Real Estate Credit Crunch*, Salomon Brothers Inc, December 1990.

In Asia, the swift development of such nations as Thailand, Indonesia and Malaysia will absorb a great deal of Japanese investment capital during the 1990s. This "second tier" of newly industrializing countries is rapidly challenging the first tier of Hong Kong, South Korea, Singapore, and Taiwan. China's huge low-wage labor force also will present key investment opportunities for Asian capitalists during the coming decade.

Altogether, these expanding foreign investment alternatives are almost certain to displace U.S. real estate markets as a destination for a large share of the capital flows from Western Europe and Japan. This will affect many aspects of economic activity besides real estate.

- **Japan's changing financial situation.** During the 1980s, the Japanese economy became the world's major producer of exportable financial capital. High domestic savings rates, together with huge and continuing export surpluses and the effects of deregulation, provided Japanese financial institutions with enormous amounts of money they could invest overseas. But two developments in 1990 significantly altered this situation. First, prices on the Japanese stock market fell by almost 50%. This directly affected Japanese banks' ability to lend, because they had invested heavily in stocks during the big stock price run-up in the 1980s. Moreover, they were permitted by financial regulators to count 45% of their unrealized capital gains on stocks as part of their basic capital. Hence, the stock market boom greatly expanded their capital bases, allowing them to extend more loans abroad. Conversely, the fall in stock prices in 1990 drastically reduced their reported net worths, slashing their ability to support loans.

Second, the rise in the exchange value of the Japanese yen versus the U.S. dollar weakened the competitive position of Japanese goods and services relative to those produced in the United States. As a result, Japan's trade surplus with the United States began to decline: After peaking at $57 billion in 1987, it had fallen to $49.7 billion by 1989 — of course, still quite large by any standards.

These factors have notably reduced the ability of Japanese financial institutions to export capital through foreign investments, including those in U.S. real estate. This will curtail not only equity purchases of existing properties but also bank loans to finance construction of new projects. For example, a Japanese bank advanced the construction loan for a giant "mega-mall" in Bloomington, Minnesota, after U.S. banks refused; that would probably not happen again today.

Sky-high real estate prices in Japan also could decline somewhat. Tokyo land prices already fell by 10%-15% in 1990 as a result of tighter lending policies by banks asked to use real estate for collateral. The huge run-up in Japanese real estate prices in the 1980s served as a foundation for borrowing from banks to finance many investments in U.S. real estate. If Japanese real estate prices stop rising and even fall somewhat, that will prevent another source of capital expansion in Japan from coming into play in the 1990s.

- **A decline in the growth of pension funds.** By 1990, the growth of private pension funds — which held about two thirds of all pension fund assets — had slowed markedly. Stock prices had risen so much that the assets of many funds were more than adequate to meet their defined future obligations. Hence, many firms financing these funds reduced their annual contributions to improve their own profit performance. Moreover, a tax law change in 1987 limited private corporations' ability to "overfund" their pension plans without paying stiff penalties.

In the 1990s, many pension funds will have to pay major benefits to retiring personnel. The number of retirees will become absolutely large enough to reduce the rate at which the total assets of many pension funds rise in the 1990s.

If U.S. pension funds (excluding those held by life insurance companies) grew at a nominal pace of only 6% per year in 1989-2000, their total assets would rise by $1.760 trillion (unadjusted for inflation) in the decade, from $2.225 trillion in 1990 to $3.985 trillion in 2000. If they invested merely 3% of those additional assets in real estate equities, they would have to spend $53 billion for such equities during the 1990s — a rise of more than 50% in their 1990 holdings of real estate equities.[8] If pension funds actually spent only half that much each year and the remaining increase in real estate asset values came from appreciation, they would still spend $2.65 billion per year to acquire real estate equities.

Thus, even if the growth in total pension fund assets slows in the 1990s to a compound annual rate less than half that of the 1980s, pension funds will still be a major source of real estate capital during the 1990s — though smaller than in the 1980s. But if pension funds assets continue growing at double-digit rates, then their spending on real estate might be larger in the 1990s than it was in the 1980s.

- **The slowing of the U.S. economy.** In 1950-90, the real gross national product (GNP) of the U.S. economy grew by 3.15% per year compounded. It grew fastest in the 1940s at 4.53% and in the 1960s at 3.79%. GNP growth slowed to 2.81% in the 1970s and 2.69% in the 1980s. During the 1990s, real GNP is likely to grow more slowly than during any decade since the 1930s. The two factors determining real economic growth — labor force expansion and productivity growth — both will remain at relatively low levels. The labor force is projected to increase at a compound rate of 1.01% per year, compared with 2.58% in the 1970s and 1.63% in 1980-88.[9] Productivity per employee in the business sector grew at a compound rate of 1.62% per year in 1980-88.[10] But overall productivity growth was only about 1.4% per year, because the 15% of all workers employed by governments posted low productivity gains. If productivity continues to expand by about 1.4% per year and the labor force grows by about 1.0%, then total real output has a potential expansion capacity — at full employment — of 2.4% per year. That is 11% less than the 2.69% per year compound growth rate of real GNP in 1980-90. These data imply that the demand for additional space from general economic growth likely will be relatively weak.

In addition, two strong forces that stimulated the demand for office space in the 1980s probably will be less vigorous in the 1990s. The rate at which more women enter the formal labor force will surely level off in the 1990s, since their participation already has reached such high levels. And so many jobs already have moved from manufacturing and other nonoffice-located activities into services and other office-housed activities that the rate at which this occurs also will slow down.

All of the above-mentioned factors have dramatically transformed the climate in real estate markets. The 1980s began with a relative shortage of space in most U.S. metropolitan areas. Subsequently, all real estate markets were flooded with billions of dollars from a variety of sources, all eager to invest in real estate equities or mortgages. At the same time, there was a major shift of activities from nonoffice locations to office space. The

---

[8] See "Separate Accounts Top Commingled Funds," *Pensions and Investments*, Steve Hemmerick, September 3, 1990.
[9] *Statistical Abstract of the United States: 1990*, p. 378.
[10] *Statistical Abstract of the United States: 1990*, p. 406.

decade also witnessed the longest peacetime economic expansion in U.S. history, from 1982 into 1990. These forces produced the greatest boom in new commercial real estate development in U.S. history, with all the consequences described earlier.

Conversely, the 1990s are beginning with a severe "credit crunch" in real estate markets. All the major sources of financial capital that swamped real estate markets with money in the 1980s have either disappeared, scaled back sharply or shifted much of their investment into other geographic and substantive areas. Moreover, the entire U.S. economy will grow relatively slowly in the 1990s, even if it manages to avoid major recessions. These fundamental shifts guarantee that real estate markets in the 1990s will be profoundly different from those of the "go-go" 1980s.

Major Consequences of the Climatic Change in Real Estate Markets

What will the major differences be? The switch from a capital surplus to a capital shortage will cause all but one of the major impacts of the flood of real estate capital in the 1980s to be reversed in the 1990s. I anticipate the following ten key results: (1) continuing high real U.S. interest rates; (2) an initial liquidity squeeze lasting no longer than mid-1991; (3) the restoration of much tougher underwriting standards for all loans and investments; (4) a drastic decline in new real estate development of all types; (5) a painful shrinkage of the development and financing industries; (6) down-and-up movements in effective rents; (7) a much closer tying of property values to their net incomes from rents; (8) a falloff, stabilization and eventual rise in property values; (9) a shift in emphasis from new development to the management, ownership and improvement of existing properties and assets; and (10) the continued dominance of real estate markets by large financial institutions.

(1) Continuing high real U.S. interest rates. The declining allure of U.S. real estate and other assets compared with foreign opportunities will keep U.S. long-term real interest rates relatively high throughout most of the 1990s. In the 1980s, foreign investors financed much of the U.S. Federal and trade deficits by buying U.S. stocks, Treasury securities and many other assets, including real estate equities and loans. If U.S. real interest rates were to decline significantly, we could not attract either the foreign or domestic capital our economy needs to continue operating with the smaller — but still large — Federal and trade deficits that are likely to persist in the 1990s.

High real interest rates will have several important consequences for real estate. First, they will prevent even fairly rapid inflation from providing much benefit to real property owners. Therefore, if the inflation rate rises in the 1990s, it will not create the windfall profits for real estate equity owners that it did in the 1970s. In that decade, rising inflation caught the financial community by surprise. Hence, many lenders had made long-term, fixed-rate loans at interest rates that proved lower than annual inflation rates in the late 1970s and early 1980s. This created *negative real interest rates*, at least for a while. In real terms, lenders were paying borrowers to borrow money! Since real estate developers typically leverage their projects heavily with borrowed funds, this situation provided them with immense profits. The market values of their properties soared with inflation, but their debt service costs remained fixed at low levels. Thus, their small or zero initial equity investments generated huge equity gains over time.

But the financial community already has anticipated rising inflation in the 1990s by demanding high real interest rates and shorter loan terms on commercial property investments. It did the same thing throughout the 1980s in reaction to its mistakes of the 1970s. So if the inflation rate rises, long-term interest rates will rise even faster, causing debt service costs to increase apace and preventing any windfall gains to borrowers like those of the 1970s.

(2) An initial liquidity squeeze lasting no longer than mid-1991. Most lenders are refusing to make what might otherwise be considered "normal" real estate loans, causing an acute liquidity squeeze in real estate markets. Yet those markets need to be lubricated by a certain amount of available credit if "normal" transactions are to occur at even relatively low transaction levels.

Real properties are long-lived assets that are extremely costly to build or buy compared with the annual net incomes they generate from rent. Hence, their annual profits cannot directly support the initial purchase or construction of such properties, because the developer or buyer must put up a multiple of the property's annual net income at the outset. This normally requires the developer or buyer to borrow much of the big initial cost, repaying it gradually over a long period using the property's future net income. Moreover, owners of existing properties frequently need to borrow funds to make major repairs or renovations. Many such improvements cost much more than a single year's net operating income after debt service; hence, they cannot be financed solely from current operations. **Thus, the "normal" healthy operation of real estate markets requires that banks and other lenders extend significant credit to the developers of new properties and the buyers and owners of existing ones.** Even when new development slows to a crawl, credit is necessary to permit the other ongoing transactions described above. Similar long-term borrowing is required to finance "normal" markets involving most long-lived assets with relatively low annual outputs, such as heavy machinery in manufacturing.

The virtual cessation of real estate lending freezes out good-quality real estate transactions, as well as bad ones. Some critics of recent real estate excesses argue that all property markets are so overbuilt that no further transactions are needed. In any market, however, a minimum level of transaction activity is necessary simply to maintain "normal" asset values. At any given moment in every type of asset market, some owners must sell for personal reasons: They need cash for emergencies, for retirement, for financing new business opportunities, or for moving elsewhere. A sufficient group of potential buyers must be both willing and able to muster the purchasing power to sustain the basic value of the assets these "mandatory sellers" are offering. If that supply of potential buyers evaporates, few or no bids will emerge when these sellers try to market their assets. Consequently, the market prices of those assets will plummet relative to their true earning power. To avoid this undesirable outcome in real estate markets, potential buyers must be able to borrow a large part of the purchase prices that they will offer sellers, for the reasons discussed earlier. If no credit is available, those buyers cannot purchase except at extremely depressed prices. Those prices must be low enough to permit purchases to be financed entirely out of the first year's earnings from the assets involved, plus whatever savings the potential buyers have accumulated.

If this severe liquidity squeeze continues long into 1991, the regulatory crackdown on bank real estate lending will prove to be self-defeating. Instead of protecting banks' capital by preventing them from making bad loans, it will be devaluing banks' existing real estate assets, thereby weakening their capital positions. The liquidity squeeze also will compel banks to foreclose on many more loans, forcing them to acquire more real estate assets that cannot be sold at anywhere near "normal" prices. To avoid this, the Comptroller will have to take some of the pressure against real estate lending off of commercial banks by mid-1991 at the latest. Hence, the period of the tightest liquidity squeeze should be over by that time. The industry should hope that commercial real estate prices across the nation have not yet collapsed.

(3) The restoration of much tougher underwriting standards for all real estate loans and investments. A by-product of the bank liquidity squeeze and the overall shortage of capital in the 1990s will be a general toughening of underwriting standards for all real estate investments by all sources of funds. Not only banks but thrifts, insurance companies, pension funds, mortgage bankers, and other capital suppliers all will reestablish traditional requirements for borrowing money for real estate deals. Borrowers will again be required to do the following: (1) furnish more genuine cash equity up front; (2) provide more adequate documentation concerning the market position of their proposed properties in relation to both existing and potential future competition; (3) get commitments from long-term "take-out" capital suppliers before they can borrow short-term construction funds; (4) provide larger debt-service coverage ratios than in the 1980s; (5) furnish appraisals of the proposed properties made by reputable appraisers in accordance with standardized methods and forms; and (6) use *pro forma* financial statements that have realistic assumptions about future rent increases and vacancy rates. The last requirement will end past ritualistic projections of desired outcomes, such as "automatic" 5% per year rent increases and "perpetual" 5% vacancy rates.

(4) A drastic decline in new development activity of all types. The dearth of financial capital in real estate markets in the 1990s will make it much harder for developers to launch new projects than at any time since the recessions of 1980-82 and 1974-75. The United States simply does not need much additional nonresidential space of any type. Existing supplies in most metropolitan areas are adequate for at least three years — and often for five to ten years — at slower future absorption rates. Of course, some new development projects will still be launched to meet special needs.

Nevertheless, at least through 1992 and probably as late as 1994, new commercial real estate development will fall to much lower levels than it has averaged at any time since 1978, including the recession years 1982 and 1983. In those two years, new commercial and industrial space placed under construction contracts fell to an average of 723 million square feet — 25% below the 965-million-square-foot average of 1978-81, the four *preceding* boom years, and 27.5% below the 998-million-square-foot average for the six *following* boom years, 1984-89. In 1990-93, however, the volume of new commercial and industrial space placed under construction will fall by as much as 50%-70% below the 1984-89 average. By July 1990, it had already plummeted to an annual rate 38% below that average.[11]

After this virtual depression, new development should recover significantly. However, new construction contracts will not return to the sustained high levels of more than 900 million square feet per year that prevailed during ten of the 12 years from 1978 through 1989. The U.S. economy simply will not grow fast enough to justify adding that much

---

[11] Data from *Economic Indicators: August 1990*, Council of Economic Advisers, U.S. Government Printing Office, Washington, D.C., October 1990, p. 19.

space, and the financial capital will not be available to fund such high levels of new construction. In most of the coming decade, therefore, new commercial property development will remain at levels substantially below its averages during the nonrecession years since 1978.

(5) A painful shrinkage of the development and financing industries. With new commercial real estate development at low levels, the need for people, firms and money in that industry will decline significantly. Many existing development firms will disappear, as will some of their consultants, architects and other suppliers; in fact, many had already done so by late 1990. These firms will simply run out of projects and therefore will lack the money to cover their overhead expenses. Some will become bankrupt; others will just close their doors. Those development firms that survive will, *without exception*, have to cut back significantly on their staffs and expenses. The lucky ones may be able to do so entirely through attrition, but most will have to lay off significant percentages of the staffs they built up during the glory years of the 1980s. The financial institutions that provided the money for the giant development boom of the 1980s — including banks, insurance companies, pension funds, and investment advisers — will experience a similar pressure to shrink. Their big staffs will not have enough transaction-based activity to justify the large expenses involved. They will shift more existing personnel into property management, but most will still have to trim their staffs notably.

These lay-offs will be unusually hard on the people who lose jobs, because they will be hard pressed to find alternative employment in the real estate industry. Nearly all development and financing firms will be laying off workers simultaneously. So where will those people who are released look for jobs? Most will have to shift outside of real estate, which will require a difficult, time-consuming and often costly period of adjustment. Yet the nation's economic efficiency requires a downsizing of the entire real estate development industry in response to lower levels of new development in the 1990s.

(6) Down-and-up movements in effective rents. Over the next two years or so, effective rents on most commercial real estate will still be heavily influenced by the large surplus of vacant space in most markets. Hence, such rents will either keep declining or stabilize at low levels.

However, new development will soon plunge below the levels required to replace obsolete property being retired from use. When the U.S. economy begins to recover, demand for additional space of all types will start rising again. This demand will outstrip the construction of new space for several years, gradually absorbing the excess space still plaguing most property markets. Rents will stabilize as vacancy rates fall.

Eventually, rents will begin to rise slowly in those markets where vacancies have fallen low. This is likely to happen first where the local population and employment both are growing rapidly, because such growth will absorb existing vacant space relatively quickly. The timing of rent stabilization and increases will vary greatly among different metropolitan areas, as well as among submarkets and property types within each metropolitan area. For example, apartment rents are already rising in the San Francisco Bay area after a rapid run-up in the early 1980s and a stable period in 1985-88, because high land costs and local government obstacles against building multifamily housing have caused a relative shortage of units there.[12]

---

[12] "Renting and Owning: A Dynamic Relationship," Bay Area Council, Housing and Development Report, Volume 3, Number 10, October 1990, p. 3.

Once rents start rising, commercial and industrial real estate ownership can again become an effective hedge against inflation. *Pro forma* statements that show rents increasing steadily by 5% per year, fictitious for the past five years, may become realistic once more. However, this will occur only if the capital to finance new real estate development remains in relatively short supply. In that case, rising rents will not immediately evoke new development activity, flooding markets with additional new space, as happened in the late 1980s. As argued earlier, the basic shift in real estate finance from a capital surplus to a capital shortage should prevent any such "perpetual oversupply" from reappearing until the second half of the 1990s.

(7) A much closer tying of property values to their net incomes from rents. In the 1980s, investors were extremely eager to purchase commercial properties. Hence, they bid up the market prices of the best such properties, even though effective rents on those properties were declining. Since prices were rising while net operating incomes were falling, capitalization rates fell substantially. This partial divorce of market prices from rental income performance spread beyond the top-quality "trophy" properties to many other good-quality ones.

In the 1990s, no crowd of eager buyers stands ready to pour capital into real estate equities. Therefore, the market prices of commercial and industrial properties will be much more closely linked to the economic profitability of those properties based upon their net rental incomes. When their effective rents are high enough to cover debt service and still provide healthy operating profits, these properties' market prices will be healthy, as well. But prices will not rise much until the operating profits from rental also rise. And assuming reasonably stable interest rates, market prices will increase commensurately with, not faster than, net rental incomes. As a result, the valuation of real estate will become much more firmly tied to the economic performance of individual properties — as it should be.

(8) A falloff, stabilization and eventual rise in property values. Since market prices will be closely linked to net rental incomes, those prices will move in tandem with net operating profits from rents and, hence, with rents themselves during the 1990s. Prices will at first decline. In fact, many properties will suffer sharp drops in price because of the current "credit crunch." But once this severe liquidity squeeze ends sometime in 1991, prices should stabilize. Then they will move roughly in accord with net operating incomes from property rents.

These considerations suggest three important conclusions. First, wise owners will avoid selling real estate during the next one to three years if they can. Instead, they will hold on to their properties and wait for market prices in general to begin moving upward in the mid- to late 1990s.

Second, a widespread collapse in commercial real estate prices is unlikely. In some markets, the prices of those few properties that are actually sold may fall sharply, especially if the current "credit crunch" persists for a long period. Hence, property prices may appear to have collapsed from the evidence of the few transactions that occur. But most owners will simply avoid putting their properties up for sale under these conditions. The rate of turnover in the total inventory therefore will drop to extremely low levels; indeed, it already has. As a result, most property owners will not suffer any adverse consequences from the apparent drop in prices. They will continue to operate their properties in the same way as before and not sell them unless absolutely necessary.

Third, this period of tight liquidity is a good time for investors with cash to search for bargains. True, there is some danger that, if you buy a property at today's low price, you might miss the chance to buy it at tomorrow's even lower price. But when a desperate seller is willing to take a price that is extremely low relative to the property's likely future earning power, it may be worthwhile to buy that property now, rather than trying to time your purchase to hit the very bottom of the price cycle. No one can be so precise as to know just when that nadir will arrive, especially since that moment will differ for each property in each market.

(9) A shift in emphasis from new development to the management, ownership and improvement of existing properties and assets. Real estate markets have two quite different basic aspects: the development of new properties and the management and ownership of existing ones. These two aspects do not have identical interests. In fact, an excessive emphasis on new development — as occurred in the 1980s — tends to undermine the profitability of existing properties by creating too much competitive space. While the 1980s were the decade of new property development, the 1990s will be the decade of existing real property management and ownership.

This shift from development to property management is already well under way. Nearly every major development firm is reallocating its resources away from planning and building more properties toward the management of existing ones. Such firms are retraining many development specialists in property and asset management. They also are trying to convince other owners of real property to hire them as professional property or asset managers.

This shift of emphasis is quite healthy for the real estate industry as a whole. During the era of super-fast growth in new development, the industry paid inadequate attention to the management and improvement of existing properties. In the 1990s, those functions will be carried out much more intensively, resulting in a more efficient and effective use of the huge capital investment that the world made in new real properties during the super-boom years of 1978-89.

(10) The continued dominance of real estate markets by large financial institutions. The only major impact of the flood of capital into real estate in the 1980s that will not be reversed in the 1990s is the increasing dominance of property markets by large financial institutions, including both domestic and foreign pension funds, commercial banks, insurance companies, and pension fund advisers. These institutions will remain important, because they will still be the principal suppliers of real estate capital, just as they were in the 1980s. However, they will be supplying a lot less capital than they did then. Hence, they will be far more selective in their choice of real property investments, giving them greater bargaining power relative to both developers and owners who want to sell existing properties.

Large institutions will use that improved bargaining power to demand better information about real estate markets. They will want developers and other potential borrowers or sellers to provide far more data about the markets they intend to serve, the specific properties they want to build or sell and the terms of any transactions they complete. A lack of comparable data about specific transactions has long plagued the real estate industry. For example, it has prevented development of any truly reliable property price index. When individuals and private firms carried out the majority of real estate transactions, they had no incentive to provide extensive data about their behavior — and some motivation to conceal such statistics. But large financial institutions are long-term players. They recognize the need to exchange detailed data over long periods to form better judgments about specific decisions. Therefore, they will try to develop standardized, detailed reporting forms for individual transactions that include many details about which market participants have long been ignorant. They will seek to impose such standardized reporting upon all transactions in which they play any part. This approach has been successful in housing mortgage markets because of the dominance of the Federal National Mortgage Association, the Federal Home Loan Mortgage Corporation, the Federal Housing Administration, and the Government National Mortgage Administration. Working together, the mortgage agencies imposed uniform data collection and reporting forms upon the entire market, although it took a long time to do so. Major financial institutions will make a similar attempt concerning commercial real estate transactions in the 1990s.

Conclusion

Economist Herbert Stein once observed that "whatever cannot go on forever, must come to an end." The record boom in new real estate development in 1978-89 created additional real property at an unsustainably high rate during ten of those 12 years. Thus, it had to end. It did so both because the flood of capital that created it slowed down dramatically and because the torrent of new property that the boom fostered undermined its continuance.

Real estate markets in the 1990s will differ vastly from those of the 1980s, in part because this decade is starting with huge space surpluses in almost every market, whereas the 1980s began with relative space shortages. The biggest reason, however, is that the flood of financial capital into real estate markets that fueled the development boom of the 1980s has slowed to a trickle. It will be replaced in the 1990s by a relative shortage of financial capital in those same markets. This radical shift will cause most of the market conditions dominant in the 1980s to reverse.

One consequence will be a major recession in the development of new properties over the next two to four years. The new development industry will suffer its worst decline since the 1930s. In the long run, that will be good for real estate as a whole. The 1980s super-boom in new development devastatingly undercut the profitable operation of existing properties by creating too much space in nearly every market. Restoring the profitability of owning and operating existing properties will require a virtual depression in new development — and that is precisely what is now occurring. Consequently, by the last half of the 1990s, supply and demand should be in much healthier balance in most U.S. real estate markets. If there is no repetition of the flood of capital into real estate that occurred in the 1980s, that balance should permit "normal" prosperity to return to the ownership of commercial real estate for the first time since the mid-1980s.

Thus, the current adverse financial conditions in real estate markets — including the bank "credit crunch" — do not portend long-run disaster. Assuming that the Comptroller eases his liquidity squeeze before mid-1991, these conditions are setting the stage for a long period of prosperous ownership and management of existing properties in the late 1990s. That prospect should inspire those members of the real estate industry who survive the current painful downsizing to persevere so they can enjoy the good times ahead.

* * * * *

[10]
What Have We Learned from the 1980s Experience?

INTRODUCTION

Since 1978, U.S. commercial and industrial real estate markets have endured a double-dip ride on an economic roller coaster of unprecedented speed and amplitude: These markets rose sharply in the late 1970s, plunged in the recession of 1980-1982, soared throughout the 1980s until about 1989, and have since plummeted into the "credit crunch" conditions of the early 1990s. During this spectacular ride, most participants in real estate investing were exposed to an unusually broad range of stimuli and market conditions. What has this experience taught us about real estate investing? This article attempts to answer that question.

LESSONS ON THE BEHAVIOR OF MARKET PARTICIPANTS

Rather than track the behavior of real estate itself, we'll begin with a series of lessons on the behavior of real estate investors and operatives. Such behavior is important because it affects the environment surrounding real estate properties and consequently their values.

Lesson One: Real estate investors usually prepare for the last financial crisis, not the current or next one. There is a saying that "The only thing we have learned from experience is that no one learns from experience." But this saying is false. People *do* learn from experience — the trouble is, they learn the wrong things. They formulate conclusions based upon recent and/or past conditions without recognizing that changes in those conditions should also change their conclusions. That is partly because it is much easier to be certain about what *has* happened than what *will* happen.

For example, in the early 1980s, most pension fund investors concluded, based upon what had happened to them in the late 1970s, that inflation was a real threat to their portfolios. During the 1970s stocks and bonds remained flat in nominal values while the general price level soared. Plan sponsors also concluded that real estate equities were excellent hedges against inflation, because the market values of real properties had risen along with — or faster than — the general price level. So they invested in real estate equities to protect themselves from another burst of rapid inflation.

But rapid inflation did not reappear after the 1982 recession, and the values of stocks and bonds skyrocketed. Moreover, the overexpansion of real estate development caused real property equities to cease being hedges against inflation, because effective rents had stalled by about 1985 and declined thereafter. So stocks and bonds greatly outperformed real estate equities during the 1980s.

Right now, many investors are rejecting real estate equities because of their poor yield performance during the 1980s. But the overbuilt real estate market conditions of the late 1980s and early 1990s will be replaced by a better balance between supply and demand in the late 1990s. Hence, real estate equities will likely do much better than they did in the late 1980s. So today may be the time to buy quality real estate at attractive prices — precisely when most pension funds and other investors are shying away from real estate.

Lesson Two: Institutional investors exhibit a herd mentality. This "group-think" occurs partly because institutional investors are primarily driven by short-run goals, such as quarterly performance reports, rather than longer-term considerations. Because each is judged in comparison with a small group of his or her peers, no one wants to behave much differently from those peers. So when office buildings were in vogue, everyone bought them; when favoritism shifted to regional malls, most investors chased after them. In the late 1980s, nearly all commercial banks were making lots of construction loans in the face of mounting vacancies. Today, nearly all banks are refusing to make real estate loans in the face of deteriorating values of their own sound real estate assets. Thus, when the herd stampedes in some direction, rational thinking about individual deals becomes completely irrelevant to the behavior of most investors.

This tendency relates to the surprising conclusion that **investors are not always swayed by objective evidence — even overwhelming evidence — if it leads to conclusions that contradict their immediate interests as perceived by "the herd."** Evidence of overbuilding in office and other markets was overwhelming by 1987, and probably even earlier. By 1987, the national office-space vacancy rate — which was under 5% in 1981 — had exceeded 19% for three years running.[1] Yet banks *accelerated* their investments in new construction loans in 1988 and 1989. Even long-term investors continued to buy real properties at rather high prices, although effective rents were falling sharply.

It might be argued that uncertainty about future conditions, plus inaccurate available data about real estate markets, permitted such behavior — that imperfect knowledge, not irrational behavior, was the root of the problem. But by 1987, even a casual observer would have known that at least office-space and hotel markets were hugely overbuilt. Yet banks increased their lending in such markets. How could so many bank lending officers have been so blind and imprudent?

One hypothesis is that U.S. commercial banking is one of the most incompetently run businesses on earth, and that most bank lending officers simply cannot distinguish between good and bad loans. They have failed to do so repeatedly with many different types of investments, including loans to foreign governments, farmers and real estate investors. Evidence supporting this unflattering view is substantial, although another hypothesis can also be based on the same facts — specifically, that huge excess capacity in banking and investing generally leads to a dilution of personnel quality that promotes incompetent behavior.

A second hypothesis aimed at explaining such irrational lending behavior is that **whenever investors are swamped with funds and are rewarded for placing them, they will keep on placing them regardless of the prudence of the deals involved**. My father used to say, "If lending officers swamped with money can't make good deals, they will make bad ones; if they can't make bad ones, they will make terrible ones; if they can't make terrible ones, they will make horrible ones — *but they will make deals*." Why? Because that is what they are paid to do. Such behavior was most blatant concerning syndicators. They earned profits mainly by financing more properties in order to gain front-end fees — regardless of the ultimate need for the space involved.

Notably, in most investment organizations, fund placement is not exercised by the same persons as those responsible for prudential caution. Moreover, fund placement creates clearer short-run gains than prudential caution. Therefore, profit-oriented top-level executives in financial institutions tend to overemphasize fund placement versus prudence. However, this conclusion is subject to the qualification that the investor herd as a whole must be moving in a deal-making direction. Once the investor herd reverses direction, as it now has, an opposite

---

[1] Coldwell Banker, *Coldwell Banker Commercial Office Vacancy Index of the United States*, various years.

form of irrational rigidity sets in with equal lack of discrimination about specific deals. This disposition rejects all real estate loans, regardless of their quality, to avoid the stigma placed on real estate by those powerful observers of the investment herd: Stock market analysts.

Another behavioral conclusion has long been well known: It concerns developers. **As long as real estate developers can "finance out" of individual deals — that is borrow, or raise as equity funds, more money than their projects cost, and have none of their own capital at risk — they will continue to construct more space, regardless of whether the market really needs it**. Why? To earn fees, to keep their organizations busy, and because each developer believes he or she can capture whatever tiny market segment remains unserved.

Such irrational pride or *hubris* is an inescapable part of real estate developers' mentality. The basic social function of developers is to do new things that haven't been tried yet — at least not in the locations where they are trying them. Success at such innovation requires overcoming the immense inertia of the world that resists all change. That in turn demands egos so strong that their possessors believe they can conquer all obstacles. In fact, individuals who lack such *hubris* rarely succeed as real estate developers even under favorable market conditions. So when market conditions turn bad, it takes a long time for these super-egotists to recognize that this change affects them, as well as all their rivals (whom they believe are much less competent). Even if the best developers recognize this ego trap and refrain from egregious overbuilding, others who are less perceptive will keep right on developing.

Hence, there is a built-in tendency for real estate developers to create excessive amounts of space, as long as they can get the money to finance it. This means that **prudent restraint in creating new space must originate with the suppliers of money, not with developers as a group**. But, as noted above, money suppliers are themselves subject to irrational and faddish movements that weaken or annihilate their prudence. That is most likely to occur if there is so much capital available that they are under great pressure to "put the money out" — as happened in the 1980s.

LESSONS ON REAL ESTATE SPACE MARKETS

We now turn to lessons on what happens to the properties and values in real estate space markets themselves. Taken together, the behavioral lessons described above imply that **the total amount of funds currently available for investment in real estate is the single most important determinant of how much new property gets built at any time**. Actual supply and demand factors in space markets hold little sway — at least in the short run. If all investors combined have a lot of funds that they want to put into real estate, they will overbuild markets as long as they still have those funds. High vacancy rates, falling effective rents, and other objective indicators of overbuilding will not necessarily deter them.

A surplus of funds available for real estate will generate new construction — even if those investing the funds initially intend to concentrate only on buying existing properties — because as competition for the best existing properties heats up, the prices of such properties are driven upward relative to their rent levels. Hence, the yields obtainable from existing properties tend to decline. This makes the yields from new properties look more attractive, because they contain an "initial development profit" absent from existing properties. Yet in reality, the higher yields obtainable from new properties result mainly from the higher risks of building new projects, rather than buying existing ones. New projects can — and do — encounter all kinds of difficulties before they become truly comparable to existing, already-occupied buildings. Hence, **on a risk-adjusted basis, new projects likely have no higher yields than existing ones**. But on paper, their projected profitability appears greater after the prices of existing properties have been bid upward. So a prolonged surplus of money seeking real estate always tends to generate increased new development, as in the late 1980s — even when most of the investors concerned claimed that they were not supporting new projects.

The next lesson is extremely simple: **Real estate prices can go down as well as up**. This seems obvious, but it was not widely believed until recently — especially concerning home prices. Investors and others had watched the market prices of their own homes rise so steadily over such a long time that they subconsciously concluded that *all* real property prices always moved only upward. Recent experience in both residential and nonresidential markets has decisively disproved that conclusion.

In fact, there exists a definite cycle of price movements in commercial real estate markets related to the three-phase real estate development cycle. Its three phases normally occur in particular relation to the broader general business cycle. The "development boom" phase begins toward the end of a general economic expansion after prosperity has absorbed all available space and driven rents upward. Property prices tend to rise in this phase. The resulting increase in new building puts a lot of additional space onto the market just as the general economy goes into a recession, cutting growth in demand for space. Hence, an "overbuilt" phase emerges in commercial real estate. Rents fall, new development ceases, and property prices drop. Then the general economy begins to recover from the recession; in turn, demand for space gradually rises and absorbs existing vacancies, eventually forcing rents upward. This "gradual absorption phase" is usually accompanied by stabilizing and then slightly rising property prices. As general prosperity intensifies, the stage is set for the next "development boom" phase. These three phases apply to commercial and industrial space; residential space is subject to a slightly different type of cycle.

Another key lesson concerning property prices is that **the market prices of commercial properties can become unhitched from their rental incomes under conditions of either extreme liquidity or extreme illiquidity in sales markets**. Only under conditions of "normal" liquidity will movements in property prices directly reflect changing net rental incomes. When real estate markets are swamped with funds looking for properties, competition among buyers loaded with money can drive property prices upward even if effective rents are falling. Such excessive liquidity and its consequences appeared in the late 1980s. Conversely, when an acute shortage of liquidity occurs, property prices can fall even if effective rents are stable or rising. This is especially likely if regulators force owners to "mark to market" all properties held, even those not in current economic difficulty.

This happens in markets for long-lived assets because "normal" transactions involving such assets require extensive use of borrowed funds. A long-lived asset like an airplane, a cargo vessel, or a factory building produces annual profits that are small in relation to the total cost of building or buying the asset. Yet owning it can still be profitable because it produces such profits for many years. But neither its initial construction nor its later purchase can be financed out of its current income; instead, the developer or buyer must borrow against its future income streams. Hence, when little or no credit is available, the number of potential buyers shrinks drastically. Yet in every time period, some owners of any kind of assets must always sell them to raise cash for their own personal or corporate reasons. Hence, a dearth of buyers creates an imbalance between the numbers of buyers and sellers, driving prices downward. This relationship is one reason why the current "credit crunch" caused by the unwillingness of banks to lend in the face of regulatory and stock-market pressure, plus the distressed state of markets, has created severe downward pressure on the prices of existing real estate — including viable properties.

Consequently, another lesson is that **it is extremely difficult to estimate reliably the market value of any property that is so loaded with debt, and so poorly occupied at such low rents that it has large negative cash flows.** If a property with a negative cash flow after paying debt service is appraised simply by capitalizing its current income, it has a negative value and is worthless to anyone who has to pay that debt service. As long as its present market situation persists, the property will have positive value only if that debt service is substantially reduced — to the point where the property throws off a positive cash flow.

The only parties that can reduce the property's legal debt service burden are the lender to whom it is owed and a bankruptcy court. Thus, restoration of positive value to such a property requires some combination of (1) raising occupancy; (2) raising average rent levels; and (3) reducing the debt against it. Achieving the first two of these changes usually requires both new management and a shift in current market conditions. Reducing the debt service — without bankruptcy — requires the lender to "take a haircut" by writing down the amount of the debt against the property — either with or without foreclosing on it. An appraiser evaluating such a property must estimate the probability that some combination of these changes will restore some positive value to it — and just how much value will be restored. Under current highly uncertain market conditions, this is extremely difficult at best, and almost impossible to do with much reliability.

Another key lesson is that **equities in commercial real property are not necessarily a hedge against inflation.** Many investors put funds into real estate equities because of what happened in the 1970s: Stocks and bonds failed to protect portfolios from real erosion due to inflation, while real estate did protect them. But that lesson proved inapplicable in the 1980s. The oversupply of properties created by the massive boom in new development prevented effective rents from rising along with the general price level. Ironically, the relationship may reverse itself again in the 1990s. Specifically, I believe that property prices will vary much more directly with rents in the 1990s than in the 1980s, and that rents will rise during the last half of this decade. Key to this assumption will be the amount of liquidity available in these markets. If liquidity in U.S. commercial real estate markets returns to a "normal" level in the late 1990s, but does not become "excessive" again as it was in the 1980s, then "true market values" can once more be reliably estimated from each property's net rental profitability.

Yet another lesson is that contrary to "market equilibrium" theory, **real estate returns do not necessarily converge geographically or by property type, even over a ten-year period.** Significant differences in yields among regions and by property types persisted through almost the entire 1980s. Regional shopping centers consistently provided higher total returns than office buildings or hotels. Returns in the Northeast from nearly all types of property remained higher than those in the Southwest until the very end of the decade, when this relationship reversed. It appears that "market imperfections" based upon the immense variability of conditions in individual real estate market areas still permit huge differences in yields and profitability over time. Such variations result not only from lack of "perfect" information, but because real properties are inherently differentiated by of the unique nature of each location in terms of both physical space and economic space. It seems that some elements of such quasi-monopolistic traits cannot be fully erased.

A related lesson is that **measures of actual property yields lag far behind actual market conditions**. It takes so long to finish a large commercial real estate project that investors must commit their funds long before accurate information about yields can be obtained. Even aggregate measures of performance lag behind current conditions. This is part of the imperfection of real estate markets, as it allows investors to continue perceiving past conditions as prevalent, even when major changes in conditions have already occurred. It is one reason why the investor herd kept charging ahead in the wrong direction far too long in the 1980s.

Accurate measures of property performance also lag behind reality because of the way appraisals are carried out. Appraisers naturally tend to look backward to obtain data for their evaluations, since no future data yet exist. Hence, they use recent sales to establish comparable prices. Even when using the income approach in trying to evaluate new properties still under construction, appraisers obtain recent data on current income flows from comparable properties already in existence. But the past performance of those comparable properties has not yet been affected by the new space still under construction. That new space includes not only the space in the project being appraised, but also that in other similar new projects underway nearby. When all that new space is in place, average occupancy levels in the market — and perhaps average rent levels — will be driven below what they have recently been. Hence, appraisers can easily overestimate future net incomes from properties they are evaluating during "development boom" periods.

Furthermore, appraisers themselves are subject to a form of "herd mentality," partly because they are influenced by the basic outlook of their clients. Every appraisal involves a personal judgment concerning the choices of a specific point within a range of plausible values that the appraiser should assign to the property. During periods when investors are anxious to make deals, they want high appraisals so they can justify paying up to obtain the properties they are seeking. Appraisers are well aware of this attitude among their clients — mainly because the clients tell them! Hence, the forward momentum of the "charging herd of investors" tends to communicate itself to appraisers, who shift toward selecting values at the high end of the range of plausible possibilities. This is true even of perfectly honest, sound appraisers — and doubly so of those few appraisers who are guilty of the old saying that "M.A.I. means Made As Instructed."[2] So appraisers have at least a slight upward bias during periods when "too much money is chasing too few good properties."

An entirely unrelated lesson from the 1980s is that **the degree of constraint on new space supplies is as important as future growth in demand for space in determining project prosperity**. If there are no constraints on supply there, the markets with the fastest-growing space demands tend to become the most overbuilt. Measures of demand growth are most impressive in fast-growing areas, such as Florida or California. But California's markets have been slightly less overbuilt than those of Florida, and substantially less overbuilt than Texas during the oil

---

[2] M.A.I. is the official designation of appraisers who are Members of the Appraisal Institute — that is, the American Institute of Real Estate Appraisers. Officially, it stands for "Member, Appraisal Institute."

boom, though California had both the greatest absolute demand growth and the greatest absolute expansion of property supply of any U.S. area. Why has it been less overbuilt? Probably because of greater local government constraints on the supply of new space there. Those constraints also have contributed to rising property prices in California, especially among single-family homes.

Still another lesson is that **expensive, high-quality properties are better investments than low-cost, lower-quality ones, in the long run.**[3] When markets become overbuilt, high-quality properties tend to retain their tenants better and are able to charge higher rents than low-cost, low-quality properties. This is a good lesson to keep in mind during this period of "bargain hunting" with low prices. Such prices are not *in themselves* enough to make a property desirable.

LESSONS ON U.S. REAL ESTATE MARKET STRUCTURE

The final group of lessons concerns the basic structure of U.S. commercial real estate markets. First, **Federal credit policies encourage funds to flow into real estate, thereby helping to increase the prices of both housing and commercial properties, as well as the size and number of insured depository institutions**. These policies include Federal deposit insurance for banks and thrifts. Such insurance enables them to attract more funds in competition with mutual funds, stocks, and bonds than they would without it. Federal deposit insurance helps keep these institutions over-expanded in relation to true social needs for them. Partly for this reason, we still have far too many banks and thrifts. In fact, gross overcapacity in the depository industry — especially among banks and thrifts — is one of the fundamental problems with U.S. financial institutions. Federal connections also decrease capital costs for the Government National Mortgage Association (GNMA), the Federal National Mortgage Association (FNMA), and the Federal Home Loan Mortgage Corporation (FHLMC). This augments the flow of financial capital into housing, as opposed to plant and equipment and other uses more likely to raise the nation's productivity.

Second, **there is no effective information system commonly available that concerns proposed or prospective development projects**. Consequently, each project sponsor proceeds as though no others were going after the same share of the market. This is a major factor encouraging overbuilding. However, even if such an information system existed, it would probably not restrain developers very much. As noted earlier, every developer believes his project is superior to those of competitors; hence, announced competition is no deterrent. Such egotism is essential to developers' mentalities. But a reliable information system about prospective developments might cause investors and lenders to exercise more restraint in financing new development projects, in spite of the inherent *hubris* of developers.

A third lesson about market structure is that **formal portfolio theory, based on historical data alone, is virtually worthless in deciding how much money to invest in real estate**. There are huge differences in price volatility between stocks and bonds, with their daily market quotations, and the infrequently appraised values of real estate. Hence, the data on these different investments are not homogeneous enough to accommodate a single theory. The low measures of price variability derived from appraised values would indicate that a high proportion of all investable funds should go into real estate, but almost no managers have followed that approach. In fact, the concept of mandatory

---

[3] I heard this lesson from Neil Bluhm of JMB Realty, to whom I am grateful.

diversification of assets for pension funds derived from ERISA does *not* necessarily mean pension funds must buy real estate equities. They did so in the 1980s because those equities had outperformed stocks in the 1970s. But stocks far outperformed most real estate in the 1980s. Real estate equities may again do well comparatively speaking in the late 1990s, but not much sooner.

The fourth market structure lesson is that **property management is a crucial factor in determining investment success, but its contribution is difficult to measure**. Moreover, writing effective incentive contracts to motivate property managers is extremely difficult. Probably the only way to provide property managers with the exact same motivation as owners is to make them owners too. The compensation of real estate operators should come more from ongoing operations than from front-end fees to insure good management. This means that real property funds run by co-owners should be better managed than those run by hired fund or property managers with no ownership stake.

A CONCLUDING LESSON

A final lesson from the 1980s is that **there is no substitute for insightful analysis of both (1) overall market conditions and trends and (2) local market conditions and trends**. Although this lesson may seem self-serving from my perspective, it is nevertheless highly relevant to looking at future investor behavior. Major differences between real estate market conditions in the early 1980s and those extant today number four: (1) Markets were undersupplied then, whereas they are now grossly overbuilt; (2) there was a flood of money available for real estate investment then — there is a drought now; (3) the U.S. economy was poised for rapid growth then — it will grow more slowly in the near future; and (4) the financial regulatory climate was highly expansive then — it is highly restrictive now. These changes mean that even the lessons learned from the 1980s must be carefully scrutinized and adjusted before they are applied to the changed conditions of the 1990s.

IMPLICATIONS FOR THE NINETIES

Lessons from the past are useful only if they can be applied toward coping with current and likely future conditions. And with regard to such conditions, four key questions about the future should be addressed: (1) What is going to happen in commercial real estate markets in the rest of the 1990s? (2) What approach to real estate should financial institutions have now? (3) Where will the capital come from to finance real estate transactions in the remainder of the 1990s? and (4) What should "smart money" do now in relation to real estate?

The Most Likely Scenario for Commercial Real Estate Markets

Two major elements with sharply varied prospects will sway U.S. commercial real estate values: (1) new development and (2) ownership and management of existing properties. The interests and health of these two elements are often in conflict. That is clearly shown by the devastatingly adverse impact that the huge boom in new development during the 1980s had upon the profitability of existing properties. Effective rents on nearly all properties fell steadily after about 1985 and especially after 1987, thanks to the immense oversupplies created by unprecedented prosperity among developers and development finance institutions.

Consequently, the new development and new development finance portions of the industry will shrink sharply by 1995 from their size at the end of the 1980s. The big excesses of supply found almost everywhere mean that little new construction will be warranted for many years in most areas. Moreover, financial institutions will refuse to put up credit for most new projects. Exceptions will be a few new office or industrial buildings constructed specifically to accomodate as major tenants large triple-A firms. Examples are new office structures built for — and solely occupied by — Fortune 500 firms moving from one metropolitan area to another. Renovations and expansions of existing properties will more easily obtain financing once this current "credit crunch" eases, but only if they produce relatively high yields with considerable developer equity.

The pain of downsizing will be shared by development firms and those financial institutions that engaged mainly in funding new development projects. Some former parts of those firms and institutions will shift to the ownership and management portions of the industry. In fact, most development firms have already relabeled themselves as "asset managers."

The ownership and management of existing properties will experience continued economic distress in the next one to three years because effective rents and property prices will keep sliding. But as the U.S. economy in general recovers from the 1990-1991 recession, demand for space of all types will rise. True, such space demand will increase less rapidly than in the early 1980s because the U.S. economy, population, and labor force all will grow more slowly in this decade. Even so, with new construction depressed to very low levels, annual space absorption should soon outpace new building. That will gradually soak up surpluses of space across the nation. Rents will stabilize by the middle of the decade, and then begin gradually rising again — assuming that new construction remains below annual space absorption.

Eventually, during the last half of the decade, new development will begin again, but at much lower annual levels of activity than those of the late 1980s. Moreover, new development projects will gain financing only if they provide far higher going-in yields than those of the 1980s. The problem facing developers and development financing institutions today is surviving until a better balance of supply and demand is restored in property markets. A great many will not do so.

What Financial Institutions Can Do to Manage Their Real Estate Assets
Many of these institutions originally put those assets — whether loans or equity positions — on their books at inflated values based upon over-optimistic pro formas. In reality, the properties concerned have experienced higher vacancies, lower effective rents, and therefore lower cash flows than expected. Many have negative cash flows after debt service. What can financial institutions do about such properties — including those they have repossessed through foreclosure?

First, they should **reposition these assets** in the market through improved management. This should be done by the developer if he is still in the deal, or by the financial institution itself if it has taken back the property. Second, they should **reprice these assets** to reflect more realistically both current adverse market conditions and the need for higher yields. However, that repricing should be based upon a realistic view of the long-term earning power of these properties, not upon comparable sales in the currently distressed market, which is plagued by abnormally low liquidity. Thus, such assets should be written down below their original, over-optimistic book values, but usually not as low as their immediate liquidation values in the current market. Third, financial institutions can try to **repackage these assets** into instruments that can attract capital from outside the banking and insurance industries. For example, consider an office building originally created at a cost of $75 million, including a $60-million mortgage. Assume that its current cash flow, *before* debt service, when capitalized at a competitive yield, produces a capitalized value of only $50 million. That is less than the original mortgage and effectively wipes out the developer's equity, as well as 16.7% of the financial institution's mortgage. But the property's value might rise in the future when overall market conditions improve.

How could the financial institution get back some of its investment soon, without sacrificing the possibility of recapturing more when market conditions get better? It could offer outside investors a new first mortgage for, say, $30 million, with a guaranteed yield of 10%-12% depending upon investor reaction, and retain the equity position in the property. Then, if future improvements in market conditions generated higher cash flows, the institution would capture the resulting increase in value. But meanwhile, it would have sold a $30-million mortgage that offered the buyer a high yield with only a 60% current loan-to-value ratio. Of course, this example assumes the institution can invest the funds it thus obtains at a higher internal rate of return than the interest it is paying on that new first mortgage.

Where will the financial capital come from to finance future real estate transactions? Currently, nearly all U.S. commercial banks and insurance companies are trying to reduce the shares of their total assets held in real estate. Why? Because the stock market has punished firms with relatively high real estate holdings by driving down their stock prices. But reducing the share of total assets held in real estate is possible for each type of firm *as a whole group* only if some other type of firm is willing to expand the share of its assets consisting of real estate. No other type of firm is now willing to do this. Nor is any other type likely to become willing in the near future. Hence, commercial banks as a group will be unable to off-load much of their $350 billion in commercial real estate loans to some other type of institution — at least in the near future. Banks will have to continue rolling over these loans, or foreclosing on them and taking over the real estate themselves, for many years. They have in essence become involuntary real estate equity investors.

The only nonbank sources of financial capital that will continue to expand in size during the 1990s are pension funds and foreign investors. Right now, pension funds also are trying to reduce or limit the fractions of their total assets held in real estate. However, pension funds have much longer-term liabilities than banks, insurance companies or most other financial institutions. And real properties need long-term financing corresponding to their relatively long economic lives. Hence, pension funds are the most logical source for future real estate finance. But logic will prevail only if real estate borrowers are willing to pay relatively higher yields than other borrowers, because of the adverse experiences investors have had with real properties in the 1980s. The difficulty of earning such higher yields on new projects is a key factor likely to keep new development activities quite low, even during the last half of the decade. As for foreign investors, they also have become reluctant to keep pouring money into U.S. real estate. Moreover, during the 1990s, they will be tempted by more profitable investment opportunities in a newly united Western Europe, an emerging Eastern Europe, and a rapidly developing Asia. Hence, they cannot be counted on to provide financing for a major share of future U.S. real estate development, even though they will not disappear from U.S. real property markets altogether.

What should "smart money" do about real estate now? Answering this question requires some preliminary exploration of the psychology of institutional investing. The most difficult thing for any investor to do is let bygones be bygones, which means writing off past losses, not mourning past mistakes, and looking *only* at future market conditions. On that basis, investment in repositioned, repriced, repackaged real estate assets is probably as smart a use of money *for the long term* as can be found today.

However, such an investment approach requires three rare qualities: (1) the ability to pick those distressed assets that are worth owning in the long run; (2) the financial strength to wait out the current period of continuing declines in values and rents; and (3) the psychological willingness to go against the herd of other investors, and to "throw good money after bad." All three abilities are extremely scarce today. Because most institutional investors have just suffered huge losses in real equities, they are extremely reluctant to start putting more of their funds into real estate. Doing so is something many big institutions cannot accept, because they operate with committee-based, share-the-blame, herd-like thinking.

Furthermore, pension funds have lost much of their past trust in the abilities of their advisors to choose good properties, manage them well, evaluate them accurately, and keep the investors well informed. Unless the advisors can somehow restore that trust, they will not be able to persuade the pension funds to use them in the next round of investing in real estate — or even to undertake such a round.

CONCLUSION

It has been said that people who do not study the past are condemned to repeat its mistakes. This article has tried to analyze the recent history of investing in real estate and derive some key lessons therefrom. I hope those lessons help future investors survive the rest of the 1990s by avoiding some of the staggeringly costly investment mistakes made during the 1980s. Then future investors will be free to make a whole new, original set of mistakes as they grapple with real estate markets in the rest of this century!

Salomon Brothers

Anthony Downs

Senior Fellow
The Brookings Institution
Consultant for
Salomon Brothers Inc

Key Trends in the External Environment of Commercial Real Properties

TABLE OF CONTENTS PAGE

Introduction	1
Summary of Conclusions	1
Technology-Based Trends	3
Demographic Trends Affecting the Demand for Space	7
Economic Changes Affecting Households	15
Trends Concerning the Needs of Commercial Space Tenants	21
Increased Public Pressures for Protecting the Environment	24
Changes in the Spatial Structure of Markets	25

FIGURES

1. Earnings of Displaced Workers from Jobs in the 1980's	7
2. U.S. Total Population Gains by Five-Year Periods, 1945-2025	8
3. Absolute Changes in Age Groups by Five-Year Periods, 1995-2020	9
4. Change in Population by Ethnic Groups, 1995-2020	10
5. Ethnic Composition of the U.S. Population, 1995 and 2020	11
6. Internal Migration Trends in the United States — 1980	12
7. Household Types and Changes from 1980-92	15
8. Increase in Number of Household Types from 1980 - 1992	15
9. Percent Changes in Adjusted Real Income, 1967-87	18
10. Real Household Income Gains in Two Twenty-Year Periods	18
11. Percent of U.S. Poor People in Each Area for Years 1970, 1980 and 1990	19
12. Percent of Each Sub-Area = Poor Persons for Years 1970, 1980 and 1990	20
13. Black/White Residential Segregation	27
14. Severely Declining Cities in the United States	29

INTRODUCTION

Recently, financial vehicles based on commercial real estate properties — such as real estate investment trusts — have been getting much more attention than the properties themselves. Yet, the ultimate success of those vehicles depends upon how well the operators of individual properties respond to key trends in their external environments. This article identifies some major external factors and discusses how each will affect investment real estate markets during the next two decades.[1]

Summary of Conclusions

- The most positive external aspect of the next two decades for the U.S. commercial real estate industry will be substantial population growth. A projected increase in total U.S. population of 60 million persons from 1995 to 2020 implies that demands for the creation of more real estate space of all types will appear again after about 2000. (That population increase is the same as the one that occurred from 1969 to 1994 — a period of immense development.) The real estate development industry — in some form — will therefore experience a resurrection after 2000, though it will probably not regain the large size it reached in the late 1980s.

- Technological innovations like the "Information Superhighway" will accelerate whatever basic trends in real estate markets are already underway for reasons other than technology. For several decades, most prevailing trends have been spatially decentralizing; so that basic movement will continue. Productivity in some service industries will increase, causing a displacement of workers into new industries or those with lower productivity. There will also be a shift to smaller production units in many parts of the economy. Rising public pressures for environmental protection are likely to greatly increase the future cost of all development.

- Huge shifts in the ethnic and racial composition of the American population will occur in the next quarter-century, partly because of continued immigration from abroad. Almost 80% of our absolute population growth will occur among minority-groups that are, on the average, much poorer and less well educated than the majority white population.[2] By 2020, about 45% of all U.S. children under 18 will be members of minority groups. Therefore, overall levels of real income and education in our society may actually decline, on the average, rather than increasing, as they have in most of our past history. That is especially likely if real household incomes among whites continue to rise as slowly as they have since 1970, and the relative income and educational status of blacks and Hispanics is not greatly improved, compared to those of whites.

The following social and demographic ethnic changes are expected to have profound implications for the global competitiveness of the American economy and the operation of almost every business in America, including all aspects of the real estate business:

- Some parts of the South, and most of the West and Southwest, will continue to grow faster than the rest of the nation, partly because of internal migration out of the Midwest and Northeast. However, immigration

---

[1] This article does not deal with how the real estate development and finance industries will be organized or operate. Those subjects were discussed in Anthony Downs, *The Structural Revolution in the Commercial Real Estate Industry* (New York: Salomon Brothers U.S. Real Estate Research, April 1992), and will be further analyzed in future publications by the author.

[2] This is true of African-Americans and Hispanics, but not of Asians. The incomes of the latter are actually higher than those of non-Hispanic whites, on the average.

from abroad probably will offset most of the losses of the latter two regions and add to the gains of the first three.

- Shifts in age distribution will strengthen the demand for home ownership in the 1990s until about 2010. After that, demands for rental units should become stronger. Also after 2010, an increasingly aging and dependent population will have to be supported by a relatively shrinking work force. This will create rising inter-generational conflicts and weaken America's political willingness to invest more heavily in the future lot of its children.

- Slow growth of household real incomes since about 1970 likely will persist in the next two decades unless productivity rises sharply. Slow income growth will be accompanied by an increasing gap between the "haves" and "have-nots" that may lead to greater social tensions. It will be especially damaging to communities with high concentrations of low-income households, such as many large U.S. cities with declining populations.

- The increasing "footlooseness" of firms and organizations of all types will cause more activities to move away from high-cost, low-amenity locations. High-cost locations include California, Hawaii, much of the Northeast, and many older big cities in the Midwest, South, and Northeast. Firms will be especially repelled by communities with poor quality public school systems, high levels of crime and violence, and high local tax rates.

- Renovation and modernization of existing properties likely will be a much larger activity than development of new projects until well past 2000. In fact, the 1990s are the decade of property management, rather than development. Even after new construction starts up again, modernization will remain significant because the existing inventory has become so large in relation to likely levels of new development.

- We expect the movement of viable activities out of big cities into the suburbs and beyond to continue, with small and mid-sized metropolitan areas and far-out fringes of larger cities being the major recipients. This withdrawal of more prosperous households and firms likely will push some older big cities into deeper fiscal decay. This will result in the concentration of more severe social problems within the minority-group and concentrated poverty neighborhoods of such cities, even though those cities will not all lose population altogether. However, not much will be done to solve these problems effectively. Doing so would be costly and is erroneously perceived by the white majority as likely to benefit mainly poor minority group members.

- Further growth of population in many metropolitan areas will generate major problems that are essentially regional in nature. They include rising levels of traffic congestion, air pollution, and infrastructure costs, plus inability to provide affordable housing or certain socially-necessary facilities (such as airports) that harm their immediate neighborhoods. In most areas, no regional institutions exist capable of dealing with those problems effectively. Moreover, none are likely to be created because of the vehement resistance of local governments to shifting any of their present authority over land uses to higher-level bodies.

- In the next two decades, the real estate industry must operate in an external environment marked by relatively slow increases in household incomes, plus intensifying social and economic cleavages in our society, with little effective action taken to remedy them. Separation between those in the top two thirds of the economy and those in the bottom one third is likely to become much greater, while the likelihood of those in the bottom of rising closer to the top will diminish. The resulting increases in social tensions will make development and property management all the more difficult and costly.

TECHNOLOGY-BASED TRENDS

Continued rapid innovations in technology likely will directly affect the external environments of real properties in many key ways.

- **Innovations in telecommunications and computers.** One of the most widely publicized trends consists of further technical advances in telecommunications and computers. The latest wrinkle is the proposed creation of an "information superhighway" linking nearly everyone in the U.S., and many people around the world, in a single network permitting broad-band two-way communications. This would allow direct interactions between households and providers of many types of information. The latter could range from retailers to publishers of dictionaries and encyclopedias to Wall Street stock brokers to renters of movies to doctors remotely diagnosing patients who remained at home. The exact nature of this "superhighway" is still ambiguous but many people expect great things from it.

- **Impacts on retail space markets.** Shopping centers are among the commercial real properties most likely to be affected by this innovation. On the demand side, an interactive network would enable people to shop from their homes with better information about products than they can now glean from catalogs or television shopping networks such as QVC. In an era of ever-increasing pressure on each person's time, such remote shopping might cut into the future growth of many regional malls.

In the long run, however, I believe that several factors will protect well-run regional malls from any devastating impacts caused by electronic or catalog shopping. For many purchases, consumers want to be able to feel or try on the goods themselves, or to ask informed salespersons questions about them. That will be difficult or impossible electronically. Comparison shopping also is likely to be more effective at a mall featuring many competing stores than over a network. Even more important, visiting malls has alluring social dimensions. It enables people to "get out of the house," to visit the "human and materialistic zoo" found in every regional mall and ogle the other people there, to engage in browsing among goods and in spontaneous impulse shopping, and to combine entertainment activities — such as attending movies or some event in the mall — with shopping. Therefore, although electronic shopping and catalog sales will slow the growth of retail sales in malls, they will not make malls an endangered species.

On the supply side of retailing, electronic advances are enabling retailers to track their sales and inventories much more closely. Wal-Mart and others have pioneered the use of laser scanners linked to computers to automate inventory control, and to develop "just-in-time" deliveries direct from product manufacturers to specific retail outlets. This may reduce the overall demand for wholesale warehouses in the industrial space market, compared to what it would otherwise have been.

- **Impacts on office space markets.** Many observers believe that recent technological innovations will reduce future growth of the overall demand for office space in three ways. More people will work at home, more workers will share spaces in headquarters' offices through the process known as "hoteling," and more mobile workers will operate mainly from their cars using portable computers with electronic links to their firms' offices. Undoubtedly, all three of these phenomena will occur much more frequently in the future. However, I do not believe that they will keep the demand for office space from growing as the work force expands, though the former will not increase in direct proportion to the latter.

Few people will want to work at home all of the time. For one thing, personally socializing with others provides one of the key rewards for working. Also, if you want to be promoted, you have to be around physically where your superiors can see you, be impressed by you, and assign added responsibilities to you. Finally, spontaneous face-to-face interactions among people provide a great stimulus to personal creativity and productivity. Therefore, though more people will work at home some of the time, the vast majority will spend at least half their time in workplaces shared with others. This will cause office space demand to grow somewhat more slowly than it would otherwise, but it will not lead to massive shifts of the work force entirely out of group quarters into their own homes.

The use of "hoteling" and remote-site mobile offices will mainly affect those workers who now spend a great deal of time on the road anyway, such as sales representatives and inspectors.

"Hoteling" — the sharing of the same office space among several persons — will also affect "telecommuters" who work at home part of the time. But most office workers will not be in these categories. Hence the impact of these practices will be very uneven across the work force, falling most heavily upon firms that already have many mobile workers or use many "telecommuters."

More common will be splitting off whole groups of office workers from present headquarters or home offices, and relocating them in less expensive space elsewhere, as discussed in more detail under changes in the nature of firms' demands for space.

- **General impacts upon real estate markets.** Electronic innovations also are going to affect nearly every other form of real estate to some extent. In general, **electronic communications innovations enable the other factors affecting behavior — whatever they are — to do so more strongly.** In other words, electronic advances are **generalized enablers** rather than **specific causes** of particular outcomes. Paradoxically, telecommunications and computer improvements can have both centralizing and decentralizing effects on businesses — sometimes simultaneously within the same firm. Such improvements enable top-level executives to gather better data faster from more activities into a single headquarters.

Therefore, they can more closely control many activities from one spot — a centralizing impact. An example is one major insurance company's issuing mortgage loan commitments nationwide by telephone from a single location.

However, the same advances also enable firms to split off certain activities from their headquarters and operate them at remote lower-cost locations — a decentralizing impact. For example, another major insurance company processes many of its claims in Ireland. Workers there have low wages and yet speak English and are well-educated. Data can be transferred to and from them by satellite instantly or by plane overnight. Because the effects of electronic innovations will be so pervasive, and yet so indeterminate in themselves, it is most fruitful to analyze those effects when answering each major trend.

- **Increased productivity among American workers.** During the past 15 years, American businesses and other organizations have spent immense amounts of capital buying and installing computers, networks, software, and other data-processing innovations. Until recently, this huge investment had surprisingly little impact in raising worker productivity. In fact, the average annual rate of overall productivity gain declined in the 1970s and 1980s to levels notably below those of the two preceding decades.

In the past few years, however, more positive effects of these technological changes upon productivity have been appearing. That is one reason large corporations have been able to cut back their work forces so drastically without significantly reducing their total outputs. Increased productivity is especially notable in service industries, which for a long time seemingly had resisted improvements in efficiency. If productivity gains in those services most susceptible to computerization continue, many service activities may undergo the same fate as both agricultural and manufacturing activities have in the past.

In those two types of production, rapid mechanization and other productivity gains caused outputs to expand at the same time that total employment was falling. This is most striking concerning agriculture. At the beginning of the twentieth century, more than one third of the U.S. population was employed in agriculture. Today, about 2% of all workers are on farms, but their total output is immensely larger in absolute terms than it was in 1900. Similarly, the **percentage** of U.S. workers employed in manufacturing reached its maximum in 1944, and the **absolute number** peaked in 1980. Yet total manufacturing output and value added have continued to rise since then. That is one reason the percentage of workers employed in services has risen sharply in the past two decades.

If many services also experience expanding output accompanied by shrinking jobs, in what types of activities will future U.S. workers be employed? Some people believe that this development would create either rising levels of long-term unemployment or a shift to very low-paying jobs not worth automating. However, past experience with thousands of innovations since the invention of the steam engine show that technical improvements do not reduce employment in the long run. Instead, they generate whole new types of activities that employ the workers freed by improved productivity in older types. For example, the computer industry did not exist at any scale until the 1960s and eventually exploded during the 1980s.

The average American works longer hours and has shorter vacations then any previous post-war generation. With technology, you are always on call. Technological improvements in productivity have three key effects that all increase the overall welfare of society. One is heightened efficiency because any given output can be produced with fewer workers and other inputs. The second is providing many workers with more leisure, because some increases in efficiency are consumed in the form of shorter working hours or more vacations. However, most Americans have not been using productivity gains to increase their leisure. The third is a shift of workers into new fields of activity that produce forms of wealth previously unknown.

However, this transition may impose serious hardships upon the persons involved if they are not trained in the skills needed in the emerging fields. That has happened to many workers released in the "downsizing" of firms during the 1980s. As depicted in Figure 1, Department of Labor studies show that about 27% of such workers have not found new jobs, 34 % found jobs that paid substantially less than their old ones, 11% found new jobs that paid about the same as their old ones, and only 28% found higher-paying jobs. Overall, although technological improvements in productivity probably will increase the welfare of society as a whole, they also will penalize some workers displaced from their original jobs.

- **A shift to smaller-sized production units.** One other likely impact of future technological changes is a shift of economic activities to smaller-sized production units. This has been made possible by the computerized control of machine tools; computerized tracking of input and output flows, inventories, and retail sales; desires among consumers for products more closely tailored to individual needs and tastes; and rapid rates of innovation producing new products, firms, and industries. These changes make relatively small production runs for certain manufactured goods just as efficient as large-scale mass production. They often raise the marketability of small-run products above those of mass-produced outputs because the former are more closely adapted to the desires of each customer.

Many smaller production units will consist of relatively small firms; but others will be owned by large firms. Since large firms will be under pressure from globalized competition to cut their work forces, there likely will be a net shift toward smaller average firm sizes (measured in terms of employees per firm), and a higher proportion of all employment in medium- and small-sized firms. These changes imply that property managers will have to deal with more firms to rent out any given total amount of office, retail, warehouse, or industrial space.

Figure 1. Earnings of Displaced Workers from Jobs in the 1980's.

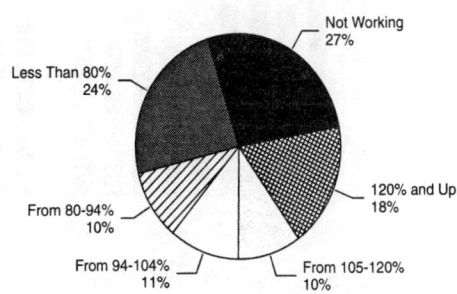

Source: CBO Tabulations from 1984-1992.

DEMOGRAPHIC TRENDS AFFECTING THE DEMAND FOR SPACE

Several population trends will affect markets for apartment units, retailing and influence future demands for office space and hotels too.

- **Total future population growth.** The rate at which the American population is likely to grow in the future is slowing down in percentage terms but not in absolute terms. The Census Bureau's middle projection assumes a lifetime fertility rate of about 2.1 births per female — the rate at which the population would exactly reproduce itself in the long run if no immigration took place. This projection, however, also assumes net immigration of 880,000 persons per year (including both legal and illegal entrants). These two assumptions indicate an overall gain of about 60 million persons in the next quarter-century (from 1995 through 2020). That is an average of 12.0 million more residents every five years — slightly higher than the actual average of 11.6 million per five years during the quarter century from 1970 to 1995, as shown in Figure 2.

This projection has two crucial implications for real estate markets. First, it means **an enormous amount of additional real property development of all types must take place during the next 25 years.** That total will be roughly the same in magnitude as all the development that occurred from 1969 through 1994 — including the boom periods of the 1970s and most of the 1980s. Therefore, the real estate development industry, which has been suffering from virtual extinction since about 1989, will experience a nearly miraculous resurrection and a vigorous future life.

Second, **the resurrection of the development industry will begin in earnest right around the year 2000 — give or take a few years.** Exactly when development will come to life again will vary, depending upon specific property types and market areas. But with total population rising by a projected 25 million persons during the 1990s, the huge surpluses of all types of space generated in the 1980s should be almost fully absorbed by 2000.

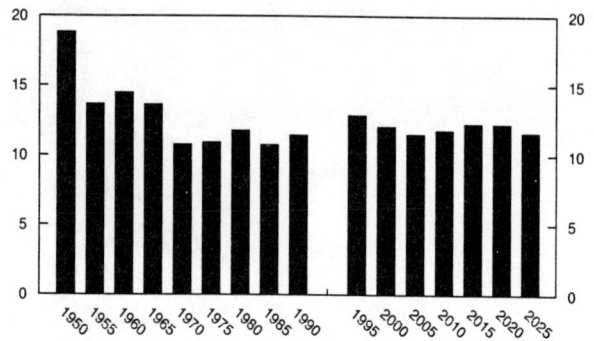

Figure 2. U.S. Total Population Gains by Five-Year Periods, 1945-2025.

Source: U.S. Census Middle Series.

These conclusions depend upon continued high levels of net immigration from abroad and relatively high fertility rates. If rates of either fertility or immigration fall notably, then new projections would be advisable. Currently, there is no compelling reason to believe those assumptions will prove wrong.

- **Shifts in age distribution.** During the 1990s, the **baby-boom generation** will be entering its 30s to 50s, causing a jump of 15 million people in the 45-64 age bracket. Those are ages in which the proportion of households owning their own homes rises to near its highest levels. Accordingly, the demand for home ownership will rise. But the **baby-bust generation** will dominate the age group from 18-34, causing it to decline by 6.4 million in the 1990s. That is the age group in which the percentage of all households renting is the greatest. **This shift will reduce the demand for rental housing, at least through about 1998.** After that, the number of young people aged 18-34 will begin to rise again, though slowly.

Changes in age distribution by five-year periods throughout the next quarter-century are shown in Figure 3. The group from 35 to 65 grows enormously in the late 1990s and continues to grow substantially through 2010 as the baby boomers pass through these ages. After 1998 and into the next century, its growth almost disappears because the baby boomers start passing age 65. The group 65 and over expands strikingly after 2010. In contrast, growth in the group from 18 to 34 begins only after 2000, increases notably from 2005 to 2010, and levels off in the last two periods.

These changes have several implications for housing markets. Demands for more home ownership will remain strong until about 2010 — **if those households have high enough incomes to afford buying homes.** (Economic trends are discussed below.) After that, the demand for home ownership will grow much more slowly. Demands for rental apartments

Figure 3. Absolute Changes in Age Groups by Five-Year Periods, 1995-2020

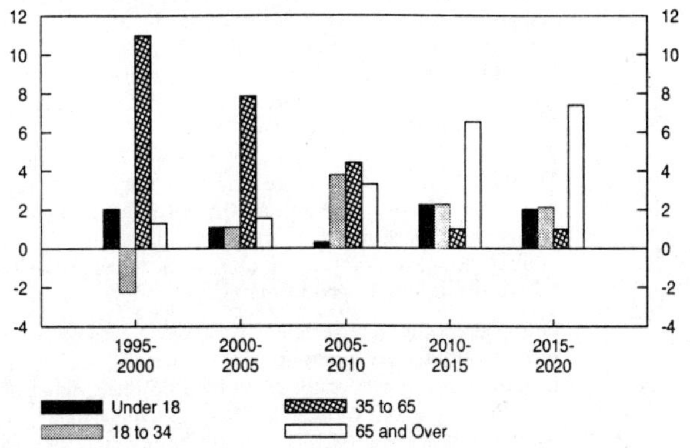

[Bar chart showing changes in four age groups (Under 18, 18 to 34, 35 to 65, 65 and Over) across five-year periods from 1995-2000 through 2015-2020]

Source: U.S. Census Middle Projections.

likely will rise notably after 2000 and especially after 2005. Also, there will be a steady increase in the school-age population under 18 requiring more educational facilities, usually heavily financed by property taxes. The housing needs of the elderly will become more important after about 2005, with a tremendous upswing after 2010.

Another important inference is that the economic burden of caring for the elderly will not rise much until after 2010, but will then increase rapidly. The number of persons in the working ages 18-64 for each person over 65 should remain around 4.8 until 2015 and 2020, when it likely will fall to 4.1 and 3.6 respectively. A similar pattern emerges when comparing the number of **all** dependent persons (those under 18 plus those 65 and over) with the number in the working ages. Hence serious strains on the Social Security system will appear in about 15 years.

- **The impacts of immigration.** A major force behind future growth of the U.S. population is immigration from abroad — mainly from Latin America and Asia. At the assumed rate of 880,000 net immigrants per year, these new arrivals will account directly for 22 million of the projected 60 million increase, or 37%. In addition, the offspring of immigrants arriving at the beginning of this quarter century will comprise millions more of the total increase during that time. Hence at least half of that total increase can be attributed to immigration, and this portion rises even higher after 2020.

Immigration will have profound impacts upon ethnic changes in the population, discussed below. It will also contribute to above-average growth rates in certain regions, especially those along the Mexican border and in Florida and California. But even inland areas are notably affected by such immigration. In the 1980s, net flows of 2.4 million immigrants from abroad into the Northeast and 1.6 million into the Midwest offset net domestic out-migration from both these regions, giving them both roughly zero change from total migratory population flows. In general, cities that already contain large clusters of Hispanic or Asian residents will continue to attract more of them.

- **Changes in ethnic and racial composition.** Perhaps the most dramatic changes in American population during the next quarter-century will involve its ethnic and racial composition. **About 47 million of the 60 million residents added during this period — or 79%— will be members of minority groups;** that is, African-Americans, Hispanics, Asians, or American Indians. Increases by ethnic and racial groups are shown in Figure 4. It indicates that non-Hispanic whites — the nation's majority group (hereafter referred to as **whites**) — will grow by only 11.1 million (up 6.4%), compared with 22.5 million more Hispanics (up 85%), 12.4 million more non-Hispanic blacks (up 35%), and 12.7 million more Asians (up 139%). Thus, minorities will outgain whites by four to one **in absolute terms**, and by more than ten to one (68% versus 6%) **in percentage terms.** In the year 2020, 36% of all Americans will be members of these minority groups, compared with about 24% today. Even more striking, **in 2020, more than 45% of all American children under 18 will be minority-group members.**

Few people now realize just how dramatic these changes will be, or how profoundly they are likely to affect American society. Every business, including all aspects of the real estate business, must become vastly more sensitive to minorities than currently practiced today. Not only will members of these groups be a much larger share of each firm's customers but also they will comprise a much bigger portion of the labor force from which each firm must draw its workers. Firms that do not recruit minority staff members and provide them with equal opportunities for advancement will find themselves severely disadvantaged in dealing with their customers.

Another impact of this ethnic and racial change will be on the levels of income and prosperity in the American economy. In 1991, median household income was $31,569 among whites, $18,807 among blacks, and $22,691 among Hispanics. Thus, the latter two groups had median incomes 40% and 28% below whites respectively — almost exactly the same as in 1970. The stability of those relationships over 20 years implies that the future incomes of these groups will remain similarly below those

Figure 4. Change in Population by Ethnic Groups, 1995-2020

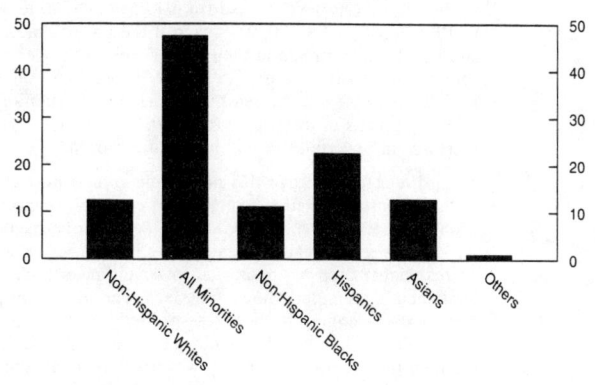

Source: U.S. Census Middle Projections.

Figure 5. Ethnic Composition of the U.S. Population, 1995 and 2020

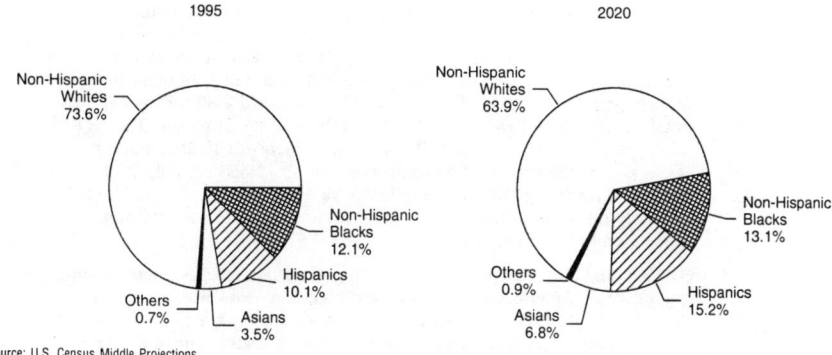

Source: U.S. Census Middle Projections.

of whites, unless major realignments occur. The greater the percentage of the total population consisting of those minority groups, the lower the overall income of the nation, assuming other things equal. In 1990, blacks and Hispanics combined comprised 21.8% of the nation's total population; by 2020, they will be 26.8%. Assuming for purposes of analysis that **real** incomes of all these groups rise from 1991 to 2020 at the same compound annual rates they did from 1970 to 1990, then the aggregate real income of the nation's households will be about 6% lower in 2020 — about $318 billion less — than it would have been if minority groups remained the same proportions of the population that they were in 1991. This projected drop in real incomes would have been 10% except for the **positive** impact of a higher percentage of Asians in 2020, since the median income of

Asian households is about 15% higher than that of whites. The same population shifts will cause the percentage of all Americans with incomes below the poverty level to rise from 13.5% in 1990 to a projected 15.3% in 1995 and 16.4% in 2020 — even if the poverty rates for each ethnic and racial group remain at their 1990 levels. The overall poverty rate has been rising slowly; it was 12.6% in 1970 but 13.5% in 1990. More than half this increase was caused by the rising proportion of high-poverty minority groups in the population from 1970 to 1990, rather than by increases in poverty rates within specific groups.

A third related impact of this population composition change may be a rise in the proportion of all workers who are poorly educated — precisely when economic needs for highly skilled workers will be rising. Both African-Americans and Hispanics have notably lower achievement test scores, higher drop-out rates, and lower ultimate levels of educational attainment than either whites or Asians. The increasing proportion of young Americans belonging to these less-well-educated groups could cause a serious deterioration in the quality of the overall American work force in the long run. That could greatly weaken the global competitiveness of American firms, or encourage more of them to locate future facilities — and jobs — overseas where workers are better educated.

These data demonstrate that **all** Americans have an immense vested interest in improving the economic and educational levels of members of our two biggest minority groups — African-Americans and Hispanics. Unless those groups are able to attain higher levels of both skills and incomes, in relation to those of whites, than they are enjoying now, the future prosperity of the entire nation will be weakened. This conclusion is especially important concerning public policies toward America's large cities, because they contain a disproportionate share of both these minority groups. The ten largest U.S. cities in 1990 contained 8.8% of the nation's total residents but 20% of all blacks and 24% of all Hispanics. The 189 U.S. cities that each had 100,000 or more residents in 1990 contained 48%-49% of the nation's black and Hispanic residents, but only 25% of its total population and 18% of its white population. So what happens to minority residents in the nation's biggest cities will have an enormous impact on the entire society.

- **Regional shifts in population.** During the 1980s, the long-term internal migration of Americans out of the Northeast and Midwest into the South, Southwest, and West continued (see Figure 6) It shows regional migration flows expressed as percentages of each region's 1980 population. Every region had a **gross internal outflow** of population of 14 to 17% of its initial 1980 population. This implies that an almost uniform proportion of people move out of each region into other U.S. regions during any given time period. However, their **gross internal flows** from other U.S. regions

Figure 6. Internal Migration Trends in the United States 1980

Item	Northeast	Midwest	South	West	Total U.S.
1980 Population in Millions	49.135	58.866	75.372	43.172	226.545
Internal Inmigrat. as Pct. of 1980 pop.	9.17%	13.65%	18.06%	20.16%	15.39%
Internal Outmigrat. as Pct. of 1980 pop	14.07	16.70	14.05	17.13	15.33
Net internal Migrat. as Pct. of 1980 pop	-4.90	-3.05	4.01	3.03	0.06
Migrat. From Abroad as Pct. of 1980 pop	4.81	2.73	5.25	10.48	5.50
Total Net Migration as Pct. of 1980 pop	-0.09	-0.32	9.26	13.52	5.56
1990 Population in Millions	50.808	59.669	85.446	52.786	248.710

Source: U.S. Census Middle Projections.

differed dramatically, thereby causing their **net internal migration flows** to differ as well. The Northeast lost about 5% of its initial 1980 population to other regions, and the Midwest lost 3%. In contrast, the South gained 4% and the West gained 3% these flows should have netted to zero nationwide, but there is a slight statistical error in the data. Net immigration from abroad was larger than net internal migration in the South and especially the West, but very similar in the Northeast and Midwest. Therefore, counting both net internal migration and net migration from abroad, the total populations of the Northeast and Midwest were almost unaffected by overall migration; whereas those of the South and West gained notably.

These regional data conceal big variations in population flows within each major region. Although the South as a whole gained 3.0 million persons from other parts of the U.S. in the 1980s, and 4.0 million from abroad, seven of its 14 states (including the District of Columbia) experienced net out-migration. The Southern gainers were Florida, Georgia, Virginia, Maryland, Delaware, and the Carolinas. Those experiencing net out-migration were Louisiana, Mississippi, Alabama, Tennessee, Kentucky, West Virginia, and the District of Columbia. The last two actually lost population in the 1980s.

In the Southwest, Texas and New Mexico had major net in-migration; whereas Oklahoma and Arkansas were exporters of population. In the West, nine states were net gainers and only Montana, Wyoming, and Idaho — the three smallest in population except for Alaska — were net exporters. All 12 Midwestern states suffered from net internal out-migration. Among the nine Northeastern states, only Vermont, Maine, and New Hampshire — three peripheral states — were net importers.

Furthermore, recent population growth — measured in absolute numbers — has been highly concentrated in just a few states. Three — California, Florida, and Texas — captured 54% of the nation's total growth in the 1980s. Two thirds of its total growth was in just six states — those three plus Georgia, Arizona, and Virginia. And 80% of the total growth was in 11 states — the preceding six plus North Carolina, Washington, Maryland, New York, and Colorado.

Will these trends continue over the next 25 years? There is no reason to predict any change in the basic pattern of net internal flows away from the Northeast and Midwest into the South and West. However, states bordering on California may increase their rates of growth as more households and firms flee from that over-regulated, highly-taxed, and natural-disaster-prone area. That means growth rates in Nevada, Arizona, Utah, Oregon, and even Idaho, Montana, and Colorado may increase. California itself will continue to gain many immigrants from abroad, even if its net inflows from the rest of the United States slow down. Texas and Florida — both huge states in total land area — will retain their positions as major destinations for immigrants from both abroad and the rest of the nation.

• **Growth of the Labor Force.** Over the next 25 years, the civilian labor force will grow more slowly than it has in the recent past. The average increase in the labor force was 1.3 million persons per year in the 1960s, but then nearly doubled to 2.4 million per year in the 1970s. It dropped back to 1.8 million per year in the 1980s, and will decline still more to 1.35 million per year in the 1990s. Annual labor force growth likely will average 1.5 million from 2000 to 2010 and 1.4 million from 2010 to 2020.

The number of potential workers determines the maximum economic output that society can attain in any specific period, given a standard productivity per worker. This means that total real output per year must grow more slowly in the 1990s and beyond than in the 1970s and 1980s, unless productivity per worker grows faster. However, total **population** will be rising somewhat more rapidly than in the recent past because growth in the non working ages will outpace that in the working ages. Therefore, real incomes **per capita** are likely to grow more slowly in the next quarter century than in the past one, unless productivity improves markedly.

That implies slower growth in the demands for all types of space supported by consumer spending. In addition, slower labor force growth implies a slower rate of increase in the use of office space, unless there is some marked rise in the percentage of all added workers employed in offices, which seems unlikely.

- **Changes in Household Composition.** From 1980 to 1992, there has been a notable change in the composition of households by major types. Married couples still comprise 55% of all households, but their number grew by only 7% in this period, compared with an overall increase in households of 18.4%. In contrast, female-headed households (other than single women) rose 37% and single persons of both sexes, 31%. So female-headed families now comprise 14% of all households and single persons, 25%.

In addition, the percentage of all households containing children under 18 declined from 38.4% in 1980 to 34.2% in 1992, as shown in the accompanying charts (Figures 7 and 8) This could lead to diminishing political support for public spending on education or radical school reforms, precisely when the rising proportion of children from minority groups will make those policies crucial for the nation's future. However, the percentage of families containing children is higher among both African-American and Hispanic households than among white households. So the rising proportion of all households in these minority-groups may offset the decline in children among white households.

The Census Bureau has not published projections of household types by ethnic and racial groups for the period 1995 through 2020. However, the rising percentage of elderly persons after 2010 indicates higher percentages of one- and two-person households from 2010 to 2020, and smaller percentages of households with children. This probably will lead to intensified inter-generational political conflicts between advocates of more aid to the elderly and those promoting more assistance to children.

The increasing proportion of single-person households will strengthen the demand for rental accommodations, although more and more single women earning good incomes are now buying their own homes. Another positive factor for rental units will be the rising proportion of households from relatively low-income groups who cannot afford home ownership.
However, many of the poorest such households will try to double-up and triple-up in order to conserve on rent, rather than occupying residences at legal densities.

ECONOMIC CHANGES AFFECTING HOUSEHOLDS

Figure 7. Distribution of U.S. Household in 1992

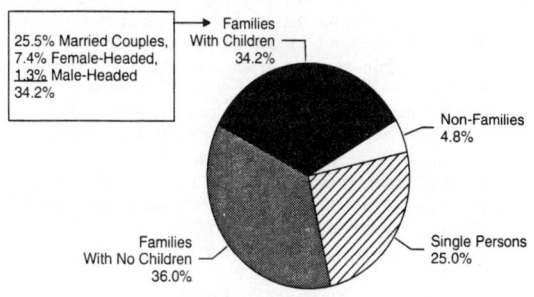

Source: U.S. Census Middle Projections.

Figure 8. Increase in Number of Households by Type from 1980-92

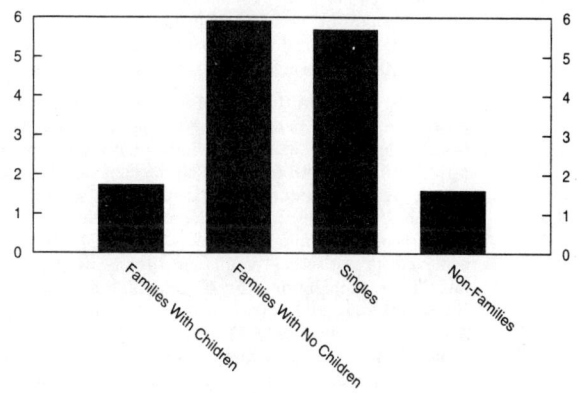

Source: U.S. Census Middle Projections.

The future economic welfare of U.S. consumer households will immensely affect all types of commercial properties. Households with strongly rising real incomes are likely to buy more goods and services, make more trips using hotels and resorts, own their own homes rather than renting, and purchase more services operated out of offices than households with stagnant or declining real incomes.

- **The rate of job growth.** Unfortunately, job growth in the first half of the 1990s has been much slower than in the preceding two decades, and it may remain so in the second half of the 1990s. In December 1993, the 1990s' general economic expansion completed its thirty-fourth month since the latest cyclical low-point in February 1991. Total civilian employment rose by about 3.5 million jobs in that period, compared with increases of 8.6 million and 8.4 million jobs in the late-1970s' and mid-1980s' expansions during periods of the same length after their low points. During the 12 months ending in March 1994, the rate of job growth has accelerated, but it is still well below that of a comparable period in the late 1970s, though similar to that of a comparable period in the mid-1980s.

The most obvious cause of this job lag is slower growth in the size of the U.S. labor force, as discussed above. In addition, the speed of the recovery from the recession of 1990-91 was cut down by at least four key factors. Two were reductions in defense industries and in the size of the armed forces resulting from the end of the Cold War. Also, many large firms slashed their work forces to reduce costs. They were motivated by intense global competition and a widespread inability to increase sales dramatically, because of the severe recession. When firms cannot add to profits by selling more or raising product prices, they try doing so by cutting costs per unit of output. Firms have also been reluctant to add permanent workers to their payrolls because of high fringe benefit costs and tons of red tape processing government requirements. That is one reason use of temporary workers has soared. This cause of slower job growth may be intensified by health care reform, if it adds to each firm's payroll costs.

The resulting slow rate of increase in employment dampened household optimism in the early 1990s, cutting back the amounts consumers were willing to spend — especially on big-ticket items like homes or cars. But consumer optimism improved in 1993 as did the rate of job growth, and it will get even better in 1994. In fact, the rate of job growth is likely to be greater in most of the last half of the decade. This will accelerate sales of automobiles and housing, compared to the low levels prevailing in the early 1990s. Some such acceleration had already appeared in early 1994.

- **Levels of skill in the work force.** Total worker incomes depend not only on how many people have jobs, but also upon how the average salary of those jobs. That, in turn, depends greatly upon the degree of skills prevalent in the work force, which depends heavily upon how well young people are trained in primary and secondary schools. Measured by college attendance and high-school drop-out rates, the education of American young people has improved somewhat since 1970—measured by achievement test scores, results are slightly worse. In a recent algebra test taken internationally **only by 17-year olds in college prep math courses the scores were as follows:** Japanese students averaged 78% right; Americans averaged only 43%. In a series of academic tests covering many subjects and taken by young people from over a dozen nations, Americans consistently scored at or near the bottom of the entire group.[3] Unless we greatly improve our schools, many future U.S. workers in our high-tech economy will not be suited to the types of jobs that pay well enough to support a family in "decent" style. More will be "stuck" in low-paying jobs. This outcome is especially likely because of the increasing proportion of all future young Americans who will be black or Hispanic, and the low average levels of educational attainment among members of those two groups, as noted earlier.

- **Basic social strategies for dealing with unemployment.** In all societies, providing people with well-paying jobs is a central goal of economic and social policy. Doing so is desirable both to increase total output, and to improve the welfare of potential workers. Yet, involuntary

---

[3] Statistical Abstract of the United States: 1992. Table 369. p. 830.

unemployment remains a key problem everywhere. How developed societies respond to such unemployment varies sharply among them, but two basic strategies seem dominant.

The American approach is to keep minimum wages low and publicly supplied unemployment benefits both low and short-lived. This creates strong pressure on unemployed workers to accept whatever jobs are available, including many that pay very low wages. American firms can therefore hire workers at low wages; so they create a lot of new jobs at all wage levels. This keeps reported unemployment rates in the U.S. relatively low, but leaves many full-time workers with incomes below the poverty line.

The Western European approach is to keep minimum wages high and publicly supported unemployment benefits both generous and long-lived. This greatly reduces the pressure on unemployed workers to accept jobs that pay less than their unemployment benefits, or not much more. They prefer to live relatively well at public expense without working. But this approach also makes private firms reluctant to create new permanent jobs. Each such job costs them too much, not only in high direct hourly wages, but also in generous fringe benefits required by law. So the Western European approach results in both higher long-term unemployment rates, and workers who have higher incomes, regardless of whether or not they have jobs. Consequently, poverty is lower among Western European populations, but the public costs of reducing it are very high. That makes European tax rates higher, and reduces income differences between the highest-income and lowest-income parts of the population. In addition, the number of private-sector jobs in Western Europe has not grown very much at all over the past two decades. And Western European firms are not nearly as flexible in their use of labor.

Each of these approaches has benefits and drawbacks opposite from those of the other. The American approach tends to bifurcate the work force more than the Western European approach, causing an ever-widening gap between its lowest-paid and highest-paid members. Since 1973, median real household incomes (adjusted for household size) have risen much faster among households in the upper 90% of the income distribution than in the lowest 10%, as shown by an accompanying chart (Figure 9). In fact, from 1979 to 1987, such incomes actually fell by 9.8% among the lowest-income one tenth of American families and unrelated individuals, while rising 14.3% among the highest-income one tenth. Contrary to statements by some conservatives, this increasing disparity is **not** exaggerated by exclusion of fringe benefits from these data. The rapid recent growth of fringe benefits has been concentrated among higher-paid workers rather than lower-paid ones.

Furthermore, overall real household income growth has been almost stagnant in the United States since 1970. In the 20 years from 1950 to 1970, median family money income, corrected for inflation, soared 84%.[4] But it rose only 6.1% in the 20 years from 1970 to 1990! That 92% slowdown in the annual rate of real household income growth was a key cause of a rise in the national poverty rate from 12.6% in 1970 to 13.5% in 1990. Thus, recent progress in improving the economic well-being of much of the nation's population has been discouragingly slow.

---

[4] This comparison uses **family** income rather than **household** income because data concerning the former are more readily available for both periods involved. However, the basic conclusion would be the same if median real household incomes were used.

Figure 9. Percentage Changes in Adjusted Real Income, 1967-87

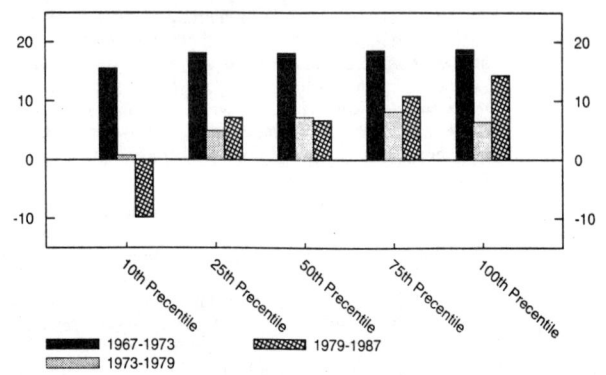

Source: Lynn A. Karoly.

Figure 10. Real Household Income Gains in Two Twenty-Year Periods

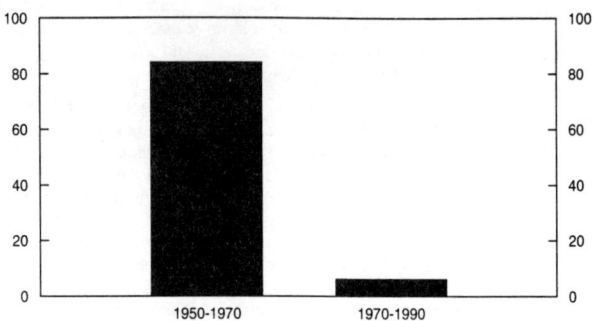

Source: U.S. Statistical Abstract.

The increasing gap between the non-poor and the poor is likely to become more pronounced in the future if the skill disparities between the worst-educated and best-educated American young people are not reduced. Yet, those disparities have been getting larger, partly because of the declining performance of public elementary and secondary schools in large cities and older suburbs. Big-city schools have performed so poorly mainly because they are plagued by many problems beyond their control. These include under-nourished students, drugs, teenage use of guns and other violence, the concentration of many destitute households with negative attitudes toward schooling in ghetto neighborhoods, and lack of family structure, discipline, and responsible values there. Poor Americans are disproportionately found in the nation's central cities. As shown in accompanying diagrams (Figures 11 and 12), in 1990, such cities contained about 30% of the total population but 42% of those with incomes below the poverty line. So 19% of all central city residents were poor, compared with about 8.7% of all suburbanites and 14% of the nation's total population.

These economic and social conditions have critical effects upon real estate markets. (Their spatial effects are discussed later.) If an increasing percentage of the population is getting worse off economically, members of this "underclass" may become more and more disaffected from society generally. That could generate more widespread crime and violence, plus greater political pressure for economic assistance to the most depressed households — paid for by the rest of society. Such rising social tensions would adversely affect many specific property markets. They might also

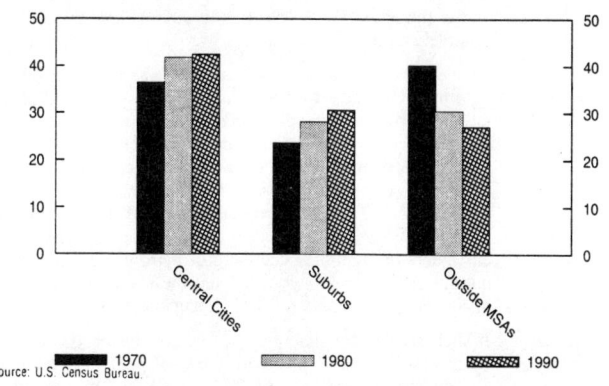

Figure 11. Percentage of U.S. Poor People in Each Area for Years 1970, 1980 and 1990

Source: U.S. Census Bureau.

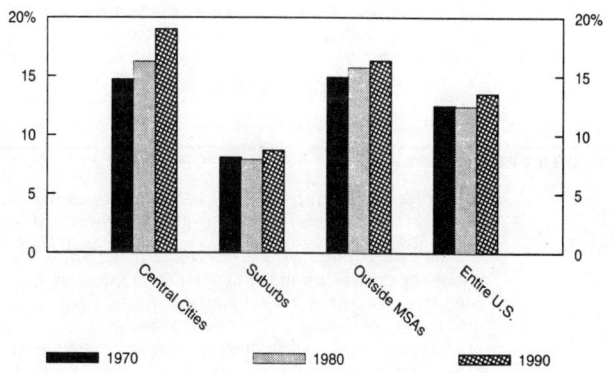

Figure 12. Percentage of Each Sub-Area = Poor Persons for Years 1970, 1980, and 1990

Source: U.S. Census Bureau

reduce the private purchasing power of both the very poor and the non-poor being taxed more heavily to finance social programs. Lower private purchasing power means lower demands for space of all types in real estate markets — except perhaps for prisons and government offices!

- **The challenge to the real estate industry.** These prospects create major challenges for private leadership in the United States generally and in the real estate industry specifically. The educational reform we need to help reverse the under-training of many young Americans will never come from public schools themselves. Both administrators and unionized teachers have too big a stake in perpetuating existing monopolistic arrangements to support the radical reforms needed to make public schools truly effective. No one in any field wants to weaken his or her monopolistic market position and support creation of a lot of new competition. Yet in many areas, reforms should include establishing direct competition among schools, both within public systems and between them and private systems. Also needed are more autonomy for individual schools and the ability of "outsiders" to set up new schools that are funded with public resources. And these reforms must occur separately in thousands of communities across the nation, since our public schools are set up and run mainly by relatively small school districts.

Such widespread and radical reform of many U.S. public school systems — which is critical for the nation's future peace and prosperity — will only take place if outside forces — mainly private-sector business and other leaders — put immense pressure on thousands of existing local school boards to change their ways. The real estate industry has an especially strong stake in such reform, because real properties are immovable. Any income properties located in a community with ineffective public schools will soon suffer from the unwillingness of tenants or customers to continue occupying or patronizing those properties. The quality of the local work-force and the resulting low incomes of local residents will discourage viable occupancy.

If such an abstract statement of this conclusion is not convincing, consider Detroit. It has the highest percentage of poor people among its residents of any major American city (32% in 1990), and the greatest concentration of poor residents in distressed neighborhoods (36%). The owners of property in the downtown area and elsewhere in Detroit have suffered immense losses of value because of the massive withdrawal from the city by both office-occupying firms and retail customers with good incomes. A similar fate, though perhaps not so extreme, threatens the owners of income properties in many other parts of the nation, including many suburbs, if we do not vastly improve the quality of education being received by our young people.

TRENDS CONCERNING THE NEEDS OF COMMERCIAL SPACE TENANTS

Also affecting commercial real estate markets during the next two decades are factors that will influence the space needs of various types of tenants.

- **Increasing footlooseness of economic activities.** By far the most important such factor is the increasing "footlooseness" of many economic activities — especially among private firms. Because of technical innovations described earlier and changes in the nature of what most firms produce and how they produce it, more and more activities will not be tied to any one location, or even any one general region. More future activities will be engaged in producing, processing, or transmitting some type of information, rather than tangible goods or services. But most information can be almost instantly transmitted electronically to nearly anyplace on earth. Therefore many people, firms, and other organizations can choose locations independent of the factors that formerly tied them to specific sites. They do not need to be near sources of raw materials, their customers, other firms they interact with, competitors, or places that have especially good transportation or other facilities. Their locational freedom has been intensified by wider ownership and use of automotive vehicles in America and by more extensive jet airline service worldwide.

Yet, attracting and holding top-quality personnel is still critical for information-oriented and other high-tech organizations. Their most important factor of production is usually technically skilled workers. Therefore, most organizations that enjoy great locational freedom of choice will pick sites that provide three key ingredients: a good supply of well-trained workers, low operating costs (including relatively low wages for those workers), and desirable amenities for personal living. These traits tend to reinforce each other. Places with desirable living amenities and relatively low costs more readily attract and hold skilled workers. The most important such amenities include natural ones like good weather and beautiful topography, and cultural ones like good-quality schools and universities. Attractive communities are also big enough to provide interesting job opportunities for both members of working couples, but small enough to keep commuting distances convenient.

These traits bode ill for communities with high operating costs and poor living amenities.

The highest U.S. operating costs are in big metropolitan areas in the Northeast, in California, in Hawaii, and inside big cities with high local tax rates and security costs. The worst living amenities are in adverse climates like those of the Midwest and Northeast, in hot and humid parts of the Southeast such as Louisiana and Mississippi, and inside big cities with low-quality schools, long commuting distances, and great personal insecurity. Tiny places far removed from metropolitan amenities are also unattractive to firms that must lure and retain sophisticated high-tech workers who need frequent professional re-training.

Even when whole firms are not footloose, many parts of them may be. Those parts can be shifted to locations with the above traits. For example, a major forest products firm moved its entire legal staff from corporate headquarters in Portland, Oregon, to Coeur d'Alene, Idaho — and not just to get away from its lawyers! Some of these "detachable departments" need not attract high-tech professionals. Such portable low-tech departments can be moved to low-cost communities that lack superior living amenities, as long as they have a supply of loyal, hard-working employees. That is why some firms have moved forms-processing activities to remote rural locations in South Dakota and Ireland, with good results.

The footlooseness of more activities increases the pressure of competition among communities to attract and hold jobs. In nearly all localities, it is much more important to hold onto the new jobs created by the growth of firms already there than to attract firms now located elsewhere. If an area lacks the characteristics described above, many firms will put their future expansion somewhere else. That is one reason California may have more difficulty regaining the jobs it has recently lost than many Golden State boosters realize.

One type of location alluring to footloose activities is a relatively small community with great weather and topography, located either on the outer fringes of a big metropolitan area, or close to a smaller one. Firms or individual executives locating there can enjoy great living amenities plus short commuting distances, without sacrificing access to metropolitan facilities and markets. A recent **Wall Street Journal** article described many semi-rural small towns as the super-growth centers of the 1990s. But most of them are growing rapidly only in percentage terms; their absolute increases in size are tiny compared with those of the suburbs around major metropolitan cities.

Two other traits conducive to rapid growth are low housing costs and access to good higher educational institutions. Most good colleges and universities are in or near metropolitan areas; that is why localities remote from such areas are not considered desirable by high-tech firms. Both these traits are most common in moderate-sized metropolitan areas, which also enjoy short average commuting distances. That may be why metropolitan areas containing from 500,000 to 999,999 residents in 1990 grew 13.9% in the 1990s — slightly faster than those in any other size group (overall, metropolitan areas grew 11.7% versus 9.8% for the entire nation).

Within large metropolitan areas, many downtowns districts will lose still more footloose firms because they lack the key attractions described above. Such central business districts have high taxes and operating costs, poorly-trained local work forces emerging from inferior public schools, long average commuting distances, and low personal security.

- **Global competition and mergers.** Avoidance of high-cost locations will be further encouraged by intense global competition that drives firms to slash operating costs. That is why foreign companies establishing factories in the United States have so often chosen sites in the rural South, rather than in established industrial states dominated by strong labor unions. As smaller and smaller U.S. firms become engaged in foreign trade, this pressure will spread to larger segments of U.S. industry.

Mergers of smaller firms into bigger ones have increased the reach of global competition, and have reduced the number of firms headquartered in many mid-sized U.S. cities. When a firm's home office is in a particular city, its leaders often engage actively in civic affairs there. They have both a personal and a corporate interest in the community's prosperity and amenities. However, when that firm is merged into a bigger one with headquarters in New York or London or Tokyo, the persons running what has now become a local branch have neither the inclination nor the parent firm's permission to spend many corporate resources improving local conditions. The "merger mania" of the 1980s thus drastically reduced the amount and quality of leadership, participation, and resources available to maintain local civic life in many mid-sized U.S. cities. Greater footlooseness encouraging more firms to locate to far-out smaller communities will intensify this effect in the future.

- **Increased flexibility of firm operations**. In this era of rapidly changing production methods, product design, and even lines of business within individual firms, a key to success is extreme flexibility of space use. Firms need to be able to shift the types of activities that they are conducting within a given space, the amount of space they occupy, its layout, and even its location at unprecedented rates of speed. Moreover, the U.S. economy is entering a phase when most occupancy growth will occur among relatively small firms, while large ones continue to cut back their work forces. These conditions place a premium on highly flexible tenant relationships with landlords.

This situation has several major implications for property management. First, it means that office, industrial, and retail space must be physically designed to accommodate a wider range of floor loads, electrical loads, wiring systems, and interior partition layouts. Second, because tenants will be changing layouts more often, higher allowances must be made for tenant improvements in relation to original building costs. Third, tenants will want shorter-term leases, except in cases where they can get exceptionally low rents because of overbuilt markets. However, amortizing higher tenant improvements over shorter-term leases means higher rents per square foot.

Fourth, the average amount of space taken by individual tenants will be smaller than in the past — at least initially—so there will be more tenants in a structure of any given size. This increases overall management costs per square foot. Fifth, landlords should be prepared to accommodate rapid growth in space consumption by at least some small to medium-sized tenants, because fast expansion will be concentrated among such firms. Such flexible space availability within individual structures is fortunately consistent with each structure's having more relatively small-scale space users, if lease terms are kept relatively short. Sixth, landlords prepared to offer tenants a choice of locations over time are less likely to lose those tenants than landlords who can only offer space in a single structure.

- **The increased importance of renovation and modernization.**

Emphasis upon renovating and modernizing existing space of all types will be much greater than emphasis upon developing new space for at least the rest of the 1990s. The record building boom of the 1980s immensely expanded the supply of relatively new space. Continuing surpluses of such space will greatly restrict the need for new development until after 2000, except for occasional "build-to-suit" projects. Yet, rapid technical innovation renders any particular space configuration obsolete at a faster pace than ever. Therefore, even though the total **amount** of space will be adequate for several years, the **technical quality** of much of it will need updating long before large-scale new development becomes economically feasible. For example, few existing buildings are wired with fiber-optic cables, but they seem likely to be a key part of the future "information super-highway."

This means that **managing existing properties well — including renovating them — is the key to real estate profitability in the rest of the 1990s,** rather than developing new ones. Even when a lot of new development begins again, the relative importance of renovating and modernizing the existing inventory will remain greater than in the past. That is inevitable because the size of that inventory is now so much larger than ever before, in relation to likely levels of new development. Thus, the renovation and modernization industries, and all activities connected with them, will be larger in scale than the new development industry until around 2000. Even after that, the absolute size of renovation and modernization activities likely will remain enormous.

INCREASED PUBLIC PRESSURES FOR PROTECTING THE ENVIRONMENT

In most elementary and secondary schools across the nation, children are being indoctrinated with the view that they have a sacred duty to protect the physical environment — **without regard to the costs of doing so.** Although teaching religion has been banned from public schools, this particular faith is being propagated by zealous teachers who have no experience in actually trying to implement the regulations they are promoting. Most do not understand the relationship between the potential benefits of more environmental protection and its costs. In addition, few people who do understand that relationship have any influence over the environmental policies being promoted in schools almost everywhere.

Public policies based upon such environmental zeal already have immensely raised the costs of developing and managing real properties of all types. No doubt, in the past two decades, there has been a great improvement in the quality of the nation's physical environment. But many particular environmental policies produce benefits that are tiny compared with their costs. An outstanding example is the Endangered Species Act. It specifically forbids policy makers to take human economic and social costs into account when developing regulations to protect endangered species, even when the latter are obscure snails or rodents that produce no detectable benefits for mankind. For example, this act has led to imposing a fee of $1,960 on each new housing unit built in large parts of fast-growing Riverside County, California, to protect the Stevens kangaroo rat. The total cost of preserving this one creature has already exceeded the total amount of money being spent on the entire homeless human population of Southern California. Yet, the only benefit defenders of this rat can cite is protecting the "universal gene pool" from further depletion. Hundreds of millions of dollars are being spent across the nation to maintain the existence of a whole set of obscure sub-species, without regard to any economic costs involved. In fact, many anti-growth interests have seized upon this law as a means of blocking new developments they oppose. This imposes huge costs upon the developers involved, or prevents them from proceeding altogether, without compensation to them or any costs to the anti-growth forces involved.

Without question, adoption of environmental regulations in America has improved the quality of the nation's physical environment in many salutary ways. It also is surely reasonable to examine the relationship between the costs and benefits of each particular regulation so as to prevent imposition of massive private and public costs far exceeding any resulting benefits. Yet this is rarely done. Moreover, when Congress passes some new environmental law, it almost never appropriates public funds to pay for that law's implementation. Consequently, almost all extensions of environmental regulations increase private-sector costs, and often local government costs, sometimes by very large amounts.

Future extensions of environmental protection legislation and regulations are certain to further increase the cost of all real estate development and management by significant amounts. This is one area where the real estate industry should exert collective legislative vigilance to protect its own interests.

CHANGES IN THE SPATIAL STRUCTURE OF MARKETS

The spatial structure of property markets is a major element in the external environment of investment real estate.

- **Continuing dispersal of economic activities away from city cores.** For at least the past 70 years, there has been a net outmovement of economically viable households and business firms from the cores of big cities into their suburbs and more remote locations. This decentralization has been caused by a combination of positive forces drawing activities outward, and negative ones repelling them from cities. One basic positive force — especially before 1970 — was rising real household incomes that enabled households and firms to consume more and better-quality space than was available in older, fully built cities. Other positive forces included immensely expanding use of cars and trucks at all income levels, construction of a huge network of expressways and other roads improving access to sites distant from downtowns, a shift to forms of structures requiring more extensive sites (such as regional shopping centers and one-floor warehouses and industrial buildings), and the technical innovations in telecommunications and computers described earlier. The negative forces include rising levels of poverty and insecurity, declining public school quality in big cities, increased commuting distances and times from fringe locations to the central business district, rising taxes, falling service levels in some big cities, the increasing obsolescence of older city homes and commercial structures, and higher rents and operating costs within downtown districts than in the suburbs.

None of these causal factors seems likely to change much in the near future; in fact, some improvements in telecommunications are intensifying. Accordingly, the net outflow of viable households and businesses away from the core portions of big cities will continue. In 1990, the central cities of all metropolitan areas combined contained about 30% of the nation's total population, but their outlying areas contained about 47%.

However, this conclusion does **not** mean that largest U.S. cities will lose population in the future. In fact, during the 1980s, among the 189 cities in the U.S. containing 100,000 or more residents in 1990, 133 gained population. They included 55 that gained more than 20% and 83 that gained more than 10% (the entire nation gained 9.8%). Only 53 actually lost population. Among the 15 largest cities in 1990, only four lost population (Chicago, Philadelphia, Baltimore, and Milwaukee); as a group, these 15 gained 8.0%. Surprisingly, the population of all central cities combined expanded by 9.9% in the 1980s; whereas that of all suburbs grew only 8.6%.

Immigration from abroad is a key reason for the continued growth of big-city populations in spite of further decentralization of activities within metropolitan areas. However, many big cities still growing in total population are experiencing net outmovement of those households and firms with the highest incomes and greatest growth potentials. Those losses likely will continue or accelerate in the future, except in newer cities in the South, Southwest, and West built mainly during the automobile era.

- **Continued racial and economic segregation**. Two other important aspects of spatial market structure involve the continuation of **racial segregation** and **economic segregation** in housing markets. These conditions are rooted in discriminatory policies and behavior by whites of all incomes and middle-class and upper-income households of all ethnic groups.

The spatial segregation of blacks from whites can be measured by the **racial dissimilarity index**. It indicates the percentage of blacks living in metropolitan areas who would have to change census tracts in order to produce the same mixture of blacks and whites in every census tract as in the region as a whole. Among the 30 metropolitan areas with the largest black populations in 1990, this index averaged 75.3 in 1970, 68.3 in 1980, and 66.5 in 1990, as shown in an accompanying chart (Figure 13).[5] Similar indices computed for whites and ethnic groups other than blacks were much lower at all three dates. Although overall black-white spatial

---

[5] Douglas S. Massey and Nancy A. Denton, *American Apartheid* (Cambridge: Harvard University Press, 1993), pp. 99-105.

segregation declined somewhat in the 1980s, most blacks still live in predominantly-black neighborhoods separated from whites. In 1990, 15 metropolitan areas (including some smaller ones) had black-white dissimilarity indices over 80. This group of severely segregated metropolitan areas included some of the nation's largest, such as Chicago, Detroit, Philadelphia, Cleveland, St. Louis, and Milwaukee.[6] Black-white spatial segregation is **not** confined to low-income groups; racial dissimilarity indices for blacks and whites are almost as large among high-income groups as among poor groups.

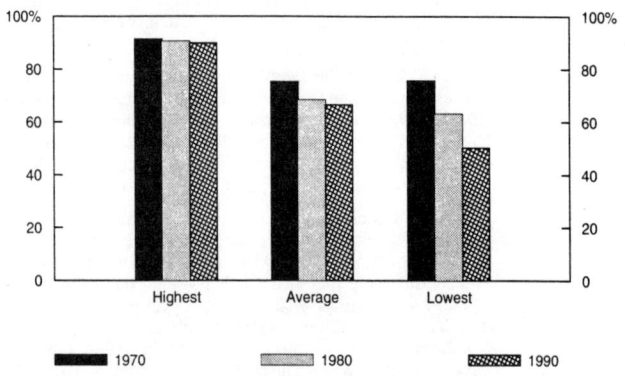

Figure 13. Black/White Residential Segregation

Source: American Apartheid.

As Douglas Massey and Nancy Denton persuasively argue in **American Apartheid,** the great spatial segregation of African-Americans from whites has powerful negative impacts upon the ability of millions of the former to attain economic, educational, and social equality with the latter. Because median household incomes are 40% lower among blacks than among whites, isolating blacks together compels many to live in neighborhoods dominated by poverty and its associated problems. Moreover, since in most of America, the school one attends is based upon where one lives, a high percentage of African-American children must attend big-city school systems that provide very low quality educations, compared with mainly-white suburban systems. These big-city school systems have become predominantly attended by minority-group children as white families with children have withdrawn to legally separate suburban systems. Among the 63 largest cities in the U.S. with minority populations of 100,000 or more each in 1990 (which include all but four of the nation's 50 largest cities), the average minority percentage in public schools was 73% in 1990. (The fraction of minorities in their combined total populations averaged 55%). In 21 of these cities, including six of the largest ten, minority-group students comprised over 80% of all public school students. So racial segregation is forcing the fastest-growing group of American young people to attend the nation's worst schools, thereby helping perpetuate their positions at the bottom of the economic and social ladder.

---

[6] Reynolds Farley and William H. Frey, *Changes in the Segregation of Whites from Blacks During the 1980s: Small Steps Toward a More Integrated Society* (Ann Arbor: Population Studies Center of the University of Michigan, 1993), Table 1.

These basic structural aspects of American metropoli areas could be changed to at least some degree by strong anti-discriminatory policies in housing markets, and by reductions in local government regulatory barriers to affordable housing. But neither of these strategies is being adopted because they are costly and threaten the desire of millions of white households to segregate themselves from blacks.

- **Increasing social and economic problems within certain central cities and older suburbs.** Many of the changes described above have combined to create increasing social and economic problems within certain central cities and older suburbs. In the 1980s, 31 U.S. cities containing more than 100,000 residents in 1990 lost 5% or more of their 1980 populations; I regard these as **severely declining cities**. They are listed in an accompanying table, along with salient facts about their populations. All but one (Denver) are older cities in the Midwest, Northeast, and South. Their average overall minority population in 1990 was 54%, and their average black population was 41% (yet for all big cities, the percentage of blacks in a city's population is **not** significantly correlated with its population loss in the 1980s). Nearly all are experiencing more widespread poverty and increasing concentrations of poor people in certain distressed neighborhoods.

Figure 14. Severely Declining Cities In The United States:
All cities with 1990 population over 100,000 that lost 4.9% or more of their 1980 population in the 1980's

Sort Rank	City	Reg.	Total Population On April 1 (In Thousands) 1970	1980	1990	Change: 1980-1990 NO.	PCT.	Change: 1970-1980 NO.	PCT.	Change: 1970-1990 NO.	PCT.	1990 Percentage Ethnic Breakdown BLACK	IND.	Amer. Asian PAC.	HISP.	1990 Total Pct. Minor.	1990 Land Area in Square Miles	1990 Density As Pop. Per Sq. Mile
1	Chicago	MW	3,369	3,005	2,784	-221	-7.4	-364	-10.8	-585	-17.4	39.1	0.3	3.7	19.6	62.7	227.2	12,254
2	Philadelphia	NE	1,949	1,688	1,586	-102	-6.0	-261	-13.4	-363	-18.6	39.9	0.2	2.7	5.6	48.4	135.1	11,739
3	Detroit	MW	1,514	1,203	1,028	-175	-14.5	-311	-20.5	-486	-32.1	75.7	0.4	0.8	2.8	79.7	136.7	7,520
4	Baltimore	S	905	787	736	-51	-6.5	-118	-13.0	-169	-18.7	59.2	0.3	1.1	1.0	61.6	80.8	9,109
5	Memphis	S	624	646	610	-36	-5.6	22	3.5	-14	-2.2	54.8	0.2	0.8	0.7	56.5	256.0	2,383
6	Washington	S	757	638	607	-31	-4.9	-119	-15.7	-150	-19.8	65.8	0.2	1.8	5.4	73.2	61.4	9,886
7	Cleveland	MW	751	574	506	-68	-11.8	-177	-23.6	-245	-32.6	46.6	0.3	1.0	4.6	52.5	77.0	6,571
8	New Orleans	S	593	558	497	-61	-10.9	-35	-5.9	-96	-16.2	61.9	0.2	1.9	3.5	67.5	180.7	2,750
9	Denver	W	515	493	468	-25	-5.1	-22	-4.3	-47	-9.1	12.8	1.2	2.4	23.0	39.4	153.3	3,053
10	St. Louis	MW	622	453	397	-56	-12.4	-169	-27.2	-225	-36.2	47.5	0.2	0.9	1.3	49.9	61.9	6,414
11	Atlanta	S	495	425	394	-31	-7.3	-70	-14.1	-101	-20.4	67.1	0.1	0.9	1.9	70.0	131.8	2,989
12	Pittsburgh	NE	520	424	370	-54	-12.7	-96	-18.5	-150	-28.8	25.8	0.2	1.6	0.9	28.5	55.6	6,655
13	Cincinnati	MW	454	385	364	-21	-5.5	-69	-15.2	-90	-19.8	37.9	0.2	1.1	0.7	39.9	77.2	4,715
14	Toledo	MW	383	355	333	-22	-6.2	-28	-7.3	-50	-13.1	19.7	0.3	1.0	4.0	25.0	80.6	4,132
15	Buffalo	NE	463	358	328	-30	-8.4	-105	-22.7	-135	-29.2	30.7	0.8	1.0	4.9	37.4	40.6	8,079
16	Newark	NE	382	329	275	-54	-16.4	-53	-13.9	-107	-28.0	58.5	0.2	1.2	26.1	86.0	23.8	11,555
17	Louisville	S	362	299	269	-30	-10.0	-63	-17.4	-93	-25.7	29.7	0.2	0.7	0.7	31.3	62.1	4,332
18	Birmingham	S	301	284	266	-18	-6.3	-17	-5.6	-35	-11.6	63.3	0.1	0.6	0.0	64.0	148.5	1,791
19	Akron	MW	275	237	223	-14	-5.9	-38	-13.8	-52	-18.9	24.5	0.3	1.2	0.7	26.7	62.2	3,585
20	Richmond	S	249	219	203	-16	-7.3	-30	-12.0	-46	-18.5	55.2	0.2	0.9	0.9	57.2	60.1	3,378
21	Dayton	MW	243	194	182	-12	-6.2	-49	-20.2	-61	-25.1	40.4	0.2	0.6	0.7	41.9	55.0	3,309
22	Knoxville	S	175	175	165	-10	-5.7	0	0.0	-10	-5.7	15.8	0.2	1.0	0.7	17.7	77.3	2,135
23	Chattanooga	S	120	170	152	-18	-10.6	50	41.7	32	26.7	33.7	0.2	1.0	0.6	35.5	118.4	1,284
24	Kansas City KS	MW	168	161	150	-11	-6.8	-7	-4.2	-18	-10.7	29.3	0.7	1.2	7.1	38.3	107.8	1,391
25	Metairie	S	136	164	149	-15	-9.1	28	20.6	13	9.6	4.9	0.2	1.8	6.2	13.1	23.3	6,395
26	Warren	MW	179	161	145	-16	-9.9	-18	-10.1	-34	-19.0	0.7	0.5	1.3	1.1	3.6	34.3	4,227
27	Flint	MW	193	160	141	-19	-11.9	-33	-17.1	-52	-26.9	47.9	0.7	0.5	2.9	52.0	33.8	4,172
28	Gary	MW	175	152	117	-35	-23.0	-23	-13.1	-58	-33.1	80.6	0.2	0.2	5.7	86.7	50.2	2,331
29	Peoria	MW	127	124	114	-10	-8.1	-3	-2.4	-13	-10.2	20.9	0.2	1.7	1.6	24.4	40.9	2,787
30	Erie	NE	129	119	109	-10	-8.4	-10	-7.8	-20	-15.5	12.0	0.2	0.5	2.4	15.1	22.0	4,955

NO: Population in thousands. Pct. Percentage change.
Note: Sorted in descending order of total population in 1990.
Source: U.S. Census Bureau.

These cities suffer from worsening fiscal strain as they try to cope with the rising costs of servicing their increasing poor populations in the face of falling total populations and often declining property values. Because they are losing viable households and firms, they are basically unable to dig themselves out of a position of continued decline without some outside financial assistance. Yet both Federal and state governments have cut back on such assistance, compared to the levels provided before the Reagan Administration took office.

Within these severely declining cities, and in many other cities with still-rising total populations, the worst conditions are found in census tracts in which 40% or more of the residents have incomes below the poverty line. Over 10 million people lived in such depressed neighborhoods nationwide in 1990; 7.5 million were in central cities.

In these areas are found the most intensive versions of four basic American social problems: (1) rising crime and insecurity, (2) the rearing of children in poverty, (3) poor quality public education, and (4) failure to integrate many workers into the "mainstream" economy. Although worst in inner-city poverty neighborhoods, all four problems are really nationwide in scope. Crime and violence now rank as America's number one problem in the eyes of a majority of citizens; 23% of **all** U.S. children under the age of six are being reared in poverty households; the quality of nearly all U.S. public elementary and secondary schools ranks below that in many other developed nations; and millions of U.S. workers at all income levels

have lost their jobs and are unable to find new ones that will support their families in decent style. If America does not energetically attack all four of these problems over the next two decades, our economic prosperity will be reduced by lessened ability to compete in a globalized economy. Furthermore, our social cohesion will be threatened by increasing distrust and hostility among ethnic and other groups, plus severe disaffection from traditional American values by a rising percentage of young people.

Clearly, members of the real estate industry — and all other Americans — have an immense stake in tackling these problems effectively. Unfortunately, there are few signs that most Americans are either willing or able to do so, despite tremendous publicity and public attention in the past decade. Moreover, we do not know how to deal with certain behavioral patterns in severe poverty areas. They include the prevalence of out-of-wedlock births, drug abuse, broken families, quick resort to violence, and the development of a "culture of opposition" hostile to traditional American values. Public policies seem weak instruments for changing such behavior patterns; yet they must be changed if these four problems are to be resolved. So private leadership will be crucial, including that from the minority groups whose members predominate in many of these neighborhoods.

The inner-city neighborhoods where these four problems occur most intensively contain less than 4% of the nation's total population. Also, most people living there are members of minority groups. As a result, there is little political support for attacking those problems effectively. So conditions in these areas are likely to become worse in the near future. That will adversely affect the reputations of many other parts of the cities in which they are located as places in which to live or do business. This does not bode well for real properties in such areas, or for the fiscal health of cities containing them. In fact, it is an ominous sign for the future of American society altogether.

Yet most Americans now live far from where such problems are most severe. They believe they can isolate and insulate themselves spatially from the impacts of all four problems without dealing with them. I am convinced that this belief is a delusion, but it is certainly the dominant one among Americans today.

- **Dealing with urban problems at the regional level.** The last spatial aspect of real estate markets discussed here is the need to confront growth-related problems at a regional scale. Rapid peripheral growth in the form of low-density sprawl with highly fragmented local governments has generated a host of problems in major U.S. metropolitan areas. These growth-related problems include traffic congestion, shortages of affordable housing, air pollution, inability to pay for adequate infrastructure, inability to find sites for region-serving facilities such as airports that have adverse impacts on their immediate surroundings, and the isolation of the poor in central city ghettos.[7]

All these problems are basically regional, because their occurrence transcends the boundaries of individual localities. This is most obvious concerning air pollution, but it is equally true of all the others. However, in each metropolitan area, authority over the laws and regulations most relevant to these problems is fragmented among hundreds of local governments competing with each other for fiscal and economic resources. Each such government makes decisions aimed at maximizing the welfare of its own residents alone, without considering possible impacts upon the rest of the metropolitan area — even though all are interdependent parts of the same economic community. In short, pure parochialism prevails, as expressed in the famous NIMBY principle, "Not in MY back yard!"

Experience throughout the nation has decisively proved that local governments structured in this manner cannot solve these growth-related problems. Therefore, none can be solved unless some strong governance powers influencing both transportation and land uses are shifted to regional-level bodies. Yet local governments universally and vehemently resist any transfer of their present authority over land-uses to higher-level bodies. So no such transfer occurs, or is even seriously contemplated, in the vast majority of metropolitan areas, and these problems grow steadily worse.

The type of regional governance necessary to cope with these problems need **not** involve replacing local governments with a single huge metropolitan-area-wide government. Rather, some agency with limited planning and coordination powers over transportation and land uses needs to be created at the metropolitan-area level. It could then help existing local governments develop coordinated plans that meet regional needs, rather than each designing its local plan solely to serve the welfare of that community considered in isolation. Congress has already recognized this need concerning transportation. In the Intermodal Surface Transportation Efficiency Act of 1991 (ISTEA, known as "Iced Tea") Congress demanded that every metropolitan area create a single regional transportation planning and coordination agency before that area can receive Federal transportation assistance. Similar requirements need to be extended to land-use controls and planning, as has been done in the states of Oregon and Florida.

---

[7] The need for regional approaches to solve such problems is dealt with in greater detail in Anthony Downs, *New Visions for Metropolitan America* (Washington D.C.: The Brookings Institution, 1994).

However, because of the passionate resistance of local government officials to any such change, it will take strong leadership from private interests such as those in the real estate industry to modify present obsolete arrangements. Private leaders need to persuade state governments to adopt a new framework for planning that creates an effective regional body in each major metropolitan area. So far, such leadership has appeared in only a very few metropolitan areas like San Francisco, New York, and Los Angeles — where not much has yet come of such efforts. Once again, the desire of most Americans to live in their own small and insulated communities, separated spatially, politically, legally and emotionally from grave national problems that in reality deeply concern their own future welfare, seems likely to prevent much effective action to solve those problems.

Chapter Two

CONTRASTING STRATEGIES FOR THE ECONOMIC DEVELOPMENT OF METROPOLITAN AREAS IN THE UNITED STATES AND WESTERN EUROPE

Anthony Downs

The economic development of U.S. metropolitan areas has occurred without much influence from overall development strategies created by governmental bodies at any level. Rather, it has resulted almost entirely from a combination of market forces plus political policies aimed at goals other than how metropolitan economies ought to develop. That is the case partly because "overall strategies" for long-range planning have long been considered almost un-American by nearly all U.S. governmental bodies.

In contrast, the economic development of most Western European metropolitan areas has occurred under the influence of explicit development strategies at both national and metropolitan-area levels. True, these strategies have not always worked as planned, but they have been implemented at least to some extent.

Comparing the results of these two fundamentally different approaches to metropolitan economic development is one of two purposes of this chapter. The other purpose is to identify and briefly analyze the major forces shaping metropolitan economic development within the United States since 1945. Since delineating these forces is a necessary prerequisite to achieving the first purpose, the chapter focuses initially on this second purpose. Owing to my specialty in urban and real estate economics, the analysis emphasizes the spatial and real estate aspects of the economic development of metropolitan areas more than, say, labor markets or macroanalysis. However, it also tries to present a broad overview of the subject.

16   Urban Change in the United States and Western Europe

MAJOR FORCES INFLUENCING U.S. METROPOLITAN-AREA DEVELOPMENT

General Approach

Economic development is a process influenced by myriad factors; thus, any selection of a few as especially important is bound to be somewhat arbitrary. Moreover, this chapter seeks to present a general overview of such factors, rather than a detailed empirical analysis of their relative significance, and is necessarily rather general in assigning relative weights to the many factors it discusses. Since the analysis also endeavors to compare U.S. and Western European experience, it focuses especially upon those factors that have exerted different influences in these two regions.

Fundamental Historical and Structural Factors

LARGE SIZE AND CULTURAL UNITY OF THE UNITED STATES

The United States contains a vastly larger spatial territory under a single national government than any Western European nation, or most such nations combined. Moreover, except for very recent immigrants, nearly all Americans speak the same language, are exposed to the same national communications media, and share one basic culture. Western Europeans, by contrast, speak many languages, are exposed to different communications media, and live under very different cultures. Hence, there is much greater population mobility within the United States than in Western Europe. Even after most economic barriers among Western European nations are removed in 1992, language and cultural factors will still make it much harder for people to move from, say, Spain to Germany than from Alabama to California. This is reflected by the much higher mobility rates among American households—about 17–20 percent move each year—than among Western European households.

DIFFERENCES IN INTENSITY OF URBAN LAND USES

Another impact of the greater size of the United States, and its much lower average density of population, is a very different attitude toward the appropriate intensity of land use than in Western Europe. For centuries, the land immediately surrounding most Western European cities has been much more intensively used for agricultural or urban purposes than that around U.S. cities. This is particularly true in smaller nations, such as the Netherlands and Denmark, where there is acute competition for every available acre. Hence, the pressure to use land intensively in the process of urban development and growth is extremely strong in Western Europe, but comparatively weak in the United States.

Since Americans regard land as abundantly available, they have historically been willing to entrust considerable authority over its use to the owners of individual land parcels. In contrast, Western Europeans regard land as an extremely scarce but vital good. So they have historically wanted to exercise much tighter control over land use by political authorities entrusted with pursuit of the common good, rather than the good of individual landowners.

Differences in Governmental Structures

This variance in general attitudes has been reinforced by a fundamental difference in governmental structure between the American federal system and Western European centralized systems. The American system entrusts to the 50 states major governmental authority; in most European nations, such authority is retained by the national government, including final control over land use. Hence, the American national government has almost never exercised any direct authority over land-use decisions, or developed any coherent national policies concerning them. Western European national governments, by contrast, have retained direct authority over some land-use decisions—at least as a court of last resort. And they have often developed coherent national policies concerning land-use patterns, both among and within their major metropolitan areas.

This difference is further accentuated by greater U.S. fragmentation of authority over land use *within* individual metropolitan areas. The 50 U.S. states have delegated most of their authority over land use to individual local governments. Each major metropolitan area contains many such local governments, sometimes over 100. Only a handful of the more than 300 metropolitan areas in the United States have any regional governmental body with general authority extending throughout most of the area that constitutes a unified urban economic and social entity. Instead, land-use control has been fragmented among many small, legally separate communities whose political authorities are elected by local residents. Such officials are therefore motivated to act primarily in the interest of their own communities, rather than in the interests of their metropolitan areas as wholes.

Western European nations have often delegated considerable power over land use within an entire metropolitan area to a single governmental body located there. This body may be the central city government or a regional government, but it has the authority and the power to implement a single coherent land-use planning strategy throughout most of the metropolitan area. This is not always the case, but it is far more often true in Western Europe than in the United States.

IMPACTS OF FRAGMENTED LAND-USE CONTROLS WITHIN
U.S. METROPOLITAN AREAS

The extreme fragmentation of land-use control and other governmental powers within U.S. metropolitan areas has had profound impacts upon the ways these areas have developed economically. For example, central city governments were prevented from blocking the development of new commercial areas outside their established downtowns. Those outlying retail and commercial districts—such as regional shopping malls—eventually undermined sales in previously dominant downtown shopping areas. In Western European nations, the dominance of such historic city centers was deliberately preserved. Central-city governments had the power to prevent construction of competitive outlying facilities, and they used that power to maintain the economic strength of their historic downtowns. Even now, there are very few outlying regional shopping malls in the United Kingdom or in Germany.

A second impact of fragmented land-use control in U.S. metropolitan areas has been their rapid sprawling into low-density suburban settlements outside the boundaries of the original central city. Private housing developers were able to buy sites some distance beyond the periphery of already-built-up areas and construct whole new residential subdivisions. They were motivated to do so by the low prices of such suburban land, which enabled them in turn to offer homes for sale at low prices. Local governments in those outlying areas had the power to permit such development, even when doing so undermined the market for housing closer in, within the boundaries of the central city. This permitted a leapfrog pattern of development that spread new housing widely across the landscape, leaving large intermediate areas of still-undeveloped land between that housing and the previously built-up areas around the central city.

In Western European metropolitan areas, such a leapfrog pattern was prevented by deliberate regional or national policies seeking to preserve agricultural uses for as long as possible in the territory immediately outside the densely settled portion of each urbanized area. This policy was enforced by regional authorities who controlled land-use decisions over wide areas. They compelled all new development to occur either as in-fill within already-settled areas, or on the immediate peripheries of those areas. The result is a striking visual difference between the edges of metropolitan areas in Western Europe and the United States. In Western Europe, travelers leaving a metropolitan area suddenly pass from densely settled urbanized neighborhoods to uninterrupted, open farmland. In the United States, there is a gradual transition from the former to the latter through a broad region of scattered patchwork subdivisions and small outlying residential and commercialized areas.

Under the U.S. pattern, at least during housing boom periods from 1950 to about 1970, developers could build single-family homes on outlying land and sell them at prices many moderate-income households could afford. That fact, plus other forces such as federal insurance for home mortgages, made homeownership widely available to U.S. households. In 1940, only 43.6 percent of all U.S. households owned their own homes, but by 1960, 61.9 percent did so. (This percentage has subsequently increased much more slowly, peaking at about 64.4 percent in 1980.)

In contrast, the Western European policy of keeping new development tightly confined to the edges of existing settlements gave landowners at those edges relatively monopolistic positions in the market. This increased land prices for new housing, relative to household incomes, and kept home prices too high for most households to afford homeownership. In addition, large subsidies were made available to renters in Western European societies, for other reasons discussed later in the chapter. These factors kept homeownership percentages lower in most Western European nations than in the United States.[1]

The more tightly circumscribed development of Western European metropolitan areas also led to much higher average residential densities in those areas than in the United States. That helped sustain widespread reliance among European households upon mass transit systems supported by large-scale public subsidies. These systems usually converged upon the traditional downtown district, thereby reinforcing its dominance within the life of its metropolitan area. Conversely, U.S. low-density settlement patterns—both caused by and contributing to greater automobile ownership and use—discouraged mass transit systems. Many public transit systems in the United States were dismantled or weakened during the period after 1945, as reliance upon automobiles accelerated.

"Nationally Dominant Cities" in Western Europe but Not in the United States

The economic, political, and social lives of several Western European nations—and of Japan—are dominated by what happens in a single city and metropolitan area that serves as the national capital. Examples are London, Paris, Tokyo, Athens, and Stockholm. No single city

20 Urban Change in the United States and Western Europe

or metropolitan area is similarly dominant within the national life of the United States, or that of several other Western European nations, such as Germany. In countries containing such dominant "super cities," both population and economic growth tend to concentrate in and around the metropolitan areas of those cities. This is true even if the national government adopts policies and programs designed to discourage growth in those metropolitan areas and to encourage it elsewhere. Such policies rarely work effectively.

The absence of any one such dominant city in the United States has certainly influenced the way its metropolitan areas have developed economically. Although a few major metropolitan areas have experienced much more growth than most others, none has yet attained the status within the United States as a whole of the Western European "super cities" just mentioned.[2]

IMPACT OF WARTIME DAMAGE IN WESTERN EUROPE

Another factor differentiating metropolitan-area development in these two regions was the extensive physical destruction and damage in most of Western Europe caused by World War II. After 1945, most Western European governments were faced with acute shortages of housing, food, and building materials that affected their entire societies. They were almost compelled to adopt more interventionist policies in housing markets than seemed appropriate to U.S. governments, where no wartime damage existed. These policies included publicly subsidizing large-scale housing construction and occupancy, and allocating access to the units so created through political processes rather than sheer market forces.

As a result, most Western European nations have housed much higher fractions of their households in directly subsidized units than the United States has—from 20 percent to 30 percent in Europe compared to less than 10 percent in the United States. Consequently, directly subsidized housing in Western Europe contains residents from a much broader socioeconomic spectrum of the entire population than does such housing in the United States, whose residents tend to be from society's poorest and most destitute groups.[3] This fact—plus the high concentration of black, single-parent households in U.S. public housing—has the effect of making publicly subsidized housing socially more acceptable to surrounding residents in Europe than in the United States. Hence, subsidized housing in Western Europe is spread throughout each metropolitan area, rather than heavily concentrated within central cities, as in the United States.

The devastation of World War II also created much stronger pressures within Western Europe than in the United States to establish extensive welfare programs aimed at raising the economic level of all persons in society to an acceptable minimum. This reinforced a similar tendency caused by another factor, as discussed next.

THE TRADITION OF SOCIALIST OR LABOR PARTIES IN EUROPE

The final historical difference between these two sets of regions mentioned here concerns the structure of their political parties. Beginning in the late 19th century, most Western European nations developed socialist or labor parties that espoused strong central governmental roles in managing their nations' economies. These parties frequently captured large fractions of the total vote and in some nations, especially Scandinavia, they were elected to office and saw many of their policies enacted. But the United States never developed a strong political movement stressing socialist themes or the rights of labor. Historically the U.S. labor movement remained weak and focused upon pragmatic economic benefits for workers, rather than ideological platforms involving strong government intervention in economic life. Even after U.S. labor unions gained more strength in the 1940s, they did not adopt anything like the economic interventionist theories typical of European labor parties. Thus, there was no American political tradition favoring national government intervention into many aspects of economic life similar to the socialist-worker party tradition in Western Europe. This difference had especially profound impacts on economic development strategies aimed at attacking poverty, rather than those explicitly aimed at spatial development patterns among or within metropolitan areas.

Population Growth and Migration Factors

Major differences in population trends in the United States and Western Europe have greatly affected the economic development of metropolitan areas in these regions. These are discussed next.

POPULATION GROWTH

The United States has experienced much greater population growth during the past few decades than has Western Europe, both absolutely and in percentage terms. In 1988, 13 major Western European nations had a combined population of 330.1 million, compared to 246.0 million in the United States and 122.6 million in Japan. From 1970 to 1988, total population grew 41.1 million in the United States, 21.1 million in the 13 Western European nations, and 18.3 million in Japan. Percentage population gains from 1970 through 1988 are shown in the accompanying figure 2.1.[4] The United States had by far the greatest percentage increase among all the larger of these nations—20.09 per-

22 Urban Change in the United States and Western Europe

Figure 2.1 POPULATION GROWTH, 1970-1988 (U.S., Western Europe, and Japan)

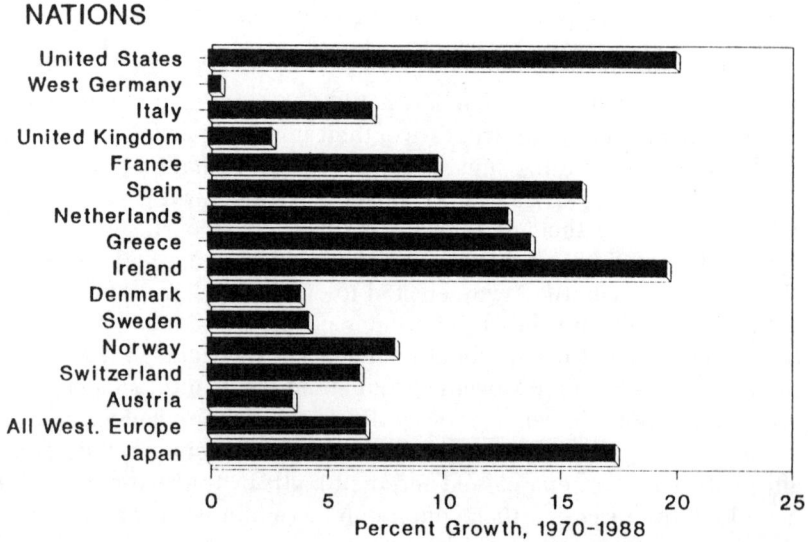

cent. Only Spain with 16.08 percent and Japan with 17.52 percent came close, except for tiny Ireland, which grew 19.73 percent. Germany had hardly any population increase during these 17 years, and the United Kingdom grew less than 5 percent. Most other Western European nations gained less than 10 percent. For all 13 Western European nations in figure 2.1 combined, the growth rate for this period was 6.8 percent, or about one-third that of the United States. Western European nations grew more slowly than the United States because of both lower fertility rates and lower immigration from abroad.

Regression analysis of the most important causes of employment growth in individual United States metropolitan areas in the 1970s has shown population increases in those areas to be the single most influential factor underlying their job growth (see Bradbury, Downs, and Small 1982; chaps. 5, 6). Hence, the greater growth of population in the United States compared to that in Western Europe has undoubtedly stimulated stronger economic growth in United States metropolitan areas than in such areas in Western Europe. This inference is confirmed by total employment data for selected nations for the period 1970-87. The United States had a net gain of 33.7 million jobs, or 42.8 percent, in those 17 years. In contrast, Germany *lost* 0.7 million jobs, or 2.7 percent; Italy gained 1.5 million, or 7.9 percent; the United

Kingdom gained 0.6 million, or 2.5 percent; and France gained 0.7 million, or 3.5 percent. Even dynamic Japan had a net gain of 8.2 million jobs, or only 16.4 percent. Thus, there was an immense disparity between the employment dynamism of the United States and that of Western Europe in this period. It is not possible in this paper to analyze the reasons for this disparity. However, greater dynamism in the United States economy surely stimulated the economic development of its metropolitan areas.

That development has also been greatly affected by four major population migration trends since 1945, discussed next.

MIGRATION FROM RURAL TO METROPOLITAN AREAS

In the 1940s, a massive movement of rural Americans into major metropolitan areas was begun as part of the recruitment of workers for wartime industries. Because housing production was essentially suspended during the war, this migration generated extensive overcrowding in the housing stocks of most major cities. After about 1950, production of new housing accelerated sharply, enabling a "decanting" of overcrowded households into new housing units, especially those built in suburbs outside central cities.[5] At the same time, the mechanization of cotton farming in the South and of farming in general created huge labor surpluses in rural areas. Millions of poor rural residents moved into metropolitan areas to find jobs in burgeoning postwar industries. This movement continued at high levels until about 1965.

Because most of the newcomers were quite poor, and many were black, this movement aggravated racial segregation patterns in many metropolitan areas, especially in the Northeast and Midwest. Black newcomers moved into neighborhoods already dominated by black households, because racial segregation and discrimination by whites prevented them from moving into mainly white areas. This generated more overcrowding in poor black neighborhoods. After the U.S. Supreme Court ruled in 1948 that racially restrictive private covenants were not enforceable, blacks began moving into previously white areas on the edges of overcrowded all-black neighborhoods. This caused most whites there to withdraw, resulting in a massive transition from white to black occupancy. As this process continued, most large U.S. central cities had rising black populations and declining white populations. Many of their white residents moved out to mainly white suburbs. Over a period of 40 years, from 1950 to 1990, this process caused many of the largest U.S. central cities to shift from a largely white population composition to a largely or even mainly black composition. Moreover, the black population in these cities is much

24 Urban Change in the United States and Western Europe

younger than the white population, on the average, and many white children attend private schools. Consequently, a majority of public school children in nearly all of the nation's 25 largest central cities consists of minority-group children, mostly black. These race-related processes were mostly absent from Western European cities, or occurred on a much smaller scale with immigrant groups of different racial backgrounds from the nationally predominant ethnic group. Thus, some such phenomena took place in London with West Indians and Pakistanis; in West Berlin with Turks; in Amsterdam with Indonesians; and in Paris with Algerians. But few Western European cities were so profoundly affected by racial segregation and transition as were a majority of the largest American cities.

MIGRATION FROM ABROAD INTO AMERICAN CITIES

Immigration from abroad has been a major source of U.S. urban development throughout the nation's history. During the past two decades, such immigration has markedly accelerated and changed in nature. Whereas most immigrants to the United States before about 1960 were from various parts of Europe, a large majority of those arriving during the 1970s and 1980s were from Latin America and Asia, most entering the United States through the West Coast and the Mexican border. Over 6 million legal immigrants *net* entered the United States during the 1980s; the total including illegal entrants may have been closer to 8 million.

This large inflow of newcomers markedly affected the population composition of certain metropolitan areas, especially those that already contained large numbers of Hispanics. The New York, Los Angeles, Miami, Chicago, Washington, D.C., San Diego, San Francisco, Orange County (Calif.), San Jose, Oakland, and Boston metropolitan areas each received over 10,000 immigrants from abroad in the year 1987. Children attending public schools in the city of Los Angeles come from homes in which over 100 different languages are spoken as "native tongues." This cultural and linguistic diversity poses an extremely difficult challenge for educators and other public officials in such communities. That challenge is absent from most Western European nations, or is at least present to a much lesser degree.

MOVEMENT OUT OF CENTRAL CITIES INTO SUBURBS

From about 1950 onward, a massive shift of population and economic activities out of central cities into surrounding suburbs occurred within U.S. metropolitan areas. This movement had actually started in the 1920s, but was interrupted by the great Depression of the 1930s and World War II in the 1940s. It was accelerated after 1950 by several key public policies. One such policy made federal mortgage insurance available to millions of homebuying households. A second policy, the Interstate Highway System program, which started in 1956, created a nationwide network of limited-access, high-speed, high-capacity roadways. These highways not only linked together most major metropolitan areas but also provided both radial and circumferential arteries within most of them. This opened up accessibility to immense areas of vacant land on the outskirts of most major cities. In addition, the federal government provided urban renewal funds to redevelop large portions of older cities, and infrastructure funds to build sewer and water systems in growing suburban areas. Large-scale construction and sale of automobiles and trucks increased the mobility of both households and business firms so they could effectively spread out over the landscape without becoming economically inefficient.

All these forces, together with huge population inflows of poor rural residents into central cities themselves, generated massive movements of households and business firms out of central cities and into the suburbs. At the same time, in the nation as a whole, more new housing units were being built each year after 1960 than new households were being formed, mostly in suburban areas. By 1965, this construction had generated a sufficient overall surplus of available housing within each metropolitan area as a whole to cause some abandonment of the worst-quality structures within central cities.[6]

This suburbanization had profound impacts upon the economic development of U.S. metropolitan areas. Manufacturing and wholesaling shifted out of older, multistory, congested neighborhoods in central cities into spacious new one-story buildings located along expressways in the suburbs. This reduced the tax bases of central cities but increased those of the suburbs. Downtown areas formerly dominated by a combination of retailing, manufacturing, and wholesaling were largely abandoned by the last two, and suffered from increasing competition from outlying shopping centers. This greatly weakened their economic viability until the office-space boom of the 1970s and 1980s restored vitality to many such central business districts. The loss of millions of middle- and upper-income households to the suburbs caused central cities to shift toward greater economic, social, and political dominance by low-income groups. Their governments were increasingly squeezed fiscally by rapidly rising demands for services but only slowly rising tax bases. Large portions of some older midwestern and northeastern central cities cleared by urban renewal programs remained vacant for decades. No viable enterprises or households wanted to move there because these sites were surrounded by neighborhoods dominated by poverty and the many adverse conditions associated with it, including high rates of crime, delinquency, drug abuse, broken families, unemployment, and mental health difficulties. This situation persists in such cities as Chicago, Detroit, New York, Philadelphia, Washington, D.C., Gary, and Cleveland.

MIGRATION OF PEOPLE AND BUSINESSES TO THE SOUTH AND WEST

The fourth major migration flow in the postwar United States has been a steady movement of both households and business firms out of the Northeast and Midwest and into the South and West. In the early postwar period, migration from the rural South to the Northeast and Midwest caused net outflows from the South. But after 1960, these flows reversed. In the 1970s, the Northeast had net outmigration of at least 2.9 million persons, and the Midwest, 2.7 million. At the same time, the South had net immigration of at least 6 million, and the West, 4.1 million. From 1980 to 1987, the figures were −363,000 for the Northeast, −2,142,000 for the Midwest, +5,000,000 for the South, and +2,481,000 for the West (U.S. Bureau of the Census 1989: 21).[7]

It is not clear exactly why these migration flows have occurred. Living costs are generally lower in the South than in the Northeast or the Midwest, as are wage levels. But living costs and wage levels are relatively high in California, which has consistently had the greatest net immigration of any state. In fact, just three states—California, Florida, and Texas—captured 41.7 percent of the nation's total population growth during the 1970s and 52.4 percent from 1980 to 1987. Yet they contained only 23 percent of the nation's total population as of 1987. Mean January temperatures are positively correlated with metropolitan area population growth rates and are statistically significant in regressions seeking to "explain" those rates (see Bradbury et al. 1982; chaps. 5, 6). So warmer climate is undoubtedly one factor luring people out of the Northeast and Midwest. Some economists have speculated that many business firms have moved out of the Midwest and Northeast and into the South to escape from high-wage and highly unionized labor markets. However, that is hard to prove statistically. Nevertheless, there is no doubt that this basic migration flow has immensely influenced economic development patterns among U.S. metropolitan areas.

DIFFERENCES BETWEEN U.S. AND WESTERN EUROPEAN MIGRATION PATTERNS

Several Western European nations have experienced population migration patterns since 1945 similar to those just described in the United States. A significant movement out of rural areas and into metropolitan areas has occurred in most Western European nations since 1945. (However, the timing of such migration has differed greatly among Western European nations; for example, it happened much earlier in the United Kingdom than in Spain.) And there has been notable suburbanization of population around most major Western European cities. But both of these movements have been smaller, relative to the total size of the central cities involved, than in the United States.

In addition, there has been sizable immigration into several Western European nations by members of ethnic groups other than the traditionally dominant groups in those nations, as pointed out earlier. However, as stated previously, such immigration has also been much smaller, in relation to the dominant group, than the immigration of either blacks or Hispanics into U.S. metropolitan areas. Hence, far less "massive racial transition" occurred in Western European cities than in U.S. cities.

The last U.S. migration trend—movement from the Northeast and Midwest to the South and West—also has some analogue in Western Europe. In the United Kingdom, economic growth has been much stronger in the South than in the North; hence, there has been some movement from Scotland and the northern regions of England into the area around London and the South. Similarly, in Germany, jobs in the industrial Ruhr area have grown much more slowly than those in industrial cities in the southern part of the country; thus, there has been another north-to-south migration flow there. And in Italy, northern regions have generated far more new jobs than southern regions; so some migration flows from the South to the North have taken place. Nevertheless, in all three instances, internal migration flows in Western Europe have been much smaller than those in the United States. (However, West Germany twice received very large inflows of immigrants from East Germany: once soon after 1945, and again immediately preceding unification.) European citizens appear much more rooted to subregions within their nations than do Americans, probably because of greater subregional cultural and other differentiation within Western Europe than within the United States, and perhaps because of longer periods of family history and connections in the former.

Also, large housing price disparities between economically stagnant and economically growing regions make it hard for homeowning households to move from the former to the latter. For example, a homeowning household in northern England that sells its home receives a relatively low price and must pay a much higher price for a similar home in southern England. This clearly discourages migration among homeowners from northern to southern England, or similarly, from the Ruhr to the southern states of Germany, even though in each case there are far more jobs available in the latter region than in the former. The people who make such moves are mainly young people unencumbered either by long-established social ties to their "native" communities or by homeownership. True, since about the mid-1970s, similar housing price disparities have developed among U.S. metropolitan areas. They may have similar impacts upon internal U.S. migration in the long run, but that has not yet been clearly established.

Technological Factors

At least four major technological forces have affected the economic development of U.S. metropolitan areas since 1945. Most of these factors have had a *centralizing* impact upon the location of economic activities in metropolitan areas compared to nonmetropolitan areas, but a *decentralizing* impact upon the location of such activities within metropolitan areas.

CREATION OF MAJOR HIGHWAY NETWORKS AND EXPANDED USE OF AUTOMOTIVE VEHICLES

The building of the Interstate Highway System and related vehicle expressways linking major metropolitan areas has already been described. It was accompanied by an "explosion" in the U.S. automotive vehicle population. From 1960 to 1988, the human population of the United States rose by 65.6 million, or 36.5 percent. But the population of cars, trucks, and buses in use skyrocketed by 104.1 million, or 152.8 percent. From 1983 to 1988, the United States was annually adding more than twice as many vehicles as people. Regardless of whether these forces should be considered technological or economic, they revolutionized the economic development of U.S. metropolitan areas.

Automotive vehicles became the overwhelmingly dominant form of transportation for both people and goods. This had a sharply decentralizing impact upon the way U.S. metropolitan areas developed, both internally and among regions. Business firms were more able to locate almost anywhere near a major expressway. Vacant land near such roads became available for new residential subdivisions, even though they were many miles from established downtown areas. Employment within each metropolitan area scattered widely around its periphery. In consequence, all established downtowns—even though most downtowns added more jobs absolutely—declined relatively as employment centers vis-à-vis their suburbs.

These forces also weakened U.S. reliance upon public transit of all types for movements *within* metropolitan areas. The percentage of workers commuting daily by mass transit, as well as the percentage of all types of trips on mass transit, declined sharply after 1945 and has remained much lower than in Western European nations.

TELECOMMUNICATIONS AND COMPUTER INNOVATIONS

Rapid technical advances in telecommunications and computers enabled firms to integrate their operations closely in function, even though they were widely separated in space. This had ambiguous impacts upon the location of economic activity. It enabled firms that wanted to more fully centralize control over spatially scattered operations to do so. But it also enabled firms to separate spatially operations that had formerly been considered too functionally linked to be located apart from each other. Because other forces in society and the economy more strongly favored decentralization than centralization, the net impact of telecommunications and computer innovations has surely been a decentralizing one.

EXPANSION OF AIR TRANSPORTATION AND AIRPORTS

U.S. air travel expanded tremendously in the postwar period, partly because of such technical innovations as jet engines, much larger aircraft, and improved radar control of flight movements. Whereas the total population of the U.S. increased 35 percent from 1960 to 1987, total passenger revenue miles flown rose from 39 billion in 1960 to 163 billion in 1975 and 404 billion in 1987—more than a 10-fold increase. Major airports became much more important modal-transfer points than railroad passenger stations, which served fewer and fewer people. By 1988, the number of passengers traveling through specific airports each year had risen to huge levels: 28 million in Chicago (at three airports), 22 million in Dallas-Fort Worth (at two airports), 22 million in Atlanta, 23 million in Los Angeles (at four airports), and 21 million in New York (at two airports) (U.S. Bureau of the Census 1989: 621–22). Airports consume considerable space for runways, taxiways, hangars, terminal facilities, and access roads; hence, they are usually built on the edges of metropolitan areas where large vacant sites are available, rather than near traditional downtown centers. As the importance of airports rose, other facilities to serve them grew up around them, including hotels, apartment clusters, industrial parks, restaurants, and office complexes.

Air travel thus had a doubly decentralizing impact upon economic activity in U.S. metropolitan areas. It enabled firms to locate branch activities in metropolitan areas distant from their main offices while still allowing them to reach those offices quickly. Hence, this dispersed economic activity more widely across the nation. In addition, the rising importance of airports *within* metropolitan areas created outlying clusters of activities rivaling traditional downtowns.

PRODUCTIVITY INCREASES IN MANUFACTURING AND AGRICULTURE

In the period from about 1950 to 1973, productivity rose rapidly in both manufacturing and agriculture, not only in the United States but around the world. As a result, the number of workers required per million dollars of output in both these economic sectors declined, compared to the analogous number in other sectors—notably both private and government services. This was a major cause of the population migration from rural to metropolitan areas already described. In 1950, 12.5 percent of all employed workers were in agriculture and 25.9 percent in manufacturing. By 1975, these fractions had declined to 3.9 percent and 22.7 percent, respectively, and by 1987, they were 2.9 percent and 18.6 percent, respectively. In 1950, agriculture comprised 7.2 percent of gross domestic product (GDP) and manufacturing comprised 30.9 percent of GDP. In 1975, these fractions were 3.4 percent and 25.1 percent, respectively; by 1987, they were 2.5 percent and 22 percent. Thus, the shares of the workforce in these sectors had declined much more than their shares of total value of output, though the latter also declined. One of the results of these changes was a marked shift in the location of jobs from farms and agricultural industries, and from manufacturing plants, into offices of all types, as service employment became a rising share of an expanding labor force. Accompanying this was a sharp increase in the need for office space, which fueled an enormous development of such space, especially after the recovery period of 1976–79 began. The biggest "explosion" of office space occurred in the 1980s under the dual impact of rising numbers of office workers and overflowing availability of investment capital for real estate development, as discussed later.

These factors stimulated rapid economic growth in those metropolitan areas well situated as locations for international, national, or regional office headquarters for firms of all types. A virtual "headquarters hierarchy" of metropolitan areas developed in U.S. office space markets. At the top of this pyramid were the "international headquarters" cities of New York, Washington, D.C., Los Angeles, and Chicago. At a slightly lower level were the "regional headquarters or gateway" cities of Atlanta, Dallas, Minneapolis, Boston, San Francisco, Miami, and Seattle. Still farther down were "industrial headquarters" cities for specific industries, such as Houston for oil and energy, and Detroit for automobiles. Their economic fate depended heavily upon what happened in their industries. But every major city enjoyed some office-space boom in the 1980s.

Although more office space was built in the suburbs than in central cities in total, the concentration of large amounts of new office space within traditional downtowns helped stimulate their revival in most of the cities just mentioned in the 1970s and especially in the 1980s. New downtown offices were accompanied by new hotels, restaurants, convention centers, stadiums, performing arts facilities, and public buildings. These injections of both capital and jobs helped offset the continuing loss of retail, wholesale, and manufacturing jobs form downtown areas.

DIFFERENCES BETWEEN THE U.S. AND WESTERN EUROPE

Many of the same technological factors that influenced the economic development of U.S. metropolitan areas also occurred in Western Europe. The biggest difference between such factors in these two major regions concerned automotive transportation. Western European nations did not experience nearly so great an expansion of either highway facilities or ownership and use of automotive vehicles as did the United States. Instead, their public policies deliberately emphasized continued reliance upon extensive networks of railroads and local mass transit systems, financing the large losses of such systems through public subsidies.[8] This reinforced the basic Western European urban development strategy of strengthening traditional downtown or other established shopping districts, encouraging relatively high-density residential living, and limiting suburban sprawl.

Moreover, Western European metropolitan areas did not experience nearly so great an increase in office space development as most U.S. metropolitan areas. This was true because of much tighter local government planning controls over new development in Western Europe, as well as two other factors discussed later in the chapter: less readily available financing for new office development and slower creation of new jobs.

Sociological Factors

At least four major sociological factors influenced economic development patterns in U.S. metropolitan areas. One factor was racial segregation and discrimination, discussed previously under population migration. A second factor was the increasing tendency of women, both single and married, to work outside the home. This tendency accelerated after 1973 because of the sudden cessation of real wage increases that had previously been sizable; more and more married women had to work to support increases in their families' standards of living, since their husbands' real wages stopped rising and even declined. Moreover, divorce rates rose sharply in the 1950s and 1960s, partly because of liberalized divorce laws. Thus, as more and more women became heads of households, they were required to support themselves and their children.

As more women took jobs outside the home, the commuting patterns of households changed. Many more households contained multiple workers who traveled to work simultaneously, but to jobs in different locations. This was a major factor causing increased use of automotive vehicles. Today, over 50 percent of all U.S. households own more than one such vehicle.

Another major sociological force was the U.S. baby boom—a period of unusually high birthrates from about 1950 to about 1965. A huge bulge in the previously "normal" age distribution was generated by this surge in births. This bulge gradually moved through succeeding ages, causing dislocations in public facilities and shifts in cultural emphasis within the entire nation. Thus, the 1960s saw a big increase in the number of school-aged children and teenagers, which produced a strong emphasis upon youth in American culture. In contrast, as the 1990s began, this bulge was entering middle age; the first baby boomers are passing their 40th birthdays, and the last ones are passing their 25th birthdays. The ensuing drop in numbers of young households being formed will reduce the demand for new housing in the 1990s, compared to the high levels of demand caused by the baby boomers in the past, especially in the 1970s, when they were entering household-formation ages.

The last sociological factor to be discussed here is the declining effectiveness of the U.S. educational system, compared to analogous systems in other nations. Dropout rates among high school students, especially in big-city public school systems, are much higher in the United States than in most other economically developed nations. Also, American students get lower scores on international tests of knowledge and ability than students from most other developed nations. Although the United States has been discussing "school reform" for over a decade, and has greatly increased spending on education, these factors have not produced any measurable improvement in the performance of U.S. schools as a whole.

This last trend could have profound impacts upon the economic development of U.S. metropolitan areas in the future, if it is not changed. Business firms that cannot hire young workers well educated enough to perform the tasks required in a high-technology society will move to other locations where such people are available.

This implies further movement out of central cities to alternative locations. It also implies that business firms may have to spend large amounts training new workers to bring their capabilities up to the levels necessary to meet their own performance standards.

In Western European nations, fewer students attend higher educational institutions than in the United States, but a higher percentage of students complete secondary school educations. Moreover, in contrast to American students, students in most developed nations spend more time in school each year, spend more time in class each day studying academic material, and do more homework each day, on average. Therefore, the quality of education received by Western European students is probably better, on average, than that received by U.S. students at any stage of the learning process up to the end of secondary school.

Financial and Economic Factors

Hundreds of financial and economic factors, other than those previously mentioned, have affected the way U.S. metropolitan areas developed since 1945. This chapter arbitrarily focuses on just a few that seem especially important.

Economic Shocks of the 1970s

The 1970s were a decade of multiple economic shocks throughout the world. Two major oil price increases, in 1973 and again in 1979, radically changed the financial balance between oil-importing and oil-producing nations. There was also a food shortage in the early 1970s that drove agricultural prices up sharply. Those factors produced rampant inflation around the world. And there were two significant recessions—one in 1974-75 and another at the end of the 1970s.

For these reasons, and others that economic analysts have been unable to identify, the growth of U.S. economic productivity that had been so strong in the 1950s and 1960s suddenly slowed and almost stopped after 1973. Average real wages per hour were actually lower in 1990 than in 1973—17 years earlier. So were average weekly earnings. In 1987, median household income in 1987 dollars was $25,986, only 1 percent higher than in 1970 (U.S. Bureau of the Census 1989: 440).

Households that had become accustomed to rising standards of living before this "plateau" arrived sought to maintain their consumption increases in spite of falling real wages. They did so by (1) saving less out of their current incomes, (2) having more members work outside the home—notably women, and (3) having fewer members on

34 Urban Change in the United States and Western Europe

the average—notably fewer children. Hence, private savings rates out of disposable income declined, especially in the 1980s, a drop that was aggravated by huge federal budget deficits in the 1980s. The overall U.S. savings rate declined sharply, and the economy became dependent upon massive borrowing from abroad to maintain the consumption standards enjoyed by U.S. citizens.

These developments had several impacts upon the economic development of U.S. metropolitan areas. Economic pressures on households in the 1970s helped cause a "taxpayers' revolt" against rising expenditures by state and local governments to accommodate metropolitan area growth. Voters in several states adopted limits on the ability of both state and local governments to raise property and other taxes, or increase expenditures. At the same time, the federal government—under pressure from rising budget deficits—cut back on financial assistance to local governments for creating new low-income housing and infrastructures. This put a double squeeze on local governments in areas experiencing rapid population growth, as in Florida and California. They had to seek new sources of revenue to build the roads, schools, sewers, water systems, and other infrastructures necessary to accommodate such growth. So they adopted "impact fees" and other taxes placed on new developments themselves to finance such improvements.

These fees helped raise the prices of newly built homes in certain fast-growth areas to very high levels. That in turn prevented low- and moderate-income households from moving into suburban new-growth subdivisions in such metropolitan areas. The result was a reinforcement of the spatial separation of low- and moderate-income households from middle- and upper-income households in most U.S. metropolitan areas, compared to most of those in Western Europe.

Another impact of the worldwide economic dislocations of the 1970s was a dramatic gyration in oil prices. A huge increase occurred from 1973 through 1979, stimulating an immense economic boom in those U.S. metropolitan areas specializing in energy exploration and processing, such as Houston, Tulsa, Oklahoma City, New Orleans, Anchorage, and Denver. Massive capital spending occurred in those cities, rapidly expanding office space and other properties in anticipation of further long-run increases in oil prices. Then oil prices suddenly collapsed in the mid-1980s under pressure from a worldwide glut of supply and conservation-generated limits on demand. The economies of those cities that had expanded rapidly in anticipation of a long-term energy-related boom were suddenly plunged into a major recession. The Houston metropolitan area, for example, lost over 200,000 jobs in less than three years. Real estate markets in these cities were devastated by these gyrations in oil prices and the fortunes of energy industries. Office vacancy rates in the cities mentioned soared to around 30 percent and stayed high for many years. Thus, a "regional recession" gripped many large U.S. metropolitan areas in the mid-1980s, in spite of overall general prosperity in the nation.

IMPACTS OF SUSTAINED PROSPERITY

The longest peacetime economic expansion in U.S. history began in 1983 with recovery from the severe recession of 1980–82. This recovery sustained itself for a record seven years, and continued into 1990. It was initially fueled by heavy federal defense spending and large federal budget deficits. In those metropolitan areas that have experienced both sustained economic prosperity and rapid population growth, residents of many communities have developed strong antigrowth attitudes that are influencing the way growth occurs there. Specifically, those attitudes cause local governments to slow down housing and commercial real estate development, raising the prices of both types. This usually does not reduce the overall growth of the entire metropolitan area concerned, even if it does reduce that of the particular communities involved. But it pushes housing prices upward and spreads development out farther over the landscape. In metropolitan areas experiencing large-scale immigration, antigrowth attitudes also create pressure on low-income households to occupy illegally overcrowded facilities, since they cannot afford to pay high housing prices.

FINANCIAL PRESSURES FOR OVERBUILDING

During the 1980s, several developments in capital markets created a "bias" favoring more investment in real estate than was economically justifiable on the basis of its competitive yields alone. This bias led to systematic overbuilding of real properties of all types, except perhaps of single-family residences. The result was a stimulation of the construction and real estate development industries, and of land prices, that greatly affected the economic development of U.S. metropolitan areas.

One element generating overinvestment in real estate markets was the Tax Act of 1981, which provided generous tax benefits for such investment. It shortened depreciation periods compared to their past lengths, thereby creating large accounting losses for new real estate projects in their early years. This permitted persons in high income-tax brackets to shield their wage and other incomes from taxes by offsetting paper real estate losses against those incomes. Syndication firms were able to raise large amounts of money from investors seeking tax shelter to invest in creating new buildings, almost regardless of whether there was an economic or space-requirement-related need for such buildings. This condition resulted in syndicators financing development of many buildings for which there was little or no market demand. This condition persisted until the Tax Reform Act of 1986 eliminated most of the tax-shelter benefits involved.

A second stimulus to overbuilding was deregulation of the banking and savings and loan industries, which reached its most complete stage in 1983. At that time, previous ceilings on the interest rates they could pay depositors were eliminated. Before that, whenever prevailing short-term rates rose above those ceilings, depositors withdrew funds from these institutions for investment in higher-rate alternatives elsewhere. This process had created periodic "credit crunches" slowing down real estate development, because these institutions had little money to lend to developers when those "crunches" occurred. But elimination of the interest ceilings permitted such institutions to raise rates so as to retain their deposits, even when short-term rates soared. This kept money in those institutions at all points during the business cycle, putting pressure on them to invest the money almost regardless of the prevailing supply-and-demand balance in space markets.

At the same time, savings and loans were able to use higher interest rates to attract massive inflows of deposits that enabled the most adventuresome to grow with astonishing speed. Depositors did not have to worry about whether their funds would be wisely invested by the institutions in which they placed those funds, because federal deposit insurance guaranteed no losses for accounts up to $100,000. So risk-oriented operators of savings and loans raised the rates they paid depositors above the prevailing levels, used "account brokers" to gather funds from across the whole nation, and expanded their liabilities to enormous levels. This put them under big pressure to make investments that would presumably pay high yields to offset the high rates they were paying to attract such funds. But high-yield investments are usually riskier than lower-yield ones—that is why they have higher *apparent* yields.

Under these conditions, many savings and loans—which had formerly invested mainly in mortgage loans for single-family homebuyers—shifted to investing large amounts in risky commercial real estate ventures, including purchase of vacant land and equity positions in new office buildings, hotels, and shopping centers. This was the second major source of "bias" toward overinvestment in real estate, since savings and loans essentially had to focus most of their investments on real estate, rather than other things.

During this same period, both foreign investors and U.S. pension funds also greatly expanded their funding of real estate projects. They were motivated by the relatively strong performance of real estate equities in the 1970s, when the stock and bond markets were languishing under the pressure of inflation and rising interest rates. So they put money into real estate to diversify against excessive concentration on stocks and bonds.

The result was an immense flow of capital into real estate markets from multiple sources. Developers had access to great amounts of money that they could "finance out" of their projects—that is, obtain more than the real cost of those projects from other investors, either as loans or equity shares. With no money of their own at stake, but able to collect large development fees, they were motivated to flood the space market with new buildings. And so they did. The prevailing vacancy rate in office space markets in major metropolitan areas rose steadily, from under 5 percent in 1981 to over 20 percent in 1986, and stayed that high for several years thereafter.

This stimulated a huge boom in real estate development, and greatly expanded the properties present in both established downtowns and outlying commercial areas. During 10 of the 12 years from 1978 through 1989, over 900 million square feet of new commercial and industrial space were placed under construction contracts annually—even though that had happened in only one previous year in U.S. history. This boom accelerated the development of outlying retail centers that expanded into multiuse "new cities" on the edges of many large metropolitan areas.

RESULTS OF STATISTICAL ANALYSES OF METROPOLITAN AREA DEVELOPMENT

Two statistical analyses of sources of metropolitan area growth have been conducted by myself and colleagues. The first was an in-depth analysis of 121 U.S. metropolitan areas conducted for the book *Urban Decline and the Future of American Cities* (Bradbury, Downs, and Small 1982: chs. 5, 6). Two multiple regression analyses of these areas were carried out, using employment growth from 1960 to 1970 and from 1970 to 1975 as dependent variables. A number of independent variables were used that had been derived from various theories about why urban decline might occur. The analysis treated central city growth separately from suburban growth, but only the results for entire metropolitan areas are cited here.

When percentage change in metropolitan area employment for 1970–75 was the dependent variable, the statistically significant factors found to influence it were (1) percentage change in metropolitan area population form 1970 to 1975, (2) a local industry mix containing fast-growing industries, (3) whether or not the area contained a state capital (if so, it enhanced job growth), (4) an estimated cost of living index for the metropolitan area (the higher the living cost, the slower the job growth rate), (5) the percentage change in the cost-of-living index from 1970 to 1985 (the greater the change, the slower the job growth rate), (6) metropolitan area income per capita in 1970 (the higher the income, the faster the job growth rate), (7) the percentage change in metropolitan area income per capita from 1970 to 1975 (the greater the rise, the faster the job growth rate), and (8) a measure of the total size of employment there in 1970 (the larger the total number of jobs, the slower the job growth rate). The R-square of this regression was 0.74.

A similar regression using the percentage change in metropolitan area jobs from 1960 to 1970 as the dependent variable produced similar results, with a few changes. Living costs did not have a significant impact, nor did whether the area contained a state capital or the absolute size of the area's total employment at the start of the period. But both population density per square mile and a measure of local government taxes per capita had negative impacts upon the rate of job growth. This regression had an R-square of 0.88.

Other regressions using population growth rates as dependent variables showed that job growth and population growth were highly interdependent. Each was the single most important factor influencing the other. People follow jobs *among* metropolitan areas, but not so much *within* metropolitan areas, as separate regressions for central cities and suburbs showed. Central-city prosperity would thus be better served by retaining residents than business firms. Using percentage change in metropolitan-area population from 1970 to 1975 as the dependent variable showed that the following factors influence that variable: (1) percentage change in metropolitan area population due to natural increase, (2) percentage change in metropolitan area job growth, (3) the metropolitan-area unemployment rate (the higher the rate, the slower the population growth rate), (4) the percentage of population in the metropolitan area's largest city consisting of Hispanics (the higher the percentage, the faster the population growth rate), and (5) the mean January temperature (the higher the temperature, the faster the population growth rate). This regression had an R-square of 0.67.

Another regression analysis was conducted in 1989 as part of a study of housing prices in different metropolitan areas (Downs 1989).[9] This study focused on levels and changes in median prices of existing homes sold as the dependent variable. But job and population growth in the 60 metropolitan areas concerned were independent variables, so they could be shifted to dependent variable status easily, thanks to computer analysis. When the absolute rise in population from 1980 to 1988 is the dependent variable, the statistically significant independent variables were (1) the median home price (the higher the price, the greater the growth), (2) median income in 1988 (the lower the income, the greater the growth), (3) the number of housing units authorized from 1980 to 1988 (the greater the number, the greater the growth), and (4) the number of units granted permits per 1,000 households (the smaller the number, the greater the growth). This regression had an R-square of 0.85. When the percentage change in nonagricultural employment from 1980 to 1987 was the dependent variable, the statistically significant independent variables were (1) the median home price (the higher the price, the lower the job growth rate), (2) the percentage increase in total population from 1980 to 1988 (the greater the percentage, the higher the job growth rate), and (3) the per capita income in the metropolitan area (the higher the income, the greater the job growth rate). This regression had an R-square of .92.[10]

I am unaware of similar analyses performed for Western European metropolitan areas. Therefore, no comparisons of these findings with analogous ones for Western Europe are presented here.

BASIC STRATEGIES FOR METROPOLITAN-AREA ECONOMIC DEVELOPMENT

Three Types of Possible Economic Development Strategies

Governments could conceivably develop at least three different types of economic development strategies affecting metropolitan areas. One strategy would aim at affecting *the regional allocation of resources across the nation*. Such a strategy would therefore have to be created at the national level, with the goal of influencing the relative prosperity of each whole metropolitan area compared to that of other whole metropolitan areas.

40 Urban Change in the United States and Western Europe

A second strategy would aim at *the allocation of resources within individual metropolitan areas.* It could be created at either the national, regional, or individual metropolitan-area level. Its goal would be to influence how development occurred among different parts of a single metropolitan area, such as the central city compared to the suburbs.

A third possible strategy would aim at *the allocation of resources among certain groups within society, regardless of their locations.* Reducing poverty and decreasing existing income distribution inequalities would be two examples of such strategies. They would aim at goals that were not inherently linked to differences among metropolitan areas or among parts of individual areas—although some such linkages might exist "accidentally." Thus, poverty might be concentrated more in certain regions, like Southern Italy, or in certain parts of metropolitan areas, like older central city neighborhoods, than in others.

The remaining analysis in this chapter examines how these three types of strategies have affected metropolitan-area economic development in the United States and Western Europe.

The American Strategy—or Lack Thereof

To speak of an "American strategy" for the economic development of metropolitan areas is almost to coin an oxymoron. Americans have traditionally never employed any public-policy strategies for urban economic development. This dearth of long-range conceptualizing has prevailed at all levels of government. In fact, as mentioned earlier, "strategies" of any kind—that is, long-range plans concerning how to achieve basic goals—are considered fundamentally un-American in most spheres of public policy, and certainly in the realm of urban development patterns. The basic American approach is to leave the allocation of resources that affect urban and metropolitan-area development to the operation of both "free" private markets and public policies aimed at entirely different goals. So the economic development patterns that arise among and within U.S. metropolitan areas are essentially accidental or random results, generated by actions taken by myriad private-sector and public-sector actors pursuing goals not explicitly related to overall economic development per se.

NATIONAL STRATEGIES FOR ALLOCATING RESOURCES AMONG METROPOLITAN AREAS

An example of this lack of an overall, integrated strategy is that of federal defense expenditures, which have huge impacts upon the economies of different metropolitan areas across the nation. But these expenditures are almost never explicitly aimed at assisting economically weak areas, or aimed away from booming areas to avoid aggravating their overheated economies. True, defense expenditures are greatly affected by the relative political power of individual members of the U.S. Congress who occupy key committee positions. But all such politicians invariably seek to steer more spending into their own districts or states, regardless of economic conditions there. In this respect, all members of Congress are totally locally oriented, rather than concerned with overall national patterns of defense spending impacts.

In the 1960s, the federal government created an agency called the Economic Development Administration (EDA) whose ostensible purpose is to help economically depressed areas improve their levels of employment and other productive activity. But this agency was created at a time when the thrust of nearly all federal policies was to stimulate massive movements of both people and jobs out of rural districts and into metropolitan areas. Rather than reshape all those other policies to change this impact, Congress created the EDA as an expression of concern for the rural areas that were being depopulated, partly through the impacts of all its other policies. This agency was deliberately given too few resources to stem the tide of other policies causing flight from rural areas. Hence, it was kept essentially ineffective, a symbolic gesture to show that Congress "cared" about the areas its other policies were undermining.

The U.S. federal government has also adopted many programs during the past 40 years aimed at improving economic conditions within large cities and other areas. Examples are the urban renewal, public housing, model cities, community block grant, and antipoverty programs. However, these programs did not form any coherent overall strategy for allocating resources among metropolitan areas to benefit the weakest disproportionately. Rather, they were a series of ad hoc responses to specific problems, coordinated at neither the federal, state, nor metropolitan-area levels—and often not even at the local level by the receiving governments.

REGIONAL STRATEGIES FOR ALLOCATING RESOURCES WITHIN INDIVIDUAL METROPOLITAN AREAS

Within individual U.S. metropolitan areas, there is also a nearly universal dearth of anything resembling a meaningful economic development strategy. One major reason is that no governmental body has authority over the general welfare of an entire metropolitan area, except in about a dozen areas that have true regional or semiregional governments. General governmental authority is fragmented among dozens or even hundreds of local governments, as discussed earlier. Many state governments have indeed created economic development agencies. But they focus on each state as a whole, not on individual metropolitan areas as wholes.

As a result, the basic American strategy for economic development within individual metropolitan areas has been to permit private firms, entrepreneurs, real estate developers, and landowners to do whatever they want, within a set of rules established by local governments for the parochial benefit of their own citizens. Hence, the way resources are allocated within metropolitan areas is basically determined by private market forces. However, the governmental rules within which such development must occur have steadily grown more complex, more restrictive, and more difficult to conform to in areas that have experienced sustained economic prosperity. In contrast, those rules have become more permissive in those areas that have experienced severe economic recessions, such as many energy-oriented metropolitan areas.

ECONOMIC DEVELOPMENT STRATEGIES AIMED AT SPECIFIC GROUPS

Concerning the third basic type of economic development strategy identified earlier—that of focusing upon assisting population groups in need rather than aiding spatial areas—the United States has adopted a relatively disjointed and partial approach. This approach is much more extensive than that of doing nothing, but much less extensive than the approaches adopted by many Western European nations. The federal government supports a series of assistance programs that provide mainly in-kind benefits to certain groups, except for extensive cash assistance to the elderly, to some disabled persons, and to very low-income mothers with children. The in-kind benefits include entitlement programs for all very low-income households, which provide them with medical assistance and food aid, plus housing aid furnished to only those households meeting eligibility requirements. These programs have different eligibility standards and are operated by several different federal departments, rather than being combined into a single coherent welfare program.

These programs have waxed and waned over time, depending upon which party has controlled the presidency and upon general economic conditions. During the administration of Lyndon Johnson in the late 1960s, antipoverty programs were greatly expanded. Several programs delivering federal financial aid to large cities containing high percentages of poor residents were passed and funded at notable levels. These programs were continued until the presidency of Ronald Reagan in the 1980s, when all federal aid to cities and states was drastically reduced. Programs aiding states and cities that redistributed incomes were especially hit by cutbacks.

The net result is that in 1987, around 13.5 percent of all U.S. residents, or 32.5 million persons, still had annual cash incomes below the official "poverty level." That level is defined as the money cost of a minimally adequate diet multiplied by three. The fraction of all U.S. children under age 18 living in households with incomes below the poverty level has steadily risen over the past two decades. In 1987, it was 20 percent for all children, 45 percent for black children, and 39 percent for Hispanic children (U.S. Bureau of the Census 1989: 454). The percentages of all households, persons, and children with analogously low incomes in Western European nations are generally considerably lower than those prevalent in the United States.

SPATIAL DISTRIBUTION OF SOCIOECONOMIC GROUPS WITHIN
METROPOLITAN AREAS

Another aspect of American economic development strategies for metropolitan areas involves the spatial distribution of socioeconomic groups within these areas. Although no centralized authority has deliberately devised and carried out any coherent strategy concerning where such groups will live, a de facto strategy has emerged from the disjointed decisions of individual local governments. These decisions reflect two widely held values of American households: (1) the desire to live in a neighborhood where most other residents are similar to oneself in income and social status and (2) the moral and legal right of households in each community to protect themselves from forces they believe might reduce either their property values or the social status of that community. The application of these principles by local governments is accomplished through their adoption of specific zoning regulations, subdivision regulations, building codes, and housing occupancy codes. These regulations are usually designed to prevent construction within each community of any housing with a market value substantially less than the homes now located there. In many areas containing predominantly single-family homes, this means either total or substantial exclusion of multifamily housing. Such exclusionary policies are only possible within suburbs, since most central cities already contain large amounts of both relatively low-valued housing and multifamily housing. However, central cities maintain some differentiation of specific neighborhoods by socioeconomic group through a combination of market forces that affect housing prices, and differential enforcement of building and other local codes.

The result of this highly decentralized process is creation within each metropolitan area of a rough and informal but nonetheless real socioeconomic hierarchy of residential neighborhoods. In this hierarchy, the wealthiest households live in high-priced neighborhoods occupied mainly by very high-income households; middle-income households live in not-quite-so-high-priced areas occupied mainly by middle-income households; and moderate-income households live in neighborhoods occupied mainly by moderate-income households. For members of these three groups, this hierarchy works well, providing them with neighborhoods that conform to the two values just mentioned, and thereby meeting their basic residential needs.

But this hierarchy has a devastating impact upon the poorest and most destitute households in each metropolitan area. Because members of such households are excluded from most parts of the hierarchy, they are compelled to live together in the oldest, most deteriorated areas. These areas are found mostly within central cities or in older, close-in suburbs. Moreover, these areas often become dominated by conditions associated with severe poverty, such as high rates of crime, delinquency, drug abuse, child abuse, broken families, unemployment, and mental illness. And the quality of education provided in these areas is markedly inferior to that provided in other parts of the hierarchy, partly because most of the children in schools there come from such destitute families. Thus, the poorest households are forced to live in a social, physical, and economic environment that offers nothing remotely approaching the "equality of opportunity" that is part of the American mythos.[11] In recent years, some sociologists have even argued that these neighborhoods are producing an "underclass" containing many members who remain in poverty from one generation to the next.[12]

The development of such a neighborhood hierarchy is not the result of a deliberate, centralized plot by a cabal of local government officials from relatively affluent suburbs. But it is not wholly accidental, either. The officials concerned are by now well-aware of the collective impact of their exclusionary behavior upon the welfare of the poorest residents of each metropolitan area. But they are elected by nonpoor residents of specific communities who do not want to have poor people living near them. And no political officials are responsible for the overall welfare of each metropolitan area as a whole. Hence, each local government adopts an essentially parochial view when it comes to deciding what land-use regulations to permit. The emergence of this neighborhood hierarchy is thus a direct result of the basic American strategy of having mainly fragmented governments determine how metropolitan areas should develop.

Western European Strategies

No single set of strategies for the economic development of metropolitan areas has been adopted by all the countries of Western Europe. Indeed, many diverse strategies have been employed in this regard. Nevertheless, many Western European nations have created and tried to implement certain basic and roughly similar approaches to metropolitan-area economic development, which are highlighted here. Most of these approaches have not been followed in the United States.

NATIONAL STRATEGIES FOR ALLOCATING RESOURCES AMONG
METROPOLITAN AREAS

Several European nations have adopted national strategies to influence the allocation of economic resources within and among their subregions. These subregions are not usually equated with individual metropolitan areas, but rather with larger territories encompassing several such areas. For example, the United Kingdom instituted several policies aimed at encouraging private firms to locate plants and other facilities in Scotland, Wales, and the North, rather than near London or in the South. Similarly, Italy adopted policies giving tax and other preferences to firms that located facilities in the South, rather than the North. A 1982 compilation by the Commissions of the European Communities of measures providing development assistance for "depressed" regions listed measures for Belgium, Denmark, West Germany, France, Ireland, Italy, Luxembourg, the Netherlands, and the United Kingdom (McAllister 1982: 72–75). Most of these measures consisted of financial aids and incentives for locating plants and other facilities in designated regions experiencing slower-than-average employment growth. Some consisted of assistance to regional or local governments to improve infrastructures in such regions.

Almost every analysis of the impacts of such regional development strategies arrives at the same two basic conclusions: First, the "depressed" regions being assisted still have demonstrably less-dynamic economies than the rest of the nation, so such strategies have failed to "solve" the fundamental problem at which they were aimed. Second, these strategies have nevertheless probably enhanced the economic situation in those regions beyond what it would have been had they not been instituted, although this supposition is hard to measure or prove. Even if public spending produces added jobs in the target regions, to what extent is this simply a diversion of jobs from other parts of the nation? True, an important goal of regional programs is to shift the overall distribution of jobs among regions. But this should preferably occur through net gains to society as a whole—not at the cost of offsetting reductions in jobs in other regions. After all, that spending has to be financed, presumably by taxing someone else. If the spending is financed by government deficits, that might increase the inflation rate, thereby producing an offsetting cost for society as a whole. Bryan Ashcroft (1979: 231–94) conducted an exhaustive evaluation of the major studies of regional growth strategies in the United Kingdom up to 1978. He concluded that (1) about 220,000 additional jobs had been created by regional development programs in "development areas" from 1963 to 1970; (2) capital investment in those areas was stimulated by these programs; (3) the national government received a net financial gain from these programs because they increased property and other taxes and reduced social expenditures more than they cost; and (4) the programs produced a significant net benefit to society as a whole, as well as to the national government. However, he also admitted that the last two of these findings rest on complex theoretical assumptions that are impossible to confirm with much reliability.

Thus, whether regional economic development policies like those used throughout Western Europe are worthwhile from the viewpoint of society as a whole has not yet been conclusively demonstrated. However, the two previously stated conclusions have been demonstrated, namely, that such policies do not remove the regional disparities at which they are aimed, but they do provide some positive benefits to at least some of residents of the "depressed" regions involved.

REGIONAL STRATEGIES FOR ALLOCATING RESOURCES WITHIN INDIVIDUAL METROPOLITAN AREAS

As noted earlier, most Western European nations have tried to confine new real estate development within their metropolitan areas to either in-fill sites or the immediate periphery of the already-built-up portions of those areas. In some cases, they have also permitted creation of planned "new cities" near large metropolitan areas, but separated from them by "greenbelts" of open space. More often, they have encouraged the expansion of existing communities separated from nearby large cities by "greenbelt" zones. Moreover, they have sought to protect the commercial dominance of established downtowns and other retail centers by prohibiting construction of major new automobile-oriented shopping centers in outlying locations. And they have supported extensive networks of public mass transit within their metropolitan areas to inhibit increases in the use of automotive vehicles.

In addition, the United Kingdom has attempted to stimulate economic development within older, inner-city areas through the creation of "enterprise zones." From 1981 through 1986, the national government spent about 400 million pounds for land acquisition, tax relief, and infrastructure improvements within 23 such zones in all parts of the United Kingdom. Barry Moore (1989) estimated that in 1986, enterprise zones contained 2,800 establishments employing 63,300 workers, 56 percent in manufacturing. However, only 35,000 of these jobs were there as a consequence of the enterprise zone policy; the rest would have located there anyway. Moreover, 29,600 of those 35,000 jobs were essentially transferred from other parts of the local economy, so they are not net gains even to the local economy. But 7,400 jobs were generated by linkages with these zones. Hence, a total net gain of 12,900 jobs was generated by this program for the local economies involved. The public cost per job in enterprise zones was 8,500 pounds, but the public cost per job gained net by the local economy was 23,000 pounds. In addition, enterprise zones produced notable nonemployment benefits, such as removal of derelict properties and improvements in the environment. Two-thirds of company representatives interviewed by Moore both in and outside the zones thought they were a positive catalyst to the local economy.

Western European economic development strategies *within* metropolitan areas have produced several important results that differ from what has happened in U.S. metropolitan areas. The economic viability of established downtowns and traditional retail districts has been more successfully sustained, especially concerning retailing. As stated, expansion of metropolitan areas has been confined mainly to in-fill sites, the immediate periphery of already-built-up areas, and planned "new cities," with one exception. There has also been substantial peripheral growth of many smaller towns and villages near major metropolitan areas, from which the new residents commute by car or train to those areas. This is the case in the South of the United Kingdom, for example.

However, not all the results of these strategies have been beneficial. Tightly confining peripheral expansion of existing metropolitan areas has increased land values within them more than in the United States on the average. Hence, the cost of becoming a homeowner is higher, relative to median incomes, in many Western European nations than in most of the United States, and homeownership percentages are lower. Also, tighter planning controls on all new development have prevented as much relative construction of new commercial space as in U.S. metropolitan areas. So vacancy rates are lower and commercial rents are much higher in many Western European cities, even though they have not experienced nearly so much population or job growth as many U.S. metropolitan areas. This benefits the owners of such properties, but not the tenants.

Also, vehicle ownership has expanded in many Western European nations much faster than the road capacity to handle those added vehicles. This results partly from the Western European strategy of discouraging use of private cars compared to public mass transit. Consequently, traffic congestion and its resultant delays are even worse in many Western European metropolitan areas—both large and small—than in most U.S. metropolitan areas. This is true even though congestion has recently increased substantially in the latter too.

Economic Development Strategies Aimed at Specific Groups

Most Western European nations have adopted more extensive welfare systems that support living standards among the poor than has the United States. As a result, the percentage of citizens with incomes below the poverty level is lower in most of those nations than in the United States, on average. This is especially true concerning children, because the United States is the only major developed nation that does not provide some type of children's allowance to *all* households with children.

A recent study using data from the years 1979 to 1982 compared the percentages of persons with incomes below the equivalent of the U.S. poverty line in the United States and five Western European nations (Smeeding, Torrey, and Rein 1988).[13] Its measure of income was after taxes and transfer payments. Concerning poverty among children, the United States, at 17.1 percent in 1979, had the highest fraction among these six nations, with the United Kingdom second-highest, at 10.7 percent in 1979. Sweden and Switzerland had the lowest poverty shares for children at 5.1 percent each, but they are very small nations. However, West Germany had only 8.2 percent of its children at that income level, and it had the largest population of any Western European nation.[14] Concerning the elderly, the United Kingdom had by far the highest fraction of elderly with poverty-level incomes, at 37 percent. Norway was second-highest at 18.7 percent, the United States next with 16.1 percent, and West Germany next with 15.4 percent. Lowest were Sweden and Switzerland, with 2.1 percent and 6.0 percent, respectively. Since those data were gathered, the percentage of persons with poverty-level incomes or lower in the United States has risen among children, but declined among the elderly. I do not have more recent data with respect to these percentages in Western European nations.

SPATIAL DISTRIBUTION OF SOCIOECONOMIC GROUPS WITHIN METROPOLITAN AREAS

Most Western European nations have adopted extensive housing subsidy programs that are used by sizable fractions of their renter populations. Moreover, they have built subsidized rental housing in all portions of their major metropolitan areas, including the suburbs. Hence, their low-income populations are not as highly concentrated in older, close-in, often deteriorated neighborhoods as in the United States. In fact, the relative scatteration of subsidized housing throughout Western European metropolitan areas has reduced the extent to which a spatial, socioeconomic neighborhood hierarchy has developed there compared to the United States.

This does not mean there is no differentiation of Western European urban neighborhoods by income and socioeconomic status. There are definite high-status, high-income neighborhoods and low-status, low-income ones in Western European cities and metropolitan areas—in fact, throughout the world's urban areas. However, the high-status neighborhoods are not so separated in distance from major downtown areas in Western Europe as in the United States. In Western European cities, many of the highest-income, highest-status neighborhoods are right next to the traditional downtown. That happens in a few U.S. metropolitan areas, too, such as the Near North Side in Chicago and the Upper East Side of Manhattan. But in general, the wealthiest households in U.S. metropolitan areas live in relatively distant suburbs, while the poorest ones live in relatively close-in central-city neighborhoods. In Western European cities, either there is no such differentiation among income groups by distance from the center, or the wealthier households live close-in and the poorer ones live in newer subsidized housing on the outskirts of the metropolitan area.

Furthermore, because so much higher fractions of the total population in most Western European nations receive housing subsidies, directly subsidized housing projects there contain households from a much broader income spectrum than do those in the United States. Hence, there is less tendency in Western Europe than in the United States to isolate the poorest households together in housing projects separated from other income groups. Such projects are consequently not considered such undesirable living environments as they are in the United States. That is one reason why neighborhood political resistance to building them nearby is much less intense in Western Europe than in America.

Relevance of Strategies to Major U.S. Metropolitan Area Problems

What difference has the absence of strategies for the economic development of U.S. metropolitan areas made to the welfare of these areas, compared to what might have happened if strategies like those in Western Europe had been used? One way to approach this difficult question is to examine key existing problems in U.S. metropolitan areas, and to try to guess whether they would have been less severe if the United States had adopted strategies like those in Western Europe. For this purpose, I have identified what I believe are the nine most serious problems in U.S. metropolitan areas relevant to their economic development. These are as follows (not necessarily in order of relative importance):

1. Regionally uneven prosperity across different metropolitan areas
2. Decaying inner-city areas that create unequal opportunities for their residents, combined with suburban labor shortages
3. Failures of the public education system, especially in big cities
4. Continuing poverty among large numbers of residents, especially children
5. Inability to cope with regionally generated problems by adopting coherent regionwide remedies
6. The physical decay of much infrastructure, such as highways and bridges
7. Low productivity growth, causing a very slow real wage rate increase
8. A shortage of low-rent housing, and a rising housing affordability problem among low-income households
9. Rising automotive traffic congestion

The first of these problems is more common in Western Europe than in the United States. Hence, it is not likely that adopting national strategies for allocating resources among metropolitan areas would have alleviated this problem in the United States. Decaying inner-city areas, the second problem, are also found in some Western European cities, but not nearly so extensively as in U.S. cities, nor as tied to racial segregation and discrimination. The United States has suffered a worse incidence of this problem in part because it had no strategy for dealing with it. But the problem would undoubtedly have been worse in the United States even if Americans had adopted such a strategy, because of basic differences between urban areas in these two regions.

The next two problems—poor education and continuing poverty—are worse in the United States than in Western Europe. However, they result more from failures of welfare strategies aimed at specific groups than from spatial strategies aimed at metropolitan areas per se.

The fifth problem, lack of regional coordination, results from the fragmented nature of governance in U.S. metropolitan areas, and is much less prevalent in Europe. The problem would have been much less severe if the United States had adopted an effective strategy for allocating resources *within* individual metropolitan areas.

The poor state of American infrastructures, the sixth problem, is not caused by the absence of suitable economic development strategies, but by the unwillingness of American governments to pay for the required improvements. Similarly, regarding the seventh problem, no one knows precisely what has caused low productivity growth, but it cannot be blamed on lack of suitable economic development strategies for metropolitan areas.

The shortage of low-rent housing and related housing affordability problems—the eighth problem—are caused by two main factors. One is the unwillingness of the U.S. federal government to finance housing subsidies for very poor households, as most Western European governments do. Hence, this is a failing of welfare-oriented strategy in the United States, compared to that in Western Europe. The second factor is the restrictive laws adopted by local governments that force housing prices upward. This factor results mainly from the fragmentation of governmental authority within U.S. metropolitan areas, which blocks development of any effective strategy for economic and other development within those areas.

The last problem is just as prevalent in Western Europe as in the United States, but for a different reason. In Western Europe, the unwillingness of national governments to finance additional highways is a major cause of traffic congestion. It is true that greater highway construction alone would not totally eliminate traffic congestion, and that European strategies of supporting more extensive public transit systems than in the United States have other advantages (such as generating less air pollution and consuming less open space). Nevertheless, the lack of expressway networks in many big Western European metropolitan areas surely contributes to intense traffic jams within them. That represents a shortcoming in their own national strategies for allocating resources both among and within metropolitan areas. In the United States, the national government is similarly unwilling to finance infrastructure improvements. But traffic congestion in U.S. metropolitan areas is also caused by the unwillingness of local governments to shift some of their powers upward to regional or state planning and governance bodies. Since automobile traffic is generated at the regional level, not at the local level, it cannot be dealt with effectively by purely local governmental policies. Hence, the absence of any strategy for dealing with resource allocation *within* metropolitan areas contributes to this problem. However, in both the United States and Western Europe, another factor generating traffic congestion is political unwillingness to impose peak-hour roadway pricing upon travelers. This results from a failure of political will more than a lack of any strategy.

In summary, the absence of strategies for metropolitan area economic development in the United States has probably contributed significantly to several major U.S. metropolitan area problems, though not to all of them. The failure of the United States to adopt an effective welfare strategy to aid its most deprived citizens is especially important in generating U.S. urban problems. Somewhat less central is the unwillingness of both the national government and state governments to fund major physical improvements—such as repairing highways and bridges—that would help all metropolitan areas develop more effectively. Finally, the fragmentation of U.S. government authority within metropolitan areas clearly contributes to several major problems in these areas.

On the other hand, adopting strategies for the economic development of metropolitan areas would not eliminate all of the problems in these areas, as experience in Western Europe shows. Even so, Americans should at least consider a more strategic approach to metropolitan area economic and other development, especially in those fast-growing metropolitan areas particularly plagued by intrametropolitan difficulties.

Notes

The views in this article are solely those of the author and are not necessarily those of the Brookings Institution, its trustees, or its other staff members.

1. The relatively recent policy of selling publicly owned housing units to their occupants, adopted in the United Kingdom under then-Prime Minister Margaret Thatcher's leadership, raised the homeownership percentage much closer to that in the United States. But homeownership rates in most other Western European nations are markedly below those in the United States.

2. The fastest economic growth in the United States in absolute jobs during the 1980s was in the Los Angeles and Washington, D.C., metropolitan areas.

3. The American Housing Survey (U.S. Departments of Commerce and Housing and Urban Development 1989) reported 32.724 million renter-occupied housing units in the United States in 1987. The median income of households in those units was $16,233, and 31.7 percent had incomes below $10,000. These units included 2.301 million owned by public housing authorities—7 percent of the total. The median income of households in public housing units was $6,821, and 71.8 percent had incomes below $10,000. About 41 percent of the public housing units were occupied by black households, compared to 16 percent of nonpublic-housing renter-occupied units. About 38 percent of all nonblack renter households were headed by females, compared to 53 percent of all black renter households.

4. I included only 13 Western European nations in figure 2.1 because of the limitations of my computer graph program; it was more important analytically to include the United States and Japan in the graph than Belgium, Luxembourg, and Portugal.

5. In U.S. census terminology, a *central city* is a single incorporated community acting as the heart of an economically integrated region containing at least 40,000 persons. These regions are referred to as *metropolitan statistical areas* (MSAs) and consist of those entire counties that are closely integrated around a central city. The areas within an MSA but outside of the central city are referred to as *suburbs* in this chapter. As of 1990, there were about 333 MSAs in the United States.

6. Abandonment of housing was also related to the deteriorated nature of the worst-quality structures and to their locations in neighborhoods exhibiting extreme poverty and high rates of crime, delinquency, unemployment, broken families, and other undesirable traits.

7. The negative figures do not add up to the positive figures because of a large unexplained statistical remainder, and the effects of net immigration from abroad.

8. Some economists consider public funding of highways to be a form of subsidy similar to public funding of the deficits from bus systems and fixed-rail transit systems. But in the United States, most highway construction and repairs are financed through taxes on gasoline and vehicle license fees; hence, they are paid for through what can reasonably be considered "user fees." That is not true of public funds provided to cover the deficits of mass transit systems.

9. Only parts of the Downs (1989) regression analysis were included or described in this study; the rest has not been published.

10. Since these regressions were adaptations from a regression designed to analyze housing prices, they did not include all the variables that might be relevant to population growth and job growth, but not housing prices. For example, they did not include mean January temperature as a tested independent variable. Hence, these results can be viewed as only approximate and partial.

11. For a more complete analysis of this situation, see Downs (1981, esp. chap. 4).

12. For example, see Wilson (1987).

13. There were eight nations in Smeeding et al.'s (1988) study, but only the United States and those in Western Europe are included in this analysis.

14. Population size may be significant, because large size is usually accompanied by greater ethnic diversity. It is politically easier to end poverty in an ethnically homogeneous nation than a diverse one, since support for income redistribution to the poor is backed by more social solidarity in the former than the latter. True, Switzerland contains several different major ethnic groups. But its diversity is small compared to that of the United States.

References

Ashcroft, Bryan. 1979. "The Evaluation of Regional Economic Policy: The Case of the United Kingdom." In *Balanced National Growth*, edited by Kevin Allen (231–94). Lexington, Mass.: Lexington Books.

Bradbury, Katharine L., Anthony Downs, and Kenneth A. Small. 1982. *Urban Decline and the Future of American Cities*. Washington, D.C.: Brookings Institution.

Downs, Anthony. 1981. *Neighborhoods and Urban Development*. Washington, D.C.: Brookings Institution.

——————. 1989. *What Will Happen to Home Prices in the 1990s?* New York: Salomon Bros.

McAllister, Ian. 1982. *Regional Development and the European Community: A Canadian Perspective*. Montreal: Institute for Research on Public Policy.

Moore, Barry. 1989. "Enterprise Zones: An Evaluation of the Experiment in the U.K." In *Policy Innovation and Urban Land Markets* (30–46). Paris: Organization for Economic Cooperation and Development, Urban Affairs Programme.

Smeeding, Timothy, Barbara Boyle Torrey, and Martin Rein. 1988. "Patterns of Income and Poverty: The Economic Status of Children and the Elderly in Eight Countries" (95–99). In *The Vulnerable*, edited by John L. Palmer, Timothy Smeeding, and Barbara Boyle. Washington, D.C.: Urban Institute.

U.S. Bureau of the Census. 1989. *Statistical Abstract of the United States: 1989*. Washington, D.C.: U.S. Government Printing Office.

——————. 1990. *Statistical Abstract of the United States: 1990*. Washington, D.C.: U.S. Government Printing Office.

U.S. Departments of Commerce and Housing and Urban Development. 1989. *American Housing Survey for the United States, 1987*. Pub. no. H-150-87. Washington, D.C.: U.S. Bureau of the Census.

Wilson, William Julius. 1987. *The Truly Disadvantaged: The Inner City, the Underclass, and Public Policy*. Chicago: University of Chicago Press.

Name index

Aaron, H. 164
Ashcroft, B. 256

Baumol, W. 24
Bear, D. 9
Bluhm, N. 190
Bowen, W. 24
Bradbury, K.L. 232, 236, 248
Buchanan, J. 1

Coleman, J.S. 87

Denton, N.A. 219, 220
Downs, A. 148, 163, 196, 223, 232, 247, 249, 263
Downs, J.C. Jr 64

Fain, W. 141

Gruen, V. 64

Haring, J. 130
Hurd, F.W. 5

Jacobs, J. 64
Javits, Senator 64
Jencks, C. 98

Karoly, L.A. 212
Kennedy, R. 64

Levin, H.M. 85, 86, 99
Lindblom, C.E. 65
Lloyd, F. 137

Maisel, S. 169
Massey, D.S. 219, 220
McElhiney, P.T. 7
Moore, B. 257
Moss, M. 128

Parkinson, C.N. 1
Percy, Senator 64
Provo, L.S. 11

Reagan, R. 253
Rein, M. 258
Rockefeller, D. 109

Sizer, T. 98
Small, K.A. 232, 247
Smeeding, T. 258, 263
Smith, W.S. 5
Stein, H. 183

Thatcher, M. 263
Torrey, B.B. 258

Watson, T.M. 5
Wilson, W.J. 263